ISBN 978-1-331-37354-4
PIBN 10180974

English
Français
Deutsche
Italiano
Español
Português

www.forgottenbooks.com

Mythology Photography **Fiction**
Fishing Christianity **Art** Cooking
Essays Buddhism Freemasonry
Medicine **Biology** Music **Ancient
Egypt** Evolution Carpentry Physics
Dance Geology **Mathematics** Fitness
Shakespeare **Folklore** Yoga Marketing
Confidence Immortality Biographies
Poetry **Psychology** Witchcraft
Electronics Chemistry History **Law**
Accounting **Philosophy** Anthropology
Alchemy Drama Quantum Mechanics
Atheism Sexual Health **Ancient History**
Entrepreneurship Languages Sport
Paleontology Needlework Islam
Metaphysics Investment Archaeology
Parenting Statistics Criminology
Motivational

RIGHTS OF COMMON

AND

OTHER PRESCRIPTIVE RIGHTS.

IGHTS OF COMMON

AND

OTHER PRESCRIPTIVE RIGHTS;

BEING

𝕿wenty-four 𝕷ectures

LIVERED IN GRAY'S INN HALL

IN THE YEAR

1877.

BY

JOSHUA WILLIAMS, Esq.,

OF LINCOLN'S INN, ONE OF HER MAJESTY'S COUNSEL,

SOR OF THE LAW OF REAL AND PERSONAL PROPERTY TO THE COUNCIL OF LEGAL EDUCATION.

LONDON:

H. SWEET, 3, CHANCERY LANE,

𝕷aw 𝕻ublisher;

C. F. MAXWELL, MELBOURNE AND SYDNEY.

———

1880.

W6736ri
1880

LONDON:

PRINTED BY C. F. ROWORTH, BREAM'S BUILDINGS, CHANCERY LANE, E.C.

PREFACE.

———◆———

THESE Lectures are many of them printed nearly verbatim as they were delivered. But the Author has not scrupled to amend where necessary. In some cases the law has been modified by recent decisions. In these cases the text has been altered in accordance with the altered state of the law. In making these amendments and alterations, and in the preparation of these Lectures for the press, the Author has received valuable assistance from his son, Mr. T. CYPRIAN WILLIAMS, of Lincoln's Inn, barrister-at-law, to whom also he is indebted for the Index.

7, STONE BUILDINGS, LINCOLN'S INN,
7th February, 1880.

79 1150

TABLE OF CONTENTS.

———◆———

Lecture XI.

Lecture XII.

LECTURE XIII.

LECTURE XVIII.

LECTURE XIX.

LECTURE XXII.

LECTURE XXIII.

INDEX TO CASES CITED.

ERRATA AND ADDENDA.

Pages 20, note (*p*), 21, note (*s*), Lord Coke does not distinctly say that the grantee of *herbagium terræ* shall have the underwood, and the ordinary meaning of the term does not go beyond herbs which may be cut with a scythe. See Du Cange, voce Herbagium.

Page 21, note (*u*). A right of common of pasture may by custom include a right to cut rushes for litter (*Beau* v. *Bloom*, 3 Wils. 456; *S. C.* nom. *Bean* v. *Bloom*, 2 Sir Wm. Black. 926), also a right to cut branches from oak trees in a park to feed the cattle in time of deep snow (1 Rolle's Abr. Customes (E) 12).

Page 78, note (*r*), *add* a reference to stat. 41 & 42 Vict. c. 56.

Page 151, note (*f*), *for Arlott* v. *Ellis, read—Arlett* v. *Ellis.*

Page 161, line 6 from bottom and in margin, *for Warwick* v. *Queen's College, read—Warrick* v. *Queen's College.*

Page 187, note (*d*), *for Dowglass* v. *Kindal, read—Dowglass* v. *Kendal.*

Page 195, note (*u*), *add* a reference to stat. 43 Eliz. c. 11.

Page 244, note (*o*), *add* a reference to *Kenrick* v. *The Overseers of Guilsfield,* L. R., 5 C. P. D. 41.

Page 256, note (*m*), *add* a reference to stat. 41 & 42 Vict. c. 56.

PRESCRIPTIVE RIGHTS.

———◆———

LECTURE I.

THE subject of the present course of Lectures is the Law of Commons and other prescriptive rights. If any person claims that he and his ancestors, whose heir he is, have, from time immemorial, or, in legal phrase, from time whereof the memory of man runneth not to the contrary, openly, uninterruptedly and as of right, used and enjoyed any incorporeal hereditament, he claims such hereditament by *prescription*, and the right which he claims is called a *prescriptive right*. In like manner, if any person is seised in fee of freehold lands or hereditaments, and should claim that he and all those whose estate he hath, from time whereof the memory of man runneth not to the contrary, have used and enjoyed, openly, uninterruptedly and as of right (a), a certain incorporeal hereditament as to such freehold lands and hereditaments belonging or appertaining, he claims a *prescriptive right*, and the title by which he claims is said to be a *title by prescription*.

A prescription differs from a custom in this—that a custom is local, is alleged in no person, but laid within some manor or other place. For example, as Lord Coke remarks (b): "I. S., seised of the manor of D. in fee, prescribeth thus, that I. S., his ancestors, and all those whose estate he hath in the said manor, have time out of mind of man had and used to have common of

---

(a) "*Nec per vim, nec clam, nec precario.*" Bract. lib. 4, c. 38,

par. 1, fol. 222 b.
(b) Co. Litt. 113 b.

W.P.   · 1   B

pasture, &c., in such a place, &c., being the land of some
other, as pertaining to the said manor. This properly
we call a prescription. A custom is in this manner:
A copyholder of the manor of D. doth plead that,
within the same manor, there is and hath been such a
custom, time out of mind of man used, that all the
copyholders of the said manor have had and used to
have common of pasture, &c. in such a waste of the lord,
parcel of the said manor; where the person neither doth
nor can prescribe but alledgeth the custom within the
manor."

No prescrip-
tion for land.

A title by prescription can only be made to incorporeal hereditaments. A man cannot by prescription
make a title to land; nor can land be appendant or
appurtenant, strictly speaking, to other land: though,
no doubt, popularly speaking, a certain field may
belong, and in this sense may be said to be appurtenant
to, a certain farm (c). Still this is popular language
only. In law that which is appendant or appurtenant
to land may be claimed by prescription, and must be

Exception.

Tenants in
common.

incorporeal in its nature. An exception to this rule is
mentioned by Littleton (d). He says that tenants in
common may be by title of prescription, as if the one
and his ancestors, or they whose estate he hath in one
moiety, have holden in common the same moiety with
the other tenant, which hath the other moiety, and with
his ancestors, or with those whose estate he hath, undivided, time out of mind of man. This is an exception
which can hardly arise at the present day; and I have
only noted it because it is contained in Littleton's
Tenures.

No prescrip-
tion for
things not
had without
record.

There are certain incorporeal hereditaments to which
a title cannot be made by prescription. For it is laid
down in Coke upon Littleton (e), that no man can make

(c) Plowden, 170, 171.   (e) Co. Litt. 114 a.
(d) Sect. 310.

a title by prescription to such franchises and liberties as cannot be seized as forfeited, before the cause of forfeiture appear of record; because that prescription being but an usage *in pais*, it cannot extend to such things as cannot be seized nor had *without matter of record*, as to the goods and chattels of traitors, felons, felons of themselves, fugitives, of those that be put in exigent, deodauds, cognizance of pleas, to make a corporation, to have a sanctuary, to make a coroner, and to make conservators of the peace. Most of these are ancient franchises, the law respecting which is of very little practical use at the present time. All these matters require record both for their grant and their forfeiture, and cannot, therefore, be gained merely by constant and uninterrupted usage.

It is a maxim of law that all things are presumed to be rightly done. When the law finds a person in the undisturbed exercise of any right, it presumes that he has a good title, or rather it does not presume that he came to possession by an unlawful act. In accordance with this principle it is, that fraud is never presumed, but always must be proved. When a person, therefore, is found in the undisturbed enjoyment of some incorporeal hereditament, and has been in such enjoyment uninterruptedly, as far as memory can extend, the law will presume that he came rightly to it, by some ancient grant which, in the lapse of time, must have been lost. Prescription, therefore, is said to imply a grant; and nothing can be gained by prescription but such incorporeal hereditaments as have always, in legal phrase, lain in grant and not in livery. You will remember that, before the passing of the Act to amend the law of real property (*f*), corporeal hereditaments did not lie in grant, but were conveyed by other means.

All things presumed to be rightly done.

Prescription implies a grant.

(*f*) Stat. 8 & 9 Vict. c. 106. See Lectures on the Seisin of the Freehold, p. 105.

A right, in order to be gained by prescription, must,
until the reign of King William IV., have existed from
time whereof the memory of man runneth not to the
contrary.   And such is still the law as regard all cases
of prescription which do not fall within an Act, to which
I shall hereafter have to call your attention, commonly
called the Prescription Act.   It is statute 2 & 3 Will.
IV. c. 71.   The memory of man originally was, as
long as the oldest person in the neighbourhood could
remember; but in early times, in order to prevent title
by prescription from being required to be carried too
far back, the time of legal memory was limited to certain
fixed periods.   The time of legal memory was fixed in
accordance with the time of limitation in a writ of right.
The time of limitation in a writ of right was a certain
time prescribed by statute, within which the demandant
in the action must prove himself or some of his ancestors
to have been seised.   Anciently the limitation in a writ
of right was from the time of Henry I.   After that,
by the Statute of Merton (g), the limitation was from
the time of Henry II.   Afterwards, by the Statute of
Westminster the 1st (h), the limitation was from the
time of Richard I., or, strictly speaking, from the first
year of the reign of Richard I.   And, as time passed
on, although the limitation of time in writs of right was
subsequently reduced to sixty years, yet, so far as prescriptive rights were concerned, no alteration was made
in the law; and, consequently, the date of legal prescription or memory continued to be reckoned from an
æra so very antiquated (as Blackstone remarks (i)) as
the first year of the reign of Richard I.

Of course, in most cases, it would be impossible to
prove by direct evidence that any right of common,
right of way, or other prescriptive right, had been

(g) Stat. 20 Hen. III. c. 8.   (i) 2 Bl. Com. 31, note.
(h) Stat. 3 Edw. I. c. 39.

enjoyed continuously ever since the first year of the reign of Richard I. And, accordingly, before the Prescription Act, and even now with respect to matters not included in the Prescription Act, the course of evidence used to be, and is as follows:—If it could be proved that the usage had lasted for the preceding twenty years, this was considered *primâ facie* evidence of the usage as far as legal memory would extend; and it threw on the party contesting the prescription the onus of showing that the right had arisen within some period later than the first year of the reign of King Richard I. But, however long the prescription may have been enjoyed, if clear evidence could be produced that it began at some period later than the first year of the reign of Richard I., there was an end of the pre-scription. The rule upon this subject was laid down by the Court of King's Bench in the case of *The King* v. *Joliffe* (k). That was a case of *quo warranto*, calling upon the defendant to show upon what authority he claimed to exercise the office of mayor of the borough of Petersfield. And the defendant pleaded in answer, that Petersfield was an ancient borough, and that from time immemorial there had been a Court leet, or view of frankpledge holden in and for the borough; and that the jury sworn and serving at that Court had presented a fit person to be mayor of the borough for one whole year, and that the person so presented had always been sworn in at that Court before the steward; and, being so presented and sworn, had executed the office of mayor for one year; and that, at the Court leet duly holden on such day, certain persons, naming them, good and lawful men, were then and there duly sworn as and for the jury, then and there to serve as the jury, and did serve as the jury of the said Court; and, being so sworn and serving, presented the defendant

Usage for twenty years.

Rex v. Joliffe.

(k) 2 Barn. & Cress. 54.

to be mayor; and that he, being so presented, was duly sworn before the steward, and by virtue of the premises claimed to be mayor. To this it was replied, amongst other things, that the Court leet of the borough had immemorially presented a fit person to be bailiff, who is always attendant upon the Court; that, at the Court mentioned in the plea, the steward nominated the fourteen persons mentioned in the plea, who served on the jury, and issued his precept to the bailiff to summon those persons, and that the bailiff did accordingly summon them; whereas, by the law of the land, the steward should have issued his precept to the bailiff to summon a jury; and the particular persons should have been selected by the bailiff. To this it was rejoined that, from time immemorial, the steward had been used to nominate the jurors. And issue was joined thereon. At the trial, before Mr. Justice Burrough, the defendant proved that, for more than twenty years, the precept to the bailiff had always contained a list of persons, whom the steward directed him to summon as jurors. No evidence was given for the crown to show that any other practice had ever prevailed in the borough. The learned judge told the jury that slight evidence, if uncontradicted, became cogent proof; and they found a verdict for the defendant. And this ruling was upheld by the Court of King's Bench. Chief Justice Abbott was of opinion that a rule which had been obtained for a new trial must be discharged. He said, "Upon the evidence given, uncontradicted and unexplained, I think the learned judge did right in telling the jury that it was cogent evidence upon which they might find the issue in the affirmative. If his expression had gone even beyond that, and had recommended them to find such a verdict, I should have thought that the recommendation was fit and proper. A regular usage for twenty years, not explained or contradicted, is that upon which many private and public rights are held, there being nothing in the usage to contravene the public policy. Taking, therefore, the issue to be properly found, we must consider that, by the immemorial custom of this Court leet, the steward has been in the habit of pointing out to the bailiff the persons who are to be summoned on the jury. If that custom be against any known rule or principle of law, it cannot stand, however great its antiquity may be; but I am of opinion that it is not." Justice Holroyd also agreed that the observations of the learned judge, and the verdict of the jury, were well warranted by the evidence in the cause.

The question, whether a right, that had long existed, did or did not commence before the time of legal memory, occurred in the case of *Addington* v. *Clode and others* (*l*). In that case the plaintiff Addington brought an action of trespass against the defendant Clode and others, for breaking and entering his close at a place called Upottery. The defendants pleaded (amongst other things) that the defendant Clode was seised of a messuage and lands in Upottery; and that he and all those whose estate he hath for the time being, had and used, and have been accustomed to have and use, and so still of right ought to have and use, common of pasture, in the place where the trespass was alleged to have been committed, for all commonable cattle *levant* and *couchant* (*m*), and he thereupon justifies; and the other defendants justified as his servants. The plaintiff traversed or denied the right of common. And, issue being joined thereon, it was tried at Exeter Summer Assizes, 1774; when, after the plaintiff had concluded his evidence, the counsel for the defendant opened two ancient grants without date (copies of which were left with the judges); by the first of which, John Beneyt

Old grant when inconsistent with prescription.

Addington v. *Clode.*

(*l*) 2 Sir W. Black. 989.   (*m*) See *post*, Lecture III.

grants to William De Verga all his land at Beneytishege, in the manor of Uppotery, to have and to hold to him and his heirs, of the chief lords of the fee, rendering to them 6s., by even quarterly payments, annually for all secular services. By the other deed Henry de la Pomereye confirms to William de Verga and his heirs, the same lands which he had of the gift of John Beneit, in the said Henry's manor of Uppoteri, rendering to the said Henry and his heirs 6s. yearly, by even quarterly payments; and then adds, "And I will and grant, for me and my heirs, that the said William, his heirs or assigns, shall have with his beasts common pasture on my mountain of Uppoteri." Upon which Justice Nares, who tried the cause, observed to the defendant's counsel, that this grant was entirely inconsistent with the plea of prescription; in which they acquiesced, and a verdict was given for the plaintiff. Afterwards, in Michaelmas term, the defendants moved for a new trial, on the ground that the grant might have only been in confirmation of an antecedent prescriptive right, and then it was not inconsistent with it. Upon this point the Court held that these grants might either have been before the time of memory, or else they might have been only in confirmation of a prior right; in neither of which cases would they have been inconsistent with a plea of prescription; and that it ought to have been left with the jury to decide, whether either of these was the case; and, this not having been done, a new trial was granted. Mr. Justice Blackstone truly observed that the *tenendum* of the chief lords of the fee afforded a strong presumption that the grants were subsequent to the statute of *Quia emptores* (n), and so subsequent to the period of legal memory. If the grants were subsequent to legal memory, and were not merely in confirmation of a prior right, then the title

(n) Stat. 18 Edw. I. c. 1. See Lectures on the Seisin of the Freehold, p. 21.

clearly was not by prescription, but by virtue of the grants, and ought consequently to have been so pleaded.

Now, with respect to the two kinds of prescription, a prescription of enjoyment by a man and his ancestors, and a prescription by a man, seised in fee, of enjoyment by himself and all those whose estate he hath, the latter prescription is by far the most common. A prescription of the former kind is seldom made by a private person. It is, however, occasionally made by corporations, that they and their predecessors have from time immemorial enjoyed such a right. With regard to private persons, I am not aware of more than two cases, in modern times, where a prescription of this kind, viz. a prescription of enjoyment by a man and his ancestors, irrespective of the possession of land, has been set up. The first of these cases is that of *Welcome* v. *Upton* (o). That was an action of trespass, for taking the plaintiff's cattle depasturing in a certain open field, and impounding the same. The defendant pleaded that, before and at the time of making the indenture thereinafter mentioned, one Thomas Brereton, *and all his ancestors, whose heir he then was*, from time whereof the memory of man was not to the contrary, had, and every of them had, been used and accustomed to have, and of right ought to have had, and the said Thomas Brereton at the time of making the said indenture of right ought to have had, for himself and themselves, his and their heirs and assigns, the sole and several herbage and pasturage of and in divers, to wit, 217A. 2R. 3P. of and in the said open field, in gross, for all manner of his and their cattle to feed and depasture thereon, from the 4th day of September in each and every year, until the 5th day of April next following; that the said Thomas Brereton, on the 19th of April, 1755, by indenture made between

Prescription of enjoyment by a man and his ancestors.

Welcome v. *Upton.*

Several pasture.

(o) 6 M. & W. 536.

him and Samuel Billingsley, granted to the said Samuel Billingsley the said sole and several herbage and pasturage of and in the said 217A. 2R. 3P. in the said field, to hold the same unto the said Samuel Billingsley, his heirs and assigns, for ever. The plea then stated the vesting of the right to the said herbage and pasturage, on the 1st of January, 1826, in J. R. F. Billingsley; and that he demised the same, on the 1st of March, 1836, to the defendant, and justified the seizing and impounding the plaintiff's cattle on the ground of their being upon and depasturing the land in question. There had been certain interruptions in the right by building and enclosing part of the 217 acres of land. And one of the questions in the case was as to the effect of these interruptions. It was held that the interruptions, being recent, did not interfere with the right of pasturage. It was also held that the plea of immemorial enjoyment by Thomas Brereton and his ancestors was proved, by showing enjoyment by those who claimed under him, particularly by a deed dated 23rd October, 1800, which related to the right of pasturage in question, and also by the deed of 1755, by which Thomas Brereton granted the right of pasturage to Samuel Billingsley. Baron Parke said it was certainly evidence of a seisin in fee of Thomas Brereton, that parties, afterwards coming in under him, enjoyed the right in the same manner in which he claimed to enjoy it. The Court also held that the plea was good, that a party may prescribe to take the sole and several herbage of land, this having been established as law by two cases, *Hoskins* v. *Robins* and *Potter* v. *North*, to which I hope hereafter to refer. Both cases will be found reported in Serjeant Williams's edition of Saunders's Reports (*p*). Another question arose whether a right of this kind, gained by the immemorial exercise of a right by a man and his ancestors, could be granted

Proof of immemorial enjoyment by a man and his ancestors.

Prescriptive right gained by immemorial enjoyment by a

(*p*) *Hoskins* v. *Robins*, 2 Wms. Saund. 320; *Potter* v. *North*, 1 Wms. Saund. 347.

away from his heirs; and, on this point, the Court was man and his ancestors may be granted by him.
of opinion that, although the right was gained by the personal user of Brereton and his ancestors, yet that there could be no doubt that he was not bound to use it by himself and his descendants only, and that the parties claiming under him were equally entitled to it, whether they claimed under him by deed or by descent.

The next case of a claim by prescription by reason of user by a person and his ancestors, is that of *Shuttleworth* v. *Le Fleming and others* (q). This was also an action of trespass against the defendants, for that they entered into a certain close of the plaintiff, being part of certain lands called the Low Bank Ground Estate, and landed and brought, unto and upon the said close, certain fishing nets, and thereby damaged the grass of the plaintiff there then growing. To this it was pleaded by the defendants, amongst other things, that, at the time when the alleged trespass was committed, the said close adjoined and was, and now is, part of the shore of an inland lake of water called Coniston or Thurston Water, and that the defendant Hughes Le Fleming *and all his ancestors, whose heir he was,* for sixty years before this suit, enjoyed as of right and without interruption, a free fishery in the said water, with the right of landing and bringing their fishing nets into and upon any part of the shore of the said water, as to the said free-fishery appertaining; and that the defendant Hughes Le Fleming, and the other defendants as his servants, and by his command, did what was complained of, in the lawful and reasonable use and exercise of the said right, and not otherwise. This you will observe was not a plea of immemorial usage, but a plea of usage for sixty years; and it had reference to the time mentioned in the Prescription

Shuttleworth v. *Le Fleming.* Claim of right of fishing in a man and his ancestors.

(q) 19 C. B., N. S. 687.

Act (r). The question which the Court decided was, that a claim of this kind was not within the provisions of the Prescription Act, and that the plea was bad, and that a demurrer which had been put in by the plaintiff to this plea ought to be allowed. The case, however, affords an instance of the claim of a right, which certainly now is rare, namely, a right of a private person, irrespective of the possession of land, and so a right in gross, as it is called, for the enjoyment of an incorporeal hereditament, founded merely on user by himself and his ancestors.

Claim by corporations of immemorial right exercised by them and their predecessors.

Johnson v. *Barnes.*

Corporations not unfrequently claim by prescription that they and their predecessors have from time immemorial exercised certain rights. An instance of this kind occurred in the recent case of *Johnson* v. *Barnes* (s). In that case the corporation of Colchester claimed, by reason of immemorial usage, an exclusive right of pasture in certain lands round the walls of the town, for all cattle, sheep and other commonable animals, levant and couchant, within the borough, from Lammas to Candlemas, save as to any part of the land sown, at or before the commencement of such period, with corn or other grain ; and, in that case, only after such crops should be harvested or otherwise removed in a due course of husbandry. This right they had on various occasions, and for valuable consideration, released to the owners of part of the lands; and, in some instances, the rights of the corporation had been conveyed to strangers, who had exercised similar rights. In some of the deeds, the right was described as a right of common. This description was erroneous; for a right to the sole pasture of lands is not a right of common ; a right of common being a right of pasturage in

(r) Stat. 2 & 3 Will. IV. c. 71, *post*, Lecture XII.

(s) L. R., 7 C. P. 592, affirmed on appeal, L. R., 8 C. P. 527.

common with the owner of the soil (*t*). But, notwithstanding this erroneous description, which was
several times repeated, the Court held that a legal
origin must, if possible, be presumed for a long established practice ; and that what the corporation was
entitled to was an exclusive right of pasturage over the
lands in question ; and that the right was established
by the immemorial exercise of such right by the predecessors of the corporation, not as appendant or appurtenant to the lands within the borough, but as a
right, irrespective of appendancy or appurtenancy, belonging in gross to the corporation by reason of the
ancient user of their predecessors.

But, although a private individual may prescribe by
reason of the immemorial enjoyment of himself and his
ancestors, and although a corporation may prescribe by
reason of the immemorial enjoyment of themselves and
their predecessors, yet the *inhabitants* of a place, who Inhabitants
are not a corporation, cannot prescribe for any right of cannot prescribe for
common, as having been enjoyed from time immemorial common.
by them as inhabitants of the place. This was decided
in *Gateward's case* (*u*). In that case an action of trespass *Gateward's*
was brought by Robert Smith against Stephen Gate- *case.*
ward, gentleman, because he broke into a close at
Horsington, in the county of Lincoln, called Horsington
Holmes, with certain cattle, viz., horses, cows and sheep.
And the defendant pleaded that the town òf Stixwold
is an ancient town, and lies contiguous to the said close
called Horsington Holmes, ; and that, within the same
town, there exists, and from all times whereof the
memory of man runneth not to the contrary there has
existed, a custom that the inhabitants within the same
town of Stixwold aforesaid, inhabiting any ancient
messuage there, by reason of their dwelling and residing

(*t*) Co. Litt. 122 a.   (*u*) 6 Rep. 59 b.

in the same, had, and were used and accustomed to have common of pasture in the aforesaid place, in which the alleged trespass was committed, for all and all manner of oxen and horses and other large commonable beasts, on their ancient messuages, within the aforesaid town of Stixwold, in manner and form following, viz., in every year at all times of the year, and also for sheep, Ievant and couchant, in every year on the first day of August and thenceforth to the feast of the Annunciation of the Blessed Virgin Mary then next following, and he pleaded that he, at the time aforesaid, was and still is residing and inhabiting in the said town of Stixwold, in an ancient house in Stixwold aforesaid, and so justified; upon which the plaintiff did demur in law. And this plea it is stated was often times argued at the bar; and now, this Hilary Term, the 4th of James I., it was openly argued at the bench by all the justices. And it was unanimously resolved by all the justices of the Common Pleas, that the custom was against law for several reasons, amongst others,-that this kind of common was not known to the law. What estate, it was asked, shall he have, who is an inhabitant, in the common, when it appears he hath no estate or interest in the house, but a mere habitation and dwelling in respect of which he ought to have his common ? For none can have interest in common in respect of a house in which he hath no interest. Such common would be transitory, and altogether uncertain; for it will follow the person, and for no certain time or estate, but during his inhabitancy: and such manner of interest the law will not suffer; for custom ought to extend to that which hath certainty and continuance. And it was said also to be against the nature and quality of a common; for every common may be suspended or extinguished; but such a common will be so incident to the person, that no person certain can extinguish it; but as soon as he who releases, &c. removes, the new inhabitant shall have it.

In addition to this objection Lord Coke remarks (*x*), that the custom, in the case at bar, was insufficient and repugnant in itself; for it was alleged that the custom of the town of Stixwold was, that every inhabitant thereof had used to have common within a place in the town of Horsington, which was another town. The custom, if valid as a custom, ought to have been alleged as a custom of the town of Horsington, and not of the town of Stixwold. This, however, was, by the bye : the main point of the case is that *inhabitants*, as such, cannot have any right of common, or any right of the same kind.

It is true that in the old books rights of common are not unfrequently spoken of as being enjoyed by *tenants and inhabitants*. This, so far as the word *inhabitants* is concerned, appears to be popular language only. If all the tenants in fee in a town, or parish, or manor, have a right of common, as they may have, this right is necessarily enjoyed by their tenants, who occupy the land ; and, in this way, it may be said that the right belongs to all the tenants and inhabitants. But in law the right in such a case is the right of the freeholder, though exercised by his tenant, who is in the actual occupation of his lands. Tenants and inhabitants.

In my next Lecture I hope to speak of rights claimed by a person seised in fee by reason of the continuous enjoyment of himself and those whose estate he has.

(*x*) Page 61 a.

LECTURE II.

I now come to the consideration of such prescriptive rights as are claimed by reason of the continuous and immemorial enjoyment thereof by the claimant, a person seised in fee, and by all those whose estate he has. This is called a prescription in a *que estate*. The phrase is taken from the Norman-French :—that he, and all those whose estate he has, have from time immemorial enjoyed the right :—*tous ceux que estate il ad*. Now one of the ancient rules of pleading with regard to a prescription of this kind was this :—that such a prescription must always have been laid in the person who was seised in fee simple. It was said that a tenant for life, for years, or at will, or a copyholder, could not prescribe in this manner, by reason of the imbecility of their estates ; for, as prescription is always beyond the time of memory, it would be absurd that those, whose estate commenced within the memory of man, should pretend to prescribe for anything. Therefore a tenant for life must have prescribed under cover of the tenant in fee simple, and a copyholder under cover of his lord. This rule is now abolished by the fifth section of the Prescription Act, 2 & 3 Will. IV. c. 71, to which I shall hereafter refer. Its principle is explained in *Gateward's case* (a), to which I called attention in my last Lecture (b). It is there said, that, by the rule in all our books, without question, tenant in fee simple ought to prescribe in his own name ; tenant for life, years, by elegit, &c., and at will, &c., in the name of him who hath the fee ; and he who hath

Prescription in a que estate.

Prescription in name of tenant in fee.

Gateward's case.

(a) 6 Rep. 60 a.   (b) *Ante*, p. 13.

no interest can have no common. The passage then concludes with a sentence which certainly conveys no meaning, and which I have ascertained to be merely a mistranslation of the original, which was written in Norman French. The words in the English copies of Coke's Reports to which I refer are these: "So none that hath no interest, if it be but at will, ought to have common; but by good pleading he may enjoy it"— words which evidently have no meaning. The true translation is as follows:—"So there is none, that hath any interest, though it be but at will, and who ought to have common, but by good pleading may enjoy it." The passage means that a person, who is merely a tenant at will, and who, as tenant at will, has a right of common, may enjoy his right by good pleading, namely, by pleading in the name of the tenant in fee simple.

Mistranslation in report of Gateward's case.

A copyholder, you may remember, is at law but a tenant at will to the lord of the manor of which he holds. According to the doctrine above laid down, therefore, if a copyholder should, as occasionally he might, have claimed a right of common in the lands of any other person than his lord, he must have prescribed in the name of his lord. The rights of copyholders, however, are usually rights of common in the lands of the lord himself; and, in respect of such rights, it is obvious that they cannot prescribe in the name of the lord himself; as the lord, any more than any other person, cannot bring an action against himself. In order, therefore, that the copyholders may have some legal remedy, an exception has been made in their favour; and they are allowed to insist upon their rights of common by alleging a *custom* within the manor, that all the copyhold tenants have such a right. This departure from the ordinary rules of pleading, appears to have been made by reason of the necessity of the case.

Copyholder prescribed in the name of his lord.

Copyholder may allege a custom as against his lord.

W.P.

Now there are a great many things, in respect of which a title may be made, by prescription of immemorial enjoyment by the claimant, seised in fee, and by those whose estate he has. One important kind of prescription is that which is called a prescription of a *profit à prendre*, or a right for any man, in respect of his tenement, to take some profit out of the tenement of another man. Borrowing from the language of the civil law, the tenement in respect of which the profit is taken, is called the *dominant tenement ;* and the tenement out of which the profit is taken is called the *servient tenement.* The most important kinds of *profit à prendre* are, rights of *sole or several vesture or herbage, and of sole or several pasture,* and rights of *common of pasture,* or to pasture in common with the owner of the soil; also rights of common of what is called in Norman French *estovers,* and in Saxon *botes ;* that is, rights of cutting timber, underwood, gorse or furze, and such like, for fuel to burn in the house, called *fire bote,* or for the repairs of the house and farm buildings, called *house bote,* or for the repairs of hedges and fences, called *hedge bote,* or for the repairs of instruments of husbandry, called *plough bote,* all of which I mentioned in one of my Lectures of last year (c). There may also be a prescription for taking *sand, gravel, clay, and loam* for the repairs of the roads or for the improvement of the soil of the dominant tenement ; also a prescriptive right of digging coals for fuel. A right of *sporting* over the lands of another, is also an instance of a right of *profit à prendre ;* so also is a right of fishing in another man's water. But a right to take water is not looked upon as a right of *profit à prendre,* but merely as an easement (d).

I propose first to consider the right of *sole or several vesture or herbage,* which, though perhaps not very

Profit à prendre.

Dominant tenement.

Servient tenement.
Several vesture or herbage.
Several pasture.
Common of pasture.
Estovers.
Botes.

Sand, gravel, clay, loam.

Coals.
Sporting.

Fishing.
Taking water.

Sole or several vesture or herbage.

(c) Lectures on Settlements, p. 230.

(d) *Race* v. *Ward*, 4 E. & B. 702.

frequent, is yet a remarkable species of prescription. The main authority with respect to such an interest as this is what is said by Lord Coke, in Coke upon Littleton (e). "If a man hath 20 acres of land, and by deed granteth to another and his heirs *vesturam terræ*, and maketh livery of seisin *secundum formam chartæ*, the land itself shall not pass, because he hath a particular right in the land; for thereby he shall not have the houses, timber-trees, mines and other real things, parcel of the inheritance, but he shall have the vesture of the land, that is, corn, grass, underwood, sweepage and the like; and he shall have an action of trespass *quare clausum fregit*. The same law if a man grant *herbagium terræ* he hath a like particular right in the land, and shall have an action *quare clausum fregit*; but by grant thereof and livery made, the soil shall not pass as is aforesaid." In this case Lord Coke evidently did not intend to say, that livery of seisin *secundum formam chartæ* was necessary in a case of this kind. His meaning is, that if there be a grant by deed, yet, notwithstanding that livery of seisin be made, no interest in the soil will pass under a grant of this kind, but the mere right to have the corn, grass, underwood and the like; and such a right is not a corporeal but an incorporeal hereditament. Lord Coke tells us in another place (f), that "a man may prescribe or allege a custom to have and enjoy *solam vesturam terræ* from such a day till such a day, and hereby the owner of the soil shall be excluded to pasture or feed there." But that for which a man can prescribe is clearly an incorporeal, and not a corporeal hereditament; and there is not in this case the slightest interest in the soil; though, during the time for which the right may be exercised, it is quite proper that the grantee should be protected in the enjoyment of the exclusive possession. The grantee of the sole or several vesture may accord-

(e) Co. Litt. 4 b.   *Sir George Sparke's Prescription,*
(f) Co. Litt. 122 a.   See also   Winch, 6.

ingly, as Lord Coke says, bring an action of trespass. And in another place (*g*), Lord Coke says, that "if a man demiseth the vesture or herbage of his land, he may reserve a rent, for that the thing is manurable (*h*), and the lessor may distrain the cattle upon the land." So the owner of the several herbage or vesture might, before the action of ejectment was abolished, have brought ejectment (*i*). But, having no interest in the soil, he cannot dig the land (*k*). He may, however, enclose (*l*). As the whole of the herbage may belong to a man by prescription, so he may prescribe for a limited

Thorns. right, as to take the whole of the thorns growing on a certain parcel of land, to expend and burn in his house (*m*). So the herbage may not only be granted as prescribed for indefinitely, but, as we have seen (*n*), a man may prescribe to take the herbage for some defined period, as from such a day to such a day. So the first

Prima tonsura. mowing, *prima tonsura*, or *prima vestura*, may be granted or prescribed for, and so may also the aftermath. These interests are all of the same character, and have

May be held by copy of Court roll. the same incidents. The herbage or vesture of land may be granted by copy of Court roll to a man and his heirs, and so may also the underwood, only without the soil (*o*). We have seen (*p*) that vesture or herbage includes the underwood. So *prima tonsura* may be held by copy (*q*). The reason why these things may be granted by copy, is that, though they are no part of the

(*g*) Co. Litt. 47 a.

(*h*) In all the printed editions which I have seen, this word is spelt *maynorable*, but there is no such word as this in the English language. Serjeant Coxe appears, from his MS. notes to Co. Litt. in Lincoln's Inn Library, to have read the word as "manurable," which is the only word that makes sense of the passage.

(*i*) *Wheeler* v. *Toulson*, Hardres,

330; *Ward* v. *Petifer*, Cro. Car. 362.

(*k*) Trin. 30 Eliz.; Owen, 37.

(*l*) Dyer, 285 b, pl. 40; Vin. Abr. tit. Herbage (a).

(*m*) *Dowglass* v. *Kendal*, Cro. Jac. 256.

(*n*) *Ante*, pp. 9, 12.

(*o*) Co. Litt. 58 b; *Hoe* v. *Taylor*, 4 Rep. 30 b.

(*p*) *Ante*, p. 19.

(*q*) *Stammers* v. *Dixon*, 7 East, 200.

soil, yet they are " things of perpetuity to which custom may extend," and, after every cutting, they grow again (*r*).

Our next subject for consideration is the right of sole or several pasture. This right appears to differ from that of sole or several vesture or herbage, in that it can only be taken by the mouths of cattle, whereas the owner of sole or several vesture or herbage may mow the grass. The underwood also belongs to the owner of the sole or several vesture or herbage (*s*) ; but it does not belong to the owner of sole or several pasture (*t*). Pasture, in its widest sense, comprises all vegetable products that may be eaten, such as grass, nuts, acorns, the mast of trees, the right to which is known by the name of *pannage*, and even leaves and boughs (*u*). The right of sole pasture often exists for a limited time, but it may be prescribed for in perpetuity. The two cases, by which the lawfulness of such a prescription is established, are those of *Potter* v. *North* (*x*), and *Hoskins* v. *Robins* (*y*). I mentioned both these cases in my last Lecture (*z*) ; but, as they are cases of importance, they deserve more than a passing remark. The case of *Potter* v. *North* was an action of trespass brought by John Potter against Henry North, for taking and unjustly detaining a horse called a nag, of him the said John. And the defendant justified the taking as bailiff of Sir Henry North, Bart., on the ground that the place called the Fenn, in which the taking of the horse was supposed to be done, contained

Sole pasture.

What pasture comprises.

Potter v. *North.*

(*r*) 4 Rep. 31 a.

(*s*) Co. Litt. 4 b.

(*t*) *Hopkins* v. *Robinson*, 1 Mod. 74; *S. C.* nom. *Hoskins* v. *Robins*, 1 Vent. 164.

(*u*) Bracton, lib. 4, c. 38, fol. 222 b ; Britton, c. 55, fol. 143 b.

(*x*) 1 Wms. Saund. 347.

(*y*) 2 Wms. Saund. 320 ; 2 Keble, 758, 842; 1 Vent. 123, 163; *S. C.* nom. *Hopkins* v. *Robinson*, 1 Mod. 74; 2 Lev. 2.

(*z*) *Ante*, p. 10.

a thousand acres of pasture with the appurtenances, in Mildenhall in the county of Suffolk, of which a certain place called the Delfe, containing one hundred acres of pasture with the appurtenances, was from time immemorial the proper soil and freehold of the said Sir Henry North, Baronet. And because the horse of John Potter was in the said one hundred acres of pasture, eating up the grass there growing, and doing damage there to the said Sir Henry North, Bart., he the said Henry, as bailiff to Sir Henry North, distrained the horse, so as aforesaid doing damage there. To this John Potter, the plaintiff, pleaded that the one hundred acres of pasture called the Delfe, were parcel of the place called the Fenn; and, for all times aforesaid, were parcel of the manor of Mildenhall, with the appurtenances in Mildenhall, of which manor Sir Henry North was lord; and that he, John, was seised in his demesne as of fee of and in an ancient messuage in Mildenhall aforesaid, being one of the freehold tenements of the manor, and held of the manor by rents and services; and that there were in Mildenhall aforesaid, divers ancient messuages, being freehold tenements held of the manor in fee simple, by several rents and services; and that there were within the manor divers ancient messuages, being customary tenements, parcel of the said manor, granted and grantable by the lord of the said manor for the time being, at the will of the lord, according to the custom of the said manor, by copy of the rolls of the Court of the said manor; and that the several tenants of the said freehold tenements, being seised of their several tenements in their demesne as of fee, and all those whose estate they severally have in the same, for all the time aforesaid have had, together with the said tenants of the said customary messuages, the sole and several pasture of the said one hundred acres of pasture, for all their cattle (swine, sheep and northern steers excepted) levant and couchant upon their said

respective freehold tenements, every year at all times of
the year, as to their several freehold tenements belonging
and appertaining. And that in the same manor there
was such a custom, that the several tenants of the said
customary messuages, together with the said free tenants,
were used and accustomed to have the sole and several
pasture of the said one hundred acres of pasture for all
their cattle (swine, sheep and northern steers excepted)
levant and couchant (a) upon their several customary
tenements aforesaid, every year at all times of the year,
as to their several customary tenements belonging and
appertaining. And the said John, being so seised of
the said messuage with the appurtenances in form aforesaid, he, the said John, before the time of taking of the
horse, put the horse in the declaration specified, being
his own proper horse, levant and couchant upon his
messuage, into the said one hundred acres of pasture
called the Delfe, to depasture the grass there and then
growing ; and the horse, at the time of the taking, was
in the said one hundred acres of pasture called the
Delfe, eating up the grass there then growing, until the
horse was taken. Henry North the defendant demurred
to the plea as insufficient in law ; but the Court seemed
to incline that the plea was good ; but they directed
that there should be a trial at Bar to try the truth of
it. And afterwards in Easter term a trial at Bar was
held ; but the tenants could not prove their title, as they
had alleged it ; wherefore the lord had a verdict, and
so there was no judgment in this case upon the demurrer. This was in the 21st year of the reign of King
Charles II. But in the 23rd year of the same reign, the
case of *Hoskins* v. *Robins* was decided (b). This was a case
of a similar kind, though claimed by copyholders only,

Hoskins v.
Robins.

(a) Literally, "rising up and
lying down" or maintained on
their premises. See *post*, Lecture III.

(b) 2 Wms. Saund. 320 ; 2
Keble, 758, 842 ; 1 Vent. 123,
163 ; *S. C.* nom. *Hopkins* v. *Robinson*, 1 Mod. 74 ; 2 Lev. 2.

and not by freeholders. The claim was, that within
the manor of Blisland, in the county of Cornwall, there
are, and from time whereof the memory of man runneth
not to the contrary, were divers customary tenements,
parcel of the said manor, and demised and demisable by
copy of Court roll of the said manor, at the will of the
lord, according to the custom of the said manor; and
that within the said manor there is, and from time
whereof, &c., there was, a custom that all the customary
tenants of the customary tenements of the said manor
have had, and have used and been accustomed to have,
sole and several pasture in the said places, in which the
cattle were seized, yearly and every year for the whole
year, at their will and pleasure, as belonging to their said
customary tenements. The plaintiff Hoskins alleged that
the said customary tenants had given him leave and
licence to put in his cattle into the land in question, for
which they were distrained by Robins. And then
Hoskins brought an action of replevin against Robins,
on the ground that the distress was illegal. Several
objections were taken to the custom which the plaintiff
set up, all of which were overruled by the Court. On one
point they doubted, viz. this, that the plaintiff ought to
have shown a licence by deed from the customary tenants
to put in his cattle, inasmuch as the right was one of an
incorporeal nature, and could not be granted without
deed. Judgment however was given for the plaintiff,
as, it being found that there was such a custom, the
Court would presume the licence to be such a good
licence as the law requires. You will observe in the
case of *Potter* v. *North* (c), the difference in pleading
with respect to the rights of the freeholders and copyholders. The freeholders prescribed as being seised in
fee, and claimed the right as having been exercised by
themselves and all those whose estate they had. As to
the copyholders, the right was properly laid as a custom

(c) *Ante*, p. 22.

within the manor of which they are tenants (*d*). You will also observe that in the case of *Hoskins* v. *Robins*, nothing was said about the cattle being Ievant and couchant upon the lands of the copyholders; because here the copyholders claimed all the herbage, and wholly excluded the lord; therefore it was not material whether all the grass was depastured by cattle Ievant or couchant, or any others; for there is no more mischief or wrong to the lord in one case than in the other.

It has however been held that if a claim for sole and exclusive pasture is confined to sheep and lambs, as appurtenant to a particular farm, there, the lord or owner of the soil, having the right to put in his cattle, other than sheep or lambs, no more sheep and lambs can be put on the land than such as are Ievant and couchant upon the farm in question. This was decided in the case of *Jones* v. *Richards* (*e*). This however is merely an instance of a peculiar right of common. *Sole pasture for sheep.* *Jones v. Richards.*

The case of *Hoskins* v. *Robins* was argued by Pollexfen for the defendant, and by Saunders for the plaintiff. Mr. Pollexfen afterwards became Lord Chief Justice of the Court of Common Pleas, and published a volume of reports. Although he lost the case of *Hoskins* v. *Robins*, yet he seems to have thought that his argument in that case was too good to be lost; and accordingly he inserted in his reports (*f*), a copy of the argument which he used on that occasion. This argument, inserted as it is in Pollexfen's Reports, seems more than once to have been mistaken for the judgment of the Court. The judgment of the Court however was against Pollexfen on all the points, except the last, which, as you will remember, related to the question as to whether a licence to use an incorporeal hereditament ought not to have been *Pollexfen's report of Hoskins v. Robins.*

(*d*) *Ante*, pp. 2, 17, 23. (*f*) Pages 13—23.
(*e*) 6 Adol. & Ell. 530.

made by deed. I mention this fact, because you will find, in some text books, the argument of Pollexfen in *Hoskins* v. *Robins*, cited in support of some of the propositions which he advocated; but which propositions were in fact all overruled by the judgment of the Court. I have also known the same mistake made by counsel in Court in the argument of cases of this kind. So much then for a several pasture : it is not any interest in the soil; if it were, it could not be claimed by prescription. It is a right which, as we have seen (*g*), may be claimed by the continuous exercise of it, either by a man and his ancestors, whose heir he is, or by a corporation and their predecessors, or by a person seised in fee and by all those whose estate he has.

Cox v. *Glue*.

I wish now to call your attention to two cases which seem to me strikingly to illustrate these propositions. The first is the case of *Cox* v. *Glue* (*h*). In that case the plaintiffs, Messrs. Cox, were seised in fee of a close called Siddals, in the parish of St. Peter, in the county of Derby; and the burgesses and freemen of the borough of Derby had the exclusive possession of the Siddals, from the 6th of July to the 14th of February in every year for the purpose of turning in their horses, cows, sheep and calves. It appeared that the county races had for some years past been run on this piece of land. And the action was an action of trespass against the defendant Glue for erecting a booth on the land, at the time of the races, in the month of August, 1845, which was during the time that the burgesses and freemen of the borough of Derby had the several pasture of the field. The question was as to the right of possession of the soil; and the Court held that the possession of the soil remained in Messrs. Cox, who were the owner of the fee simple in the land, and that such possession enabled them to bring an action of

(*g*) *Ante*, pp. 9, 12, 21.   (*h*) 5 C. B. 533:

trespass against Glue, in consequence of his having driven the posts of his booth some depth into the soil. The soil was theirs, and Glue, by driving the posts into the soil, injured the land of which they had possession, and rendered himself liable to an action of trespass. The Court at the same time held that the burgesses and freemen of the borough of Derby, had such a right of possession of the mere surface as would enable them to bring an action of trespass against persons who damaged the grass by walking or riding over it. It is evidently necessary for the protection of the rights of a person, whose cattle, and whose cattle alone, have a right of feed in a certain field, that he should be enabled to bring an action against any person who may interfere with his exclusive right to possess the field. And in his case an action of trespass is the proper action, because, so long as his cattle have a right to eat the grass, so long have he and his servants only the right to possess the field. The law therefore vests the possession of the mere surface in them; but that circumstance is consistent with the owner of the land still remaining in possession of the soil immediately under the surface, and of everything below it. Chief Justice Wilde in his judgment observes as follows:—"It cannot be denied that the possession of the surface may be in one person, and the possession of and the right to the subsoil in another. Such rights may be derived by grant, or may be inferred from a long and uniform course of enjoyment, which will be supposed to correspond with the interest created by some grant. It is found, in the present case, that the burgesses had a right, during a certain portion of the year, to take the herbage by the mouths of their sheep and cattle: and it is not found that they ever had any more extensive right. In order to give them that limited right, it was not necessary that the owner of the soil should part with more than the mere right of pos-

session, during the time of the exercise of such right of
pasturage.   If, then, it is competent to the owner of
the soil to grant such a limited interest, and to retain
all his rights in the subsoil, what are the proper
materials whence we are to infer what the grant was
but the course of enjoyment?   Here, all that the
burgesses and freemen were shown to have enjoyed
was, the pasturage from the 6th of July to the 14th of
February, and there was nothing in the case to lead to
the conclusion that the owner of the soil ever parted
with more than was necessary to the exercise of that
limited right.   There is no doubt that different strata
of the soil may be the subjects of separate and distinct
rights.   A difficulty might have arisen as to the depth
to which the right of the burgesses extended; but that
is excluded by the finding of the jury, which may be
assumed to mean that the holes made in the close were
dug to such a depth as to interfere with the subsoil, which the owners of the fee had not parted
with.   What then is there to prevent the latter from
maintaining an action for that trespass?   In the case
of mines no question could arise.   If the owner of the
fee retains the right to the mines and minerals, and
has also the possession, he may maintain an action for
any invasion of his rights.   Here the plaintiffs have
the fee; and they retain the possession of the subsoil.
They never granted anything more than the herbage,
leaving all their other rights just as complete and full
as if they had granted nothing.   It therefore seems to
me that the learned judge was right in saying that the
exclusive possession of the surface by the burgesses was
consistent with the right and possession of the subsoil
in the plaintiffs, and that taking the finding of the
jury to mean that the burgesses had the exclusive
possession of the surface at the time the alleged trespasses were committed, and that the exclusive possession of the subsoil was then in the plaintiffs, the

verdict was properly entered for the plaintiffs for the trespass done to the subsoil."

There was another action brought at the same time by the same plaintiffs against one Mousley. And the evidence against him was that he rode on horseback to the races, and that was the only actual trespass which he committed in the field. The Court held that this was not an interference with the soil of the plaintiffs, Messrs. Cox, but was merely an interference with the right of the burgesses to the exclusive possession, for the purpose of the exercise of their right of several pasture; and, as it was found that the right of possession and the actual possession of the mere surface were both out of the plaintiffs at the time of the committing of the alleged trespass by the defendant Mousley, which consisted merely of riding over the close, it was held that the verdict in this case was properly entered for the defendant. The jury in this case found that the burgesses and freemen had the exclusive right of possession from the 6th July to the 14th of February in every year. And one of the learned judges, Mr. Justice Vaughan Williams, remarked that he thought the finding of the jury must be taken to be equivalent to a finding in the burgesses of a right of *prima vestura* or *prima tonsura;* and with respect to the case of *Cox v. Mousley*, it was unnecessary to say what would have been the result if, instead of finding a right to *prima vestura* or *prima tonsura* in the corporation of Derby, the jury had found merely an exclusive right of pasturage. The other judges, however, do not seem to have taken this distinction. The right of *prima tonsura* clearly belonged to Messrs. Cox, for it was expressly found that they had "been in the habit of taking the forecrop and of having exclusive possession of the Siddals from the 14th of February to the 6th of July in each year." The learned judge no doubt referred to

the fact that the burgesses and freemen were found to
have had the *exclusive possession* during the remainder
of the year. And the ground of the learned judge's
doubt probably was, that as the owner of the sole right
of pasture could only take so much grass as the mouths
of his cattle could consume within a limited time, the
owner of the soil had such an interest remaining in the
grass as might warrant him in bringing an action of
trespass for treading it down. I apprehend, however,
that the owner of an exclusive right of pasturage would
be entitled to bring an action of trespass with respect
to the possession of the surface during the time limited
for the exercise of .his exclusive right, and that the
owner of the soil could not bring such an action, except
in respect of the soil, or of the trees or bushes, in which
the owner of an exclusive right of pasturage has no
interest.

Rights of
several herb-
age and pas-
ture, though
tenements,
are not cor-
poreal.

There are some cases (*i*) in which it has been held
that rights of several herbage and pasture are "tenements" within one of the old poor law acts. And these
decisions have been sometimes cited to prove that these
rights are corporeal hereditaments. But this is not so.
A right of common, which is clearly incorporeal, is
included by Lord Coke within the term "tenement" (*k*). And incorporeal hereditaments were long
ago held to be "tenements" within the act in question (*l*).

(*i*) *Rex* v. *Stoke Inhab.*, 2 T.
Rep. 451 ; *Rex* v. *Piddletrenthide
Inhab.*, 3 T. Rep. 772; *Rex* v. *Tol-
puddle Inhab.*, 4 T. Rep. 671.

(*k*) Co. Litt. 6 a.
(*l*) *Rex* v. *Hollington Inhab.*, 3
East, 113, 114.

LECTURE III.

I now proceed to consider the important subject of common of pasture. A right of common of pasture may be either appendant, appurtenant, or in gross. And first, of common appendant. Common appendant is said to be of common right, and it is defined to be the right, which every freehold tenant of a manor possesses, to depasture his commonable cattle, levant and couchant on his freehold tenement anciently arable, in the wastes of the manor. Commonable cattle are either beasts of the plough, such as horses and oxen, or animals which manure the land, as cows or sheep. Swine, goats, donkeys, and geese are none of them commonable animals; although by long usage a prescriptive right to put such animals on a common may, no doubt, be maintained. If a man claims common of pasture for all commonable cattle, and the evidence shows that he has turned on all the commonable cattle that he has, but that he has never kept any sheep, this has been held evidence to go to the jury of a right for all commonable cattle, including sheep (a).

The commonable beasts, which the tenant has a right to put upon the common are said to be *levant* and *couchant* on his land. Levant and couchant means rising up and lying down on the land; that is, in fact, being upon the land by night and by day; and it denotes the number of animals which the land, to which the right of common belongs, can maintain by its winter eatage or produce,—that is, during the season in which, the grass not growing, the right of common is of no

Margin notes: Common of pasture. Common appendant. Commonable cattle. Evidence of enjoyment. Levant and couchant.

(a) *Manifold* v. *Pennington*, 4 Barn. & Cress. 161.

benefit to the cattle. With regard to levancy and couchancy, it is held that the cattle need not necessarily be the property of the tenant or occupier of the land who puts them on. He may borrow the cattle of a stranger, if he pleases. Common appendant was no

Arable land. doubt originally enjoyed in respect only of arable land; for, in former days, the tenant lived on the produce of his farm; and, as a rule, a portion of every tenant's land was arable land. But although the land has been converted into pasture or wood, or even become waste, still the right of common appendant, once belonging to it, may continue to exist. And even the conversion of the land into garden and orchard will not destroy the right of common, if it is continued to be exercised in respect of the premises. This was decided in the case

Carr v. *Lambert.* of *Carr* v. *Lambert* (b). The action was an action of trespass for breaking and entering the plaintiff's land, and pulling up the plaintiff's posts and rails thereon. The defendants pleaded a right of common of pasture over the land, in which the alleged trespass was committed, for all cattle levant and couchant upon the premises of one of the defendants. And on the trial of the case the verdict was entered for the plaintiff, leave being reserved to the defendants to move to enter the verdict for them, if the Court should be of opinion, on the facts appearing in evidence at the trial, that there was evidence to support the right of common set up in the pleas. The facts as proved were that, at the time of the alleged trespass, John Woodall, one of the defendants, was possessed of a toftstead, consisting of a cottage and stable, with a garden and orchard, of the extent of about two acres. Evidence was given that, about fifty years before the commencement of the action, this had been planted with fruit trees, but that before that time it was swarth, and had been depastured with cattle. No direct evidence

(b) 3 Hurlst. & Colt. 499, affirmed L R., 1 Ex. 168.

was given as to the number of cattle which it had then
supported, or was capable of supporting ; and no point
was raised at the trial on either side as to the necessity
of proof on this subject. After a great deal of evidence
had been given, the learned judge suggested that the
fact seemed clear that the owners of the toftstead had,
as of right, turned the cattle, housed on the toftstead,
but not deriving their sustenance therefrom, on the *locus
in quo* for more than thirty years, and that the only
question was one of law, viz., whether such a right of
common was legal, or, in other words, if such cattle
were levant and couchant. Both sides assented to this
suggestion ; and no other question was required to be,
or was in fact, left to the jury ; and thereupon the
learned judge directed a verdict to be entered for the
plaintiff, and reserved leave to move to enter a verdict
for the defendants as above stated. A rule was afterwards obtained accordingly, and made absolute in the
Court of Exchequer ; and from this the plaintiff ap-
pealed. The Court of Exchequer Chamber however
affirmed the judgment of the Court below. The judgment was delivered by Mr. Justice Willes. His judgment was as follows :—" In this case, which was argued
before us yesterday, and in which we postponed our
judgment, we are of opinion that the judgment of the
Court of Exchequer is right and ought to be affirmed.
The main point of my brother Hayes's argument was
this : he insisted that the character of the dominant
tenement had been so altered from its character of
pasture, by means of a building being placed upon it,
and the rest turned into orchard ground, that thirty
years' user of common by cattle housed upon, but not
fed off it, was not evidence of any right which could in
point of law exist. His argument had considerable
force with reference to a total change of character ; but
much less force can be allowed to it with reference to
the facts of the present case. If he could on the facts

have established the conclusion, that the character of the dominant tenement was so altered that it could not be applied to the purpose of producing fruits, on which to keep cattle,—if, for instance, a town of considerable extent had been built upon the land and its neighbourhood, or if it were turned into a reservoir, as was suggested in the argument, it might be a question whether the right of common were not extinguished or suspended. We do not express any opinion on that question because, on the facts stated, it seems that the toftstead, which was the dominant tenement, consisted of a cottage and a stable, with a garden and orchard of two acres. It had therefore land in a state in which it might have been laid down for pasture, or for meadow, or cultivated so as to produce artificial plants and roots for the support of cattle. This is, therefore, not the case of a dominant tenement so changed in character as that cattle might not be fed off its produce. If, then, my brother Hayes had succeeded in satisfying us, that the expression of levancy and couchancy is not a mere measure of the capacity of the land to keep cattle out of artificial or natural produce, grown within its limits, but that it is further necessary to show that it could, in its actual state, produce such food, he would still not have succeeded in showing facts negativing the capacity of the land to do this; for the evidence is quite consistent with the following state of facts—land in a state of cultivation suitable for the support of cattle, afterwards in part built upon, and the rest cultivated, not with a view to the support of cattle, but in a state in which it might easily be turned to that purpose. There is no authority, either in the class of cases relating to the abandonment or loss, or to the suspension of rights, by the destruction, absolute or temporary, of the necessary measure of enjoyment, which would justify us in holding that a right, once created and existing, was, under these circumstances, destroyed by the act of the proprietor. The acts of use, which have been proved, ought to be referred to a legal origin, if they are consistent with it, rather than treated as a series of trespasses; and their inconsistency with legal right is not to be assumed, unless they could not be attached to a legal origin, or the right to which they were attached has been since extinguished or suspended. Our judgment proceeds on this proposition, that facts appear which show their referribility to a legal origin; and that it has not been shown that the right was suspended or extinguished; and whoever has heard cases of this nature tried will think that the direction usually given on their trial is in accordance with our present decision. That direction refers to levancy and couchancy rather as the measure of capacity of the land, than as a condition to be actually and literally complied with, by the cattle lying down and getting up, or by their being fed off the land. The judgment of the Court of Exchequer is therefore affirmed."

It appears, therefore, that levancy and couchancy is rather the measure of the capacity of the land, than a condition to be actually and literally complied with, by the actual lying down and getting up of the cattle, or by their being fed off the land. There can, however, be no right of common in respect of a house, which has no homestead connected with it, in which cattle may be housed. And when a right of common is claimed in respect of a messuage, it is presumed that that messuage *Messuage.* has annexed to it some outbuilding in which the cattle may be housed; otherwise there can be no right of common in respect of the messuage. And I apprehend *Land built over.* that if land be built over in such a way, as that no cattle can possibly be kept there, any right of common of pasture which formerly belonged to the land, must be considered as having been extinguished.

Common appendant is of common right.

Earl Dunraven v. Llewellyn.

Explained by Sir R. Palmer.

I observed that common appendant is of common right. There is, however, a case decided by the Court of Exchequer Chamber, in which this view was denied. I allude to the case of *Earl Dunraven* v. *Llewellyn* (c). I have, in Appendix (C.) to my Principles of the Law of Real Property (d), stated the reasons which induce me respectfully to differ from the view of the Court in that case. The decision in the case itself is thus explained by Sir Roundell Palmer, now Lord Selborne, in his argument in the case of *Warrick* v. *Queen's College, Oxford* (e). He remarks that that case was not the case of a bill of peace, nor was the question there between the lord of a manor and his tenants; but it was between the lord and a stranger, the lord trying to establish his right by means of the declaration of parties in the same interest as himself; and all that was decided was, that the matter in dispute was not such a matter of public reputation as to allow such declarations to be admitted in evidence. The case was this. The plaintiff, Lord Dunraven, brought an action against the defendant for breaking and entering the plaintiff's close, claiming the close in question as part of the wastes of the manor of Ogmore, of which the plaintiff was lord. The plaintiff offered no evidence of any exercise of rights by the lord, or any of the tenants of the manor, over the close within the period of living memory; but he tendered evidence of what had been said by certain deceased tenants of the manor, who were all acquainted with the common and waste and its neighbourhood, and who had exercised and enjoyed rights of common over the waste. These tenants had declared that the close in question was part of the common and waste of the manor. This evidence was rejected, and the Court held that the rejection was right. They agreed that the want of proof of actual

(c) 15 Q. B. 791.   (e) L. R., 10 Eq. 105, 119.
(d) Page 489, 12th ed.

user affected only the value of the evidence; but the decision was that the evidence under the circumstances was inadmissible. In support of this opinion, however, the Court seems to have thought it necessary to deny, or at any rate to explain away, the doctrine of the books, that every tenant of a manor has, of common right, a right of common appendant in the lord's wastes. I venture to think that it was unnecessary to the conclusion at which the Court arrived to deny this doctrine.

We now come to consider the question of the historical origin of the right of common appendant; and the opinions which have been long entertained on this subject, founded as they are upon the authority of Lord Coke, have been in modern times much shaken by the investigations of modern historians, particularly by Mr. Kemble, Sir Henry Maine and other writers. The explanation of the matter given by Lord Coke is to be found in *Tyrringham's case* (*f*). Lord Coke says, "The beginning of common appendant by the ancient law was in such manner, when a lord enfeoffed another of arable land to hold of him in socage, that is, *per servicium socæ*, as every such tenure at the beginning (as Littleton saith) was that the feoffee *ad manutenendum servicium socæ*, should have common in the lord's wastes for his necessary cattle, which ploughed and manured his land, and that for two reasons—first because it was, as it was then held, *tacitè* implied in the feoffment; for the feoffee could not plough and manure his land without cattle, and they could not be kept without pasture; *per consequens* the feoffee should have, as a thing necessary and incident, common in the lord's wastes and land; and that appears by the ancient books in the time of Edward the First, and by the rehearsal of the statute of Merton, Chapter IV. The second reason was for the maintenance and advancement of tillage, which is much

Origin of common appendant.

Tyrringham's case.

(*f*) 4 Rep. 38.

respected and favoured in law ; so that such common appendant is of common right and commences by operation of law, and in favour of tillage ; and therefore it is not necessary to prescribe therein, as it is held in 4th of Henry VI. and 22nd of Henry VI., as it would be if it was against common right ; but it is only appendant to ancient land arable, hide and gain, and only for cattle, viz., horses and oxen to plough his land, and cows and sheep to manure his land, and for the bettering and advancement of tillage."

This explanation refers common appendant to the original grants by lords of manors to their tenants ; and what is now denied is that it is historically true. I apprehend that in some cases it certainly is historically true that such grants have been made, at the time when the lord of the manor enfeoffed another of lands to hold of himself. An instance of such a grant is to be found in Madox's Formulare Anglicanum (*g*). I have noticed it in the Appendix (C.) to my Principles of the Law of Real Property (*h*). And it is referred to by Lord Hatherley in his judgment in the case of *Warrick* v. *Queen's College, Oxford* (*i*). His lordship observed (*k*) as follows :—" The argument which was pressed upon me very much by Mr. Manisty, fortified by the case of *Earl Dunraven* v. *Llewellyn*, was that a number of freeholders could not join together as plaintiff and assert a common right, for they had no such right at all. The persons who claim by a custom prevailing over the whole district, all come under one uniform custom ; but persons claiming by prescription necessarily claim by grant ; and how can we tell what would appear in each grant ? Each grant may have a separate right connected with it ; nor could hearsay evidence be admitted, on the very ground that this was not a common right, but a

(*g*) No. 303, p. 184. See also *ante*, p. 8.

(*h*) Page 497, 12th ed.

(*i*) L. R., 6 Ch. 725, 726.

(*k*) Page 725.

case of each single person claiming by prescription. I think there is very considerable fallacy in those arguments." And then, after referring to the case of *Powell* v. *Earl Powis* (*l*), which was before the Chief Baron Alexander, his Lordship goes on, " What is there to prevent these persons who claim by prescription from having had a grant common to all, with perhaps different privileges contained in their respective grants ? It is curious enough that in a valuable note on the case of *Earl of Dunraven* v. *Llewellyn*, made by Mr. J. Williams, a grant in Wales is mentioned by which a person granted land to certain tenants, with all the uses, privileges and advantages which had been granted to other tenants. This is an instance of what may be possible and legal." The land granted does not appear to have been in Wales, but that is immaterial.

But that, in a great number of cases, the origin of common appendant was not manorial, is I think equally true. I believe that, in many, if not in most, cases, the origin of common appendant is to be traced to the vill, Vills. town or township, which is aptly styled by Canon Stubbs in his Constitutional History of England (*m*) as the unit of the constitutional machinery, the simplest form of social organization. In the valuable Lectures given by Sir Henry Maine on Village Communities Sir H. Maine you will see this subject discussed at large. The origin on Village Communities. of common appendant is there traced to the original unit of a village community, and to the system of village communities which has prevailed, not only in England, but in Prussia and Russia, and, as Sir Henry Maine has shown, also in India, among nations of the Aryan stock, in such a manner as strongly to confirm the identity of race already proved by similarity of language.

Now there are two things which strongly support

(*l*) 1 You. & Jerv. 159.　　　(*m*) Vol. 1, p. 82.

this view, viz. the importance which has always been
attached by the law of England to the vill or township,
and also the system of cultivation of common fields, as
distinguished from waste or common pasture land, which
so extensively prevailed in England until the numerous
Enclosure Acts of the last and present century, in so
Importance of many places, swept it away.   And first, with regard to
vills. a vill or township.   Although the Ecclesiastical division
into parishes is now, as we all know, well established,
still the importance of the vill or township is seen in
this:—If a man is described, say as John Freeman of
Fairfield, this description in law still implies that John
Freeman lives in the vill or township of Fairfield; and
if it should happen that the vill of Fairfield and the
parish of Fairfield are not co-extensive, then the word
Fairfield is in law applied to the vill of Fairfield, and
not to the parish of Fairfield; although by intendment
of law, every parish is a vill, unless it be shown to the
The Statute contrary.   There is in an old statute called the Statute
of Additions. of Additions (*n*), upon which Lord Coke comments in
his second Institute (*o*).   This statute shows the preference which the law gives to vills or towns over parishes.
It ordains that, in personal actions, additions shall be
made to the name of the defendants of their estate or
degree or mystery, and of the towns or hamlets, or places
and counties, of the which they were or be, or in which
they be or were conversant.   On this Lord Coke
remarks (*p*), that the addition of the parish, if there be
two or more towns within it, is not good;   but, if there
be one town, the addition of the parish is good within
the statute, and it shall not be intended, if it be not
pleaded, that there be more towns than one in the
parish.

The law on this subject is curiously illustrated by

(*n*) Stat. 1 Hen. V. c. 5.   (*p*) Page 669.
(*o*) Page 665.

a case decided by Lord Eldon in the year 1819, viz.
Gibson v. *Clarke* (*q*). In that case there was a parish or *Gibson* v.
chapelry of Belford in the county of Northumberland, *Clarke.*
which contained within it the vill or town of Belford,
together with several other hamlets, villages or townships. A common recovery (*r*) had been suffered of
one-third of the tithes in the parish of Belford; but the
deed, which made the tenant to the præcipe, for the
purpose of suffering the recovery, conveyed only one-
third of the tithes of the village of Belford; and Lord
Eldon held that, if there be a tenant of the præcipe of
a third part of the tithes of the vill, and the recovery
was suffered of a third of the tithes of the parish, the
tithes of the lands that were in both the vill and parish
would pass, but those in the parish and not in the vill
would not pass. This is in accordance with an old
decision of *Stork* v. *Fox* (*s*). In this case it appeared *Stork* v. *Fox.*
that there were two vills, viz. Walton and Street, both
in the parish of Street. A fine was levied of lands in
Street; and the question was, whether the lands in the
vill of Walton, and which were in the parish of Street,
passed by that fine. And it was adjudged they could
not pass, Street being a distinct vill by itself, and
Walton being a distinct vill by itself. Although Street
the parish comprehends both, yet, in the fine, the lands
in Walton shall not be said to be comprised, unless
Walton had been a hamlet of Street, and that the fine
had been levied of lands in the parish of Street, and
then all had well passed.

It is laid down by Lord Coke (*t*) that every town or *A vill has or*
vill either has, or in time past had, a church and cele- *had a church.*
bration of divine service, sacraments and burials; and

(*q*) 1 Jac. & W. 159. (*s*) Cro. Jac. 120.
(*r*) See Lectures on the Seisin (*t*) Co. Litt. 115 b.
of the Freehold, pp. 157 *et seq.*

he states that there are in England and Wales 8,803 towns or vills, or thereabouts. And Sir Henry Spelman has been to the pains of making an alphabetical list of the vills in England in his work entitled Villare Anglicum, or a View of the Towns of England, collected by the appointment of Sir Henry Spelman, Knight.

A constable.
Every vill also had a constable, otherwise it was said to be but a hamlet.

Blackstone's account of vills.
The account which Blackstone gives of vills, towns, or townships in his well-known Commentaries, places the subject in a clear light. He says (*u*) : " Tithings, towns, or vills are of the same signification in law; and are said to have had, each of them, originally a church and celebration of divine service, sacraments, and burials: though that seems to be rather an ecclesiastical than a civil distinction. The word town or vill is indeed, by the alteration of times and language, now become a generical term, comprehending under it the several species of cities, boroughs, and common towns. A city is a town incorporated, which is or hath been the see of a bishop: and though the bishoprick be dissolved, as at Westminster, yet still it remaineth a city. A borough is now understood to be a town, either corporate or not, that sendeth burgesses to parliament. Other towns there are, to the number, Sir Edward Coke says, of 8,803, which are neither cities nor boroughs, some of which have the privileges of markets, and others not, but both are equally towns in law. To several of these towns there are small appendages be-

Hamlets.
longing, called hamlets, which are taken notice of in the Statute of Exeter, which makes frequent mention of entire vills, demi-vills, and hamlets. Entire vills Sir Henry Spelman conjectures to have consisted of ten freemen or frank pledges, demi-vills of five, and hamlets

(*u*) Vol. 1, p. 115.

of less than five. These little collections of houses are
sometimes under the same administration as the town
itself, sometimes governed by separate officers, in which
last case, they are to some purposes in law looked upon
as distinct townships. These towns, as was before
hinted, contained each originally but one parish and
one tithing, though many of them now, by the increase
of inhabitants, are divided into several parishes and
tithings; and sometimes, where there is but one parish,
·there are two or more vills or tithings."

LECTURE IV.

Common of pasture belonging to vills.

I NOW come to mention the numerous scattered indications which exist in our law books of common of pasture having in the first place belonged rather to vills or townships than to manors. They occur in the old forms of writs, in the old abridgments, in the year books, in the old text writers, including Coke himself, in the reports of decided cases, and in some acts of parliament. Some of these indications are very curious. If

Bracton's form of writ of novel disseisin.

we go back to the time of Bracton, who wrote in the reign of Henry III. (a), we shall find that the form of writ, which he gives as proper to be used by a person who has been disseised of his right of common, does not refer to the land, in respect of which the right of common is claimed, as being held of any manor, nor does it refer to the land, over which the right of common is claimed, as waste land of any manor. On the contrary the writ is as follows: "The King to the sheriff, greeting: A. complains to us that B. unjustly and without judgment disseised him of his common of pasture in such a vill, which belongs to his free tenement in the same vill, or in another vill." And the form of writ for the same purpose given in the second volume of

Form of writ of novel disseisin in Fitzherbert's *Natura Brevium.*

Fitzherbert's *Natura Brevium* (b) is to the same effect: "The King to the sheriff, &c.: A. hath complained unto us that B. unjustly, &c. hath disseised him of his common of pasture in N., which belonged to his freehold *in the same town, or in another town.*" Again,

Bracton's form of writ of admeasure-

in describing the old writ of admeasurement of pasture, which lay betwixt commoners who had common

(a) Bracton, lib. 4, c. 38, par. 6, p. 224.   (b) Page 179.

appendant to their freeholds, Bracton (c) gives this ment of pasture. form: "The King to the sheriff, greeting: Such a one complains to us that such a one unjustly surcharged his common of pasture *in such a vill*, so that he has in it more cattle and sheep than he ought to have, and than belonged to him to have; and therefore we command you that justly and without delay you cause that pasture to be measured, so that the said such a one shall not have in it more cattle and sheep than he ought to have, and than belonged to him according to his free tenement, which he has *in such a vill;* and that the said such a one have in that pasture so many cattle and sheep as he ought to have, and as belonged to him to have, and no more." The form given in Fitzherbert's *Natura Brevium* (d) is to the same effect.

In a note to Fitzherbert's *Natura Brevium* (e) it is Explanation of note to Fitzherbert's *Natura Brevium*. stated that if the defendant has common appendant to his freehold in three vills, it may be admeasured for the lands in one of the vills. This is a very vague statement, but on reference to the authority cited the meaning becomes clearer. It was the freehold that was in the three vills, and the common was over a large waste common to all the vills. Reference is made to Fitzherbert's Abridgment, tit. Admeasurement (f). It appears, on referring to the Abridgment, that a writ of admeasurement was brought against the prior of M., (wherever that place was,) and it was stated that the moor, in which the admeasurement was sought, was a great moor belonging to several vills, and that the prior had lands in B., to which common is appurtenant, and in two other vills named in the writ. But the plaintiff by the writ only wished to prevent the surcharge of the common of pasture by

(c) Book 4, c. 39, par. 2, p. 229.

(d) Vol. 2, p. 125.

(e) Vol. 1, p. 125.

(f) Page 15, par. 15.

the prior in respect of his lands in the same vill in which the plaintiff had lands. And it appears to have been holden that a writ of admeasurement would lie, in that case, with respect to the defendant's lands in the vill in which the plaintiff's lands were situate, although the defendant had lands in two other vills which commoned on the same waste. I mention this case because in the case of *Hollingshead* v. *Walton* (*g*) the passage in the note of Fitzherbert's *Natura Brevium* was cited as àpropos to the case there, which was a claim by the owner of lands in one township to common over two distinct wastes,—one within the township in which his lands lay, and the other in another township. It seems to have been thought that in the case in Fitzherbert the defendant's land was in one vill only, and that he had common of pasture over lands in three vills. And Mr. Justice Lawrence (*h*), thinking that this was the meaning of the passage, endeavoured to explain it, by suggesting that it might be taken that the freeholder claimed common appendant in the three vills under the same lord, and it might happen that other tenants of the lord had only common in one of the vills, in which case, if he, who had common in all three, turned on all his cattle in one of them, it would prejudice those whose right of common was confined to that one, and they might sue out their writ of admeasurement to apportion the number of his commonable cattle in that one vill. We have seen however that the case put in the Abridgment is not the case of a freeholder, in respect of one tenement claiming common in three vills ; but the case of a freeholder having lands in three vills, all of which commoned in the same large moor. What was held was, that the fact of his having lands in two other vills, in respect of which he might put cattle on the moor, did not prevent a writ of admeasurement lying

Hollingshead v. Walton.

(*g*) 7 East, 490, 492.   (*h*) Page 492.

against him at the suit of the owner of lands in one
of the vills, in which he the defendant had lands, in
respect of which he put on more cattle than he ought.
I do not know that this correction is very material, and
I cite the case rather with a view to showing how, in
ancient times, commons are spoken of, rather as be- Commons be-
longing to
vills.
longing to vills, than as belonging to the tenants of
manors. Undoubtedly the tenants of manors had
rights of common appendant; but the modern theory
is, and it seems to me that ancient documents support
it, that in the first instance there generally existed a
vill or township; and subsequently the lordship of that
vill or township, including the soil of the waste lands,
was granted to some person, who thereby became the
lord of the manor, the vill or township being, as it so
frequently is, co-extensive with the manor, and also
with the parish.

Commons belonging to townships are occasionally Mention in
Year Books of
commons of
vills.
mentioned in the Year Books. Thus, in the Year Book
11 Henry VII. (*i*), it is laid down, that a vill may make
bye-laws between themselves, as that every one, who
puts on his beast in such a common, shall pay ten
shillings. This is good, and shall bind them, but not
a stranger. So, in the Year Book 21 Henry VII (*k*),
it is laid down, that a vill may make a bye-law between
themselves, that he, who puts on his beast in the common before such a day, shall forfeit such a sum. This
is good, and shall bind them, but it cannot bind a
stranger. So the commons of a town are spoken of in Commons of
a town in
Corbet's case.
Sir Miles Corbet's case (*l*). It was there resolved that,
if the commons of the town of A. and of the town of
B. are adjoining, and that one ought to have common
with the other by reason of vicinage, and in the town
of A. there are 50 acres of common, and in the town
of B. there are 100 acres of common, in that case the

(*i*) Page 14 a.   (*k*) Page 40 b.   (*l*) 7 Rep. 5 b.

inhabitants of the town of A. cannot put more cattle into their common of 50 acres than it will feed, without any respect to the common within the town of B., *nec è converso.* Again, in Viner's Abridgment.(*m*) several instances are given of commons belonging to vills. Thus it is said of common by reason of vicinage (*n*), that one cannot put his beasts into the land of another; for there those of the other vill may distrain them damage feasant, or shall have action of trespass; but they shall put them in their own fields, and if they stray into the fields of the other vill, they ought to suffer them. Again (*o*), a great field lies between two adjoining vills, and one that has land in the one vill has common there with the tenants of the other vill. The question was, if he be to make title to this common, whether he shall make it as to common appendant, or by reason of vicinage. And the Court held that this was common by reason of vicinage. Lord Chief Baron Comyns in his Digest (*p*) thus describes common by reason of vicinage : " Common *pur cause de vicinage* is when two or more *towns* have common in the fields within their *towns*, which are open to the fields of the neighbouring *towns*, and the cattle, put to use their common there, escape into the fields of the neighbouring *towns*, and *è contra.* And therefore this common is but an excuse for a trespass." Blackstone also, in his Commentaries, speaks of common of towns in like manner. In Vol. 2, Chap. 3 (*q*), he says : " Common because of vicinage or neighbourhood is where the inhabitants of *two townships*, which lie contiguous to each other, have usually intercommoned with one another: the beasts of the one straying mutually into the other's fields without any molestation from either. This is indeed only a permissive right, intended to excuse what

Commons of vills in Viner's Abridgment.

Commons of towns in Comyns' Digest.

Commons of towns spoken of by Blackstone.

(*m*) Title Common (K), par. 9 to 14.

(*n*) Par. 10.

(*o*) Par. 12.

(*p*) Tit. Common (E).

(*q*) Page 33.

in strictness is a trespass in both, and to prevent a multiplicity of suits ; and therefore either *township* may enclose and bar out the other, though they have intercommoned time out of mind. Neither hath any person of *one town* a right to put his beasts originally into the other's common : but if they escape, and stray thither of themselves, the law winks at the trespass." Here commons belonging to towns are spoken of as well known to the law. So Lord Coke himself in his Commentary on Littleton (r), states, that an *upland town* may allege a custom to have a way to their church, or to make byelaws for the reparation of the church, *the well ordering of the commons*, and such like things. Here the commons are spoken of generally as the commons of the town ; and the town, he says, may make bye-laws for the ordering of the commons. Unless the commons belonged to the town, the town surely could not make bye-laws with respect to such commons.

Commons of a town spoken of by Lord Coke.

Claims of common in respect of vills or townships sometimes occur in the different law reports. Thus in the case of *Ellard* v. *Hill* (s) there is an instance of a claim of common for every yardland within a vill. A yardland is a Saxon term, and comprises a number of acres, which varies in almost every place. What the exact origin of the term is I do not know. However this case was an action of replevin of a cow, which had been distrained ; and issue was joined on a prescription that every yardland within such a vill ought to have common, in such a place, for twelve cows ; and for a quarter yard for three cows, and for half a quarter, one cow and a half. And after verdict, it was moved, in arrest of judgment, that one cannot prescribe to have common for half a cow ; but it was answered, and so resolved by the Court, that this, being found by the Court, shall be intended to be as follows—viz., half a year, or that

Ellard v. Hill, claims of common in respect of a vill.

(r) Co. Litt. 110 b.   (s) Siderfin, 226.

W.P.   E

Pate v. *Brownlow*, common of vills.

two shall join, when each one of them has half a cow. Again there is in Keble's Reports (*t*) a case of *Pate* v. *Brownlow* as follows. " In ejectment for a marsh the plaintiff claimed as parcel of the manor of Cressy Hall, the defendant as parcel of the manor of Newbery in Surflet in the county of Lincoln; but it appeared to be a marsh in common to *two vills* between them and their tenants by prescription for their sheep, being salt."

Lord of a vill. Mentioned in the Year Books.

In some of the old books the lord of a vill is spoken of as a personage known to the law. Thus, in the Year Book, 21 Hen. VII. 20, it is said: " If the tenants abiding in a certain vill wish to establish for law that every one of them who holds so many lands should yearly pay to the church of the same vill a certain sum, and for every default 20s. forfeiture *to the lord of the same vill*, although this constitution has been used from time immemorial, yet this custom is invalid, because on account of the non-payment of the said sum to the church the lord sustains no damage, because it follows

Mentioned in Viner's Abridgment.

in reason that by it he had no gain." So it is laid down in Viner's Abridgment (*u*), that if there be a lord of a vill, and another has a leet (*x*),—that is, a Court leet,—but no land beside the leet, and he claims, by cause of the leet, to be lord of the waste of the said vill by prescription, this is a void prescription. Again,

Lord of the town mentioned by Fitzherbert.

in the second volume of Fitzherbert's *Natura Brevium* (*y*), it is said that none shall claim common by vicinage but the lord who hath the possession of the town—meaning, I apprehend, that it was the lord who was the immediate lord of the town, which had become his manor, who alone could claim common by vicinage; but that the superior lord, of whom he may have held his manor, and who had therefore only an incorporeal seignory,

(*t*) Vol. 1, p. 876.

(*u*) Title Prescription, K. 3.

(*x*) See Lectures on the Seisin of the Freehold, p. 16.

(*y*) Page 180.

could not claim any common by vicinage. Here, again,
you have the lord in possession of the town mentioned,
the town being to all intents and purposes the same
thing as a vill.

I have very little doubt but that further research
would bring to light other instances of common of
pasture being spoken of as attached to vills or towns as
such. And those which I have been able to discover
appear to me to raise a very strong presumption that, *Early origin of common appendant.*
in most cases, the right of common of pasture, ap-
pendant of common right to arable lands, was of very
early origin, and commenced in the times when the
different families or communities which composed the
vills or towns settled in their respective places of habitation, cultivated the arable lands, divided the good
pasture amongst themselves, and turned their cattle on
the adjoining wastes. The waste in the first instance
would seem to have been unappropriated, belonging in
fact to nobody in particular. But in process of time,
as land became more valuable, each vill or township
appears to have been confined to the commons or waste
grounds within the boundaries of its own territory,
except in cases where the tenants of the land of the vill
may have had rights of common over any adjoining
park or forest. In fact, if the origin of rights of
common was, as is supposed, the placing by ancient
vills or communities of their cattle on the adjoining
waste lands, we shall probably find that, in places
which have been kept waste for the purpose of sporting,
rights of townships or communities to common on such *Rights of township to*
wastes would be found to exist. And such in truth is *common in*
the case. There is an old statute of Henry VIII. in *parks and forests.*
which common is spoken of as belonging to a vill or
township, viz., stat. 27 Hen. VIII. chap. 6. The act *Stat. 27 Hen. VIII. c. 6,*
is concerning the breed of horses, and it provides that *speaks of*
the owners of parks are to keep a certain quantity of *common of townships.*

E 2

mares, according to the size of the parks, each of them of the height of 13 hands at the least—a curious enactment, showing incidentally that in all probability at that time, horses, as well as other cattle, were much smaller than they are at present. And the 5th section provides that the act shall not extend to charge the lords, owner or owners of any park or parks, or grounds inclosed, with the finding of any mares, the herbage of which park is common to the tenants and inhabitants (z) of the *township* next adjoining to the same park ; thus speaking of the tenants and inhabitants of a *township* as having a right of common within a park adjoining. I

Forest of Bernewood.

have also been furnished with a note of an old case in the Exchequer (a), in which, on the disafforesting of the forest of Bernewood, in the county of Bucks, three towns, namely, Brill, Boarstall and Oakley were held entitled to rights of common of pasture throughout the forest.

Again, we shall find rights of common exercised by parishes, (which, as you will remember, are presumed to be co-extensive with vills or townships, unless the contrary is shown (b),) over part of the wastes of the Great Forest of Essex, one portion of which was called

Rights of common of parishes in Hainault Forest.

by the name of Hainault Forest. The case *In the matter of the Hainault Forest Act*, 1858 (c), shows this to have been the case. An Act of Parliament was passed for disafforesting the forest of Hainault. The forest of Hainault comprised certain open commonable lands, called The King's Forest or King's Woods, in the parishes of Barking and Dagenham, in the county of Essex, containing 2,842 acres, and another tract of waste in other parishes. The rest of the forest consisted of inclosed lands in the several parishes of

---

(z) See *ante*, p. 15.   (b) *Ante*, p. 40.
(a) *Att.-Gen.* v. *Dynham and*   (c) 9 C. B., N. S. 648.
others, Exch. 7 Nov. 1632, MS.

Barking, Dagenham, Stapleford Abbotts, Lambourne
and Chigwell. The evidence as to the rights of common of the commoners in these five parishes consisted
of acts of user for more than sixty years previously
to and down to the time of disafforestation, and was to
this effect :—That a reeve was appointed for each of the
five parishes whose duty it was to mark the cattle of
the persons entitled to common in their respective
parishes; that the marking usually took place near the
boundary of the King's Forest or King's Woods, and
within the parish to which the cattle so marked belonged ; that the cattle were generally turned out at
the spot where they were marked, and then went where
they pleased. The Commissioner by his Award found
that the rights of common which were exercisable in
respect of those parts or districts of the several parishes
above mentioned which lay within the boundaries of
the said forest, were exercised exclusively over the
commons or commonable land situate within such last-
mentioned parishes, including the King's Forest or
King's Woods; and that the last-mentioned rights of
common or any of them were not limited to the commons in the particular parish, district or place, in which
were situate the lands, in respect of which the said
rights are claimed, but that the said rights claimed for
each of the last-mentioned parishes, districts or places
extend indiscriminately and generally over all the commons or commonable land in each and every of the
same parishes, districts or places, including the King's
Forest or King's Woods. It was held upon a case
stated for the opinion of the Court, that the decision of
the Commissioner was warranted by the evidence, and
that the matter was within his jurisdiction. Here you
observe that each parish represented a distinct township
or community, had a reeve, who marked with a distinct
mark the cattle belonging to his own parish or township, and that those cattle so marked had a right of

common over the whole of the district mentioned, including such parts of the district as lay within the boundaries of the other parishes. I take this to be an instance of what was originally and commonly the ancient right of commoning, preserved up to modern times by reason of the royal right of chase having prevented the wastes from being inclosed. The same thing occurred in the recent Epping Forest case, which related to the other and remaining part of the great Forest of Essex, or Waltham Forest ; part of which was called Hainault Forest, and was inclosed by Act of Parliament, and the remainder was called Epping Forest. In the Epping Forest case, the Commissioners of Sewers of the City of London were seised in fee of lands within the forest, and they filed a bill on behalf of themselves and the owners and occupiers of lands in the forest against the lords of the several manors within the forest, who were seised in fee of the waste grounds, claiming to be entitled, in right of and as appurtenant to their several lands and tenements, to common of pasture for cattle levant and couchant on their respective tenements over all the waste lands of the forest. The case is reported as *The Commissioners of Sewers* v. G*lasse* (d). Now the evidence in that case was, in respect of the marking of the cattle, very much the same as in the Hainault Forest case. It appeared that the cattle, before being put upon the waste, were marked by the reeve of the parish, in which the lands were, in respect of which the cattle were put on ; and that each parish had a distinct mark of its own. The mark was called the forest mark ; and it was the duty of the reeve of each parish to mark all the beasts that were brought to him from any part of the parish to which he belonged ; and the forest mark was then a passport to the whole forest. Here, again, you have common rights over wastes exercised by parishes, repre-

Right of common of pasture in Epping Forest.

Commissioners of Sewers v. Glasse.

(d) L. R., 19 Eq. 134.

Parish of
Waltham Holy Cross

Parish of
Woking

Parish of
Theydon Bois

Parish of
Chingford

Parish of
Chigwell

Parish of
Barking

Parish of
Dagenham

Parish of
Woodford

Parish of
Leyton

Parish of
Harrow

Parish of
Wanstead

Parish of
Stanford Rivers

senting vills or communities, putting their cattle on to any part of the forest or waste, amidst which the community was situate. The contest in this case was, whether the right of common was not a manorial right, and as such confined to the wastes or commons within the boundaries of each several manor. But it was held that it was not a manorial right, but a forestal right. The fact of the separate marking by each separate parish with a different mark does not very clearly appear in the report of the case; but it was distinctly in evidence in the case; and pictures of most of the marks were given in evidence (e). In this case the claim of the commoners was proved very much by ancient documents, and entries at the old courts of the forest; but the rights proved remarkably corresponded with the rights in the Hainault Forest case, which were proved only by acts of user.

There is an old statute of the reign of Henry VIII. (f), intituled "An Act for the abuses of the forests of Wales," in which the marking by the foresters of stray cattle *with the mark of their forest*, and seizing them as forfeited to their own use, are spoken of as unlawful customs. And the following extract from a treatise on Surveying by Fitzherbert, written in the year 1539 (g), shows how usual the right of vills to

Forest marks mentioned in stat. of Hen. VIII.

(e) I am enabled by the kindness of Mr. Hunter, one of the solicitors in the cause, to present the reader with copies of the marks used by most of the parishes. See the plate annexed. It was proved in the cause that the mark for Roydon hamlet (the rest of the parish of Roydon being outside the forest) was a C and a crown, that the mark of Loughton parish was F and a crown, that the mark of Lambourne parish was I and a crown. With regard to the parish of Navestock, a bar of iron with three prongs representing a crown and parallel to the top of the P had been broken off. The mark of the Manor of West Ham was a modern mark. It will be seen that the marks were rude representations of a crown with a distinctive letter of the alphabet under it.

(f) Stat. 27 Hen. VIII. c. 7.

(g) Fitzherbert on Surveying, c. 15.

Forest marks of townships and hamlets mentioned by Fitzherbert. have common of pasture in open wastes then was; and how the cattle of each vill were usually branded with a distinct mark:—"And there me semeth the surveyor may syt with the iustices of the forestes for one thing specially, and that is this, that no townshyppe, nor hamell [hamlet] entercomen within the forestes, chases, wastes, hethes, moors, and such other great commens, but all such that of ryghte ought to have comen within the same. Wherefore it wolde be ordneyned that every townshyppe and hamell, that ought to have any such comen in any forestes, chases, wastes, moores, heythes, and such other great comens, where duers townshypps and hamels entercommon togyther, every township and hamell ought to have a dyuers brennynge yron [burning iron]; and every beaste, horse, mare and colte, that is put upon the comen, ought to be brenned in some part of his body with the said yron, and then shall euery beaste be knowen, of what townshyppe he is. And that were a great redyness to the kepers, and also a great sauegarde for stealynge of the cattle. And than may the keepers, régarders, goysters, and other officers of such forestes and chases, have perfytte knowledge what townshyppe the cattel is of. And if any of these sayd officers fynde any manner of cattel hauing no such brennynge, they may attache them and seise them as strays (h), and put them in sauegarde to the lordes use, tyll they be yered [yeared] and dyed [dayed]. And they ought to ask theym thre Sondayes in thre or foure next paryshe churches, and also cry them thre tymes in thre the next market townes. And if no man com within the yere and the day, and to make sufficient profe that the catell is his, than it is forefayt to the lorde as a strey; and in lyke maner the swyne and shepe of every township and hamell, ought to be pytched with the said brennynge yron, or such an other lyke the same."

(h) See *post*, Lecture XX.

LECTURE V.

IN my last Lecture I mentioned several notices scattered about in our law books of commons belonging to vills or townships; and I now proceed further with the subject. I will endeavour to explain the modern doctrine of the origin of common appendant from village communities, existing as societies, with arable land cultivated in common, and also common rights of pasture in the adjoining waste. I do not know that I can express the views of modern writers on this subject more concisely and accurately than in the words of Canon Stubbs in his Constitutional History of England (a). The system, which it appears has prevailed much more universally than our ancient lawyers dreamt of, is called the mark system, and it is thus explained by Canon Stubbs:—"The laborious investigations of recent scholars have successfully reconstituted the scheme of land tenure, as it existed among the Germanic races, by careful generalisations from charters, records of usages, and the analogies of Scandinavian law and practice, which at a later date reproduces, with very little that is adventitious, the early conditions of self-organising society. This scheme has been already mentioned more than once, under the name of the mark system. Its essential character depends on the tenure and cultivation of the land by the members of the community in partnership. The general name of the *mark* is given to the territory which is held by the community, the absolute ownership of which resides in the community itself, or in the tribe or nation of which the community forms a part. The mark has been

Village communities.

Canon Stubbs.

The mark system.

(a) Vol. 1, pp. 48—51, 2nd ed.

formed by a primitive settlement of a family or kindred in one of the great plains or forests of the ancient world; and it is accordingly, like any other clearing, surrounded by a thick border of wood or waste, which supplies the place or increases the strength of a more effective natural boundary. In the centre of the clearing the primitive village is placed; each of the markmen has there his homestead, his house, courtyard, and farm buildings. This possession, the exponent as we may call it of his character as a fully qualified freeman, entitles him to a share in the land of the community. He has a right to the enjoyment of the woods, the pastures, the meadow, and the arable land of the mark; but the right is of the nature of usufruct or possession only, his only title to absolute ownership being merged in the general title of the tribe, which he of course shares. The woods and pastures being undivided, each markman has the right of using them, and can turn into them a number of swine and cattle: under primitive conditions this share is one of absolute equality; when that has ceased to be the rule, it is regulated by strict proportion. The use of the meadow land is also defi-

Apportionment of land under the mark system. proportion. The use of the meadow land is also defi- nitely apportioned. It lies open from hay harvest to the following spring, and during this time is treated as a portion of the common pasture, out of the area of which it is in fact annually selected. When the grass begins to grow, the cattle are driven out, and the meadow is fenced round and divided into as many equal shares as there are mark-families in the village; each man has his own haytime, and houses his own crop; that done, the fences are thrown down, and the meadow becomes again common pasture—another field in another part of the mark being chosen for the next year. For the arable land, the same regulative measures are taken, although the task is somewhat more complex, for the supply of arable cannot be supposed to have been inexhaustible, nor would the markmen be likely to spend their strength in bringing into tillage a larger area than they could permanently keep in cultivation. Hence the arable surface must be regarded as constant, subject to the alternation of crops. In the infancy of agriculture the alternation would be simply that of corn and fallow, and for this two divisions or common fields would suffice. But as tillage developed, as the land was fitter for winter or spring sowing, or as the use of other seed besides wheat was introduced, the community would have three, four, five or even six such areas, on which the proper rotation of crops and fallow might be observed. In each of these areas the markman had his equal or proportionate share; and this share of the arable completed his occupation or possession. This system of husbandry prevailed at different times over the whole of Germany, and is in complete harmony with the idea of a nationality constituted on a basis of personal rather than territorial relations. As the king is the king of the nation, not of the land, the land is rather the sign or voucher for the freedom of its possessor than the basis of his rights. He possesses his land as being a full-free member of the community; henceforth the possession of it is the attestation, type and embodiment of his freedom and political rights. For every such mark becomes a political unit; every free markman has his place in the assembly of the mark, which regulates all the internal business of the partnership and of the relations that arise from it. The choice of the meadow, the rotation of the crops, the allotment of the shares from year to year are determined in this council; and without its consent no man may settle in the territory, build himself a house, or purchase the share of another. It is unnecessary to suppose that there was a period when the village marks administered justice among themselves; for within historical times they appear only as members of larger communities: but even these communities may have been originally constituted on the same prin-

Personal constitution of the polity in which this system prevails.

The political adjuncts of the mark system.

The village court or mark-moot.

ciple, and have possessed common woods and pasture grounds, in which the village marks have their definite shares. But the initiatory stage of legal proceedings may well have been gone through, complaints heard, and presentments drawn up in the village council. On such a hypothesis also it may have elected its own annual president; although, again, within historic times such magistrate seems to have been imposed by the king or governing council of the nation."

Kemble's Saxons in England.

Mr. John Mitchell Kemble in his Saxons in England has a chapter on the mark (b), from which I propose to read a few extracts, showing how the mark system was used in this country by the Saxons. "However far," he remarks (c), " we may pursue our researches into the early records of our forefathers, we cannot discover a period at which this organization was unknown.

Condition of German tribes.

Whatever may have been the original condition of the German tribes, tradition and history alike represent them to us as living partly by agriculture, partly by the pasturing of cattle. They had long emerged from the state of wandering herdsmen, hunters or fishers, when they first attracted the notice and disputed or repelled the power of Rome." Again (d), "without commerce, means of extended communication, or peace-

Corn grown for consumption.

ful neighbours, the Germans cannot have cultivated their fields for the service of strangers; they must have been consumers, as they certainly were raisers of bread corn; early documents of the Anglo-Saxons prove that considerable quantities of wheat were devoted to this purpose. Even the serfs and domestic servants were entitled to an allowance of bread, in addition to the supply of flesh; and the large quantities of ale and beer which we find enumerated among the dues payable from the land, or in gift to religious establishments, presume a very copious supply of cereals for the purpose

(b) Vol. 1, chap. 2.   (c) Page 37.   (d) Page 38.

of malting. But it is also certain that our forefathers Cattle used for subsistence. depended very materially for subsistence upon the herds of oxen, sheep, and especially swine, which they could feed upon the unenclosed meadows, or in the wealds of oak and beech, which covered a large proportion of the land. From the moment, in short, when we first learn anything of their domestic condition, all the German tribes appear to be settled upon arable land, surrounded with forest pastures, and having some kind of property in both."

Again (e) : " The word *mark* has a legal as well as Meaning of word *mark*. a territorial meaning ; it is not only a space of land, such as has been described, but a member of a state also ; in which last sense it represents those who dwell upon the land, in relation to their privileges and rights, both as respects themselves and others. But the word, as applied even to the territory, has a twofold meaning : it is properly speaking employed to denote not only the whole district occupied by one small community ; but more especially those forests and Word *mark* applied to wastes by which arable land was enclosed. wastes by which the arable is enclosed, and which separate the possessions of one tribe from those of another. The mark or boundary pasture land, and the cultivated space which it surrounds, and which is portioned out to the several members of the community, are inseparable ; however different the nature of the property which can be had in them, they are in fact one whole ; taken together they make up the whole territorial possession of the original *cognatio*, kin or tribe. The ploughed lands and meadows are guarded by the mark ; and the cultivator ekes out a subsistence, which could hardly be wrung from the small plot he calls his own, by the flesh and other produce of beasts, which his sons, his dependents or his serfs mast for him in the outlying forests."

(e) Page 42.

The mark is also a community.

Again (*f*): "In the second and more important sense of the word, the mark is a community of families or households settled on such plots of land and forest as have been described. This is the original basis upon which all Teutonic society rests, and must be assumed to have been at first amply competent to all the demands of society in a simple and early stage of development; for example to have been an union for the purpose of administering justice, or supplying a mutual guarantee of peace, security and freedom for the inhabitants of the district. In this organization the use of the land, the woods and the waters, was made dependent upon the general will of the settlers, and could only be enjoyed under general regulations made by all for the benefit of all. The mark was a voluntary association of free men, who laid down for themselves, and strictly maintained, a system of cultivation by which the produce of the land on which they settled might be fairly and equally secured for their service and support; and from participation in which they jealously excluded all who were not born or adopted into the association. Circumstances dependent upon the peculiar local conformation of the district, or even on the relations of the original parties to the contract, may have caused a great variety in the customs of different marks; and these appear occasionally anomalous, when we meet with them still subsisting in a different order of social existence; but with the custom of one mark, another had nothing to do; and the mark-men within their own limit were independent, sufficient to their own support and defence, and seised of full power and authority to regulate their own affairs as seemed most conducive to their own advantage.

Court of the markmen.

The Court of the markmen, as it may be justly called, must have had supreme jurisdiction at first, over all the causes which could in any way affect the interests of the whole body or the individuals composing it: and

(*f*) Page 53.

suit and service to such Court was not less the duty than the high privilege of the free settlers."

There is an interesting article in the Archæologia (*g*), by Henry Salusbury Milman, Esq., on the Political Geography of Wales, which throws some light upon this subject. He remarks (*h*) that the political boundary of Wales originally coincided with its physical or geo- logical boundary as laid down by modern science : namely, the line of the rivers Severn and Dee. But this was soon over-stepped by the Anglo-Saxon in- vaders, who gradually forced the Welch further to the westward, and established a new boundary—at first in- determinate, but at length defined by Offa's Dyke. The frontier territory traversed by the Dyke, was then and long after known as the Marches of Mercia (or England) and Wales. The precise relation of the Dyke to the Marches, and the peculiar political and legal character of the latter, are derivable from the nature of the Anglo-Saxon mark or march. And then, after quoting some passages on the subject from Mr. Kemble's Saxons in England, he proceeds (*i*), " The kingdom of Mercia, emphatically the mark country, chiefly formed out of the original mark against the Britons, and always, and at length exclusively, bordering upon them, falls under peculiar considerations. Down to the reign of Offa, its western limit seems to have been left undefined, and in fact was perpetually advancing as the Britons receded ; while, on the other hand, the Britons were ever withdrawing their settlements to some distance within their line of defence, leaving the intervening space as a protection against their encroaching enemies. And thus the mark of Mercia toward the Britons ever adjoined a district corresponding in its main features, namely the mark of the Britons toward Mercia." Again (*i*) : " The district, being of great extent, and

Milman's Political Geography of Wales.

Original boundary of Wales.

The marches or marks of Mercia and Wales.

(*g*) Vol. 38, p. 19.　　　(*h*) Page 19.　　　(*i*) Page 21.

The mark
partly inac-
cessible.
partly of inaccessible character, and little controlled by
the governments which claimed authority over it, early
became the receptacle of lawless and predatory bands,
which perpetually disturbed, plundered and oppressed
their more settled and civilized neighbours, and almost
with impunity. It further served to conceal the advances and cover the retreat of the more regnal in-
vasions; by which the Welch princes constantly avenged
the wrongs of their race, and endangered the power or
checked the conquests of the Mercian kings. It became
in short a standing menace to the Mercian people and
government, daily more intolerable, and calling more

The mark
reduced by
authority.
loudly for repression. The primitive mark was from
time to time, as social or political causes arose, reduced by public authority, and, to the extent of such
reduction, deprived of its character as mark—that
is, parcelled out among private owners; and, if the
marks of two communities adjoined, such a measure,
on the part of either, was preceded by an agreement
as to their common limit. The remedy applicable
to the condition of the marches of Mercia and Wales
was analogous, namely, to reduce and so far *unmarch*
them—to plant regular settlements and extend efficient
government in the waste and lawless district—to
confer upon civilized bodies of Mercian subjects a personal as well as national interest in its preservation
and improvement, and so to constitute them a firm and
enduring bulwark on the frontier. The first step
towards this policy was the establishment of a common

Offa's Dyke.
limit of these marches, and such a limit was Offa's
Dyke." Again (*k*) : "The construction of the Dyke was
immediately followed by the occupation of the Mercian

The reduced
mark filled
with Saxons.
march. Offa drove the Welch beyond the Dee and
Wye, and filled with Saxons the plain and more level
regions lying between these rivers and the Severn.

(*k*) Page 23.

The accounts of the gradual occupation of the land on the eastern side of the dyke and the river Wye by the English, show that the same policy was continued by the rulers of Mercia and subsequently of England." "Again (*m*), such was the recognized character of the dyke at the time of the Norman Conquest of England. Neither then, nor ever during the period that Wales remained separate from England, was any other limit of the two countries laid down. Subsequently to the Conquest, the marches of England and Wales, and lastly the remainder of Wales itself, fell under a peculiar system of occupation and government, which superseded this national boundary line, and almost effaced it from history. Offa's Dyke no longer obtained express mention, because no historical or political event turned on the common limit of the marches, which came to be regarded as one district of uniform character, and to be called, by an obvious abridgment, the marches of Wales. The practical distinction for legis- lative and administrative purposes was between the shires of Chester, Salop, Hereford and Gloucester, according to their ancient bounds, on the one hand, and the marches on the other. Yet the ancient character of the dyke continued to be recognized in matters of local description."

The marches of Wales.

Mr. Milman then notices the Act for laws and justice to be administered in Wales in like form as it is in this realm (*n*), which Act recites, "And forasmuch as there be many and divers lordships marchers within the said county or dominion of Wales, lying between the shires of England and the shires of the said country or dominion of Wales, and being no parcel of any other shires, where the laws and due correction is used and had, by reason whereof hath ensued and hath been practised, perpetrated, committed and done, within and

Marches formerly no parcel of any shires.

(*m*) Page 24. (*n*) Stat. 27 Hen. VIII. c. 26.

W.P. F

among the said lordships and countries to them adjoining, manifold and divers detestable murders, burning of houses, robberies, thefts, trespasses, routs, riots, unlawful assemblies, embraceries, maintenances (*o*), receiving of felons, oppressions, ruptures of the peace, and manifold other malefacts, contrary to all laws and justice, and the said offenders thereupon making their refuge from lordship to lordship were and continued without punishment or correction;" for the due reforma-

Some marches annexed to English shires. tion thereof the Act enacts, that some of the said lordships marchers shall be united, annexed and joined to divers of the shires of England; and divers of the

Some to Welch shires. said lordships marchers shall be united, annexed and joined to divers of the shires of the said country or

The rest made into new shires. dominion of Wales. And the residue of the lordships marches was divided into certain particular counties or shires, namely,—the county of Monmouth, the county of Brecknock, the county of Radnor, the county of Montgomery, and the county of Denbigh. Thus a district, which in ancient times was all mark or march, in the strict sense of the word, namely, a mere unenclosed waste, became in process of time settled and civilized.

We see then that in this country, and in some of the counties of Wales, the same process appears to have

Gradual settlement of land by small communities. gone on. The gradual settlement of land by small communities, vills or townships formed the commencement of civilization. Of the existence of such communities there is ample trace in our law in the

Common fields. numerous common fields, which long existed until the passing of the various Enclosure Acts of the last and present century; though I believe some are still to be found. A common field is a very different thing

(*o*) Embracery is the unlawful tampering with or frightening a jury; maintenance is the unlaw- ful maintaining the suit of another person.

Map of a portion of Coate Common Field

from what is ordinarily called a common. What are ordinarily called common or waste grounds are open pasture lands, on which the tenants of a manor, or other persons, have a right to put their cattle to feed. But a common field is a field belonging to numerous owners; whose lands, as far as I know, invariably assume a remarkable shape, viz. that of very narrow strips, sometimes not more than 30 or 40 feet or even less in width, running parallel to one another, with no fence between (*p*). These strips of land are cultivated in common to this extent; that, by the rules of the community which the owners form, the lands must generally be sown with wheat one year, with barley or oats the next year, and the third year must lie fallow, or in some other similar rotation. Each owner cultivates his own lands according to the rules thus laid down. When the crops are taken off, the land being open and undivided by any fence, the owners put in their cattle, each according to the extent of his land, who range over the whole, feeding on the stubble that is left not only on the lands of their owners, but also on all the other lands in the same field. The consequence of this evidently is, that no person can cultivate his land otherwise than as his neighbours do. If, in the year that the land is fallow, any person should attempt to sow wheat or green crops, or anything else on his lands, the cattle of his neighbours would at once eat it up and destroy it; for, during the year in which the field is fallow, the neighbours put in their cattle to range over the whole. Now it is remarkable how, as

Difference between common fields and commons.

Common cultivation of common fields.

(*p*) The annexed map represents a portion of the common field belonging to the hamlet of Coate, in the parish of Bampton, Oxon, as it existed in 1854. It is extracted from the map made for the purpose of the enclosure of the common fields and commons in that parish. The broken lines represent the unfenced boundaries of the different parcels which together compose the common field. The system was evidently formed before the high road was made, as it cuts through some of the parcels.

F 2

time rolls on, one's knowledge of antiquity in some
cases rather increases than diminishes. The right of
common in these common fields was sometimes desig-
nated as *common of shack*, particularly in the county of
Norfolk, and Lord Coke, in *Sir Miles Corbet's case* (q),
informs us that he thought that case " fit to be reported
(the case being one respecting a common field), because
it is a general case in the said. country," meaning the
county of Norfolk; " and at first the Court was altogether ignorant of the nature of this common called
shack."   Now it is abundantly clear that common
fields, of the kind which I have just mentioned, have
long existed, not only in the county of Norfolk, but in
many other counties in England ; I believe in almost

Ignorance of
the judges in
the reign of
Elizabeth as
to common
fields.

every, if not in every county. But the judges of the
Court of Exchequer in the 27th year of the reign of
Queen Elizabeth, were so ignorant of what was going
on in country parts, that they knew nothing of this
kind of common ; much less were they aware that the
same thing took place in Germany ; still less did they
know that village communities of a similar nature had
long existed in India amongst races originally of the
same stock as ourselves. There is a note by Serjeant
Wilson in his edition of Coke's Reports that the like
intercommoning is in Lincolnshire, Yorkshire and
other counties. But it seems strange, and I hardly
know how to account for it, that a system of agriculture, which was undoubtedly prevalent throughout
the kingdom, should be so little known to the judges of
those days. And it is hardly to be wondered at, that
with so few materials from which to draw a conclusion,
they should have attributed the origin of common
appendant universally to the manorial system, rather
than to the more ancient system of vills, townships or
communities cultivating their arable land in common,
and using in common the adjoining waste not culti-

(q) 7 Rep. 5.

vated for the pasture of their cattle and sheep. In *Sir Miles Corbet's case* (r), it is laid down that this kind of common was originally but in the nature of a feeding because of vicinage, for avoiding of suit. I apprehend, however, that this is not the true explanation. The true explanation is, I venture to think, that on which modern researches have thrown so much light, namely, that common of this nature arose from the common cultivation by the township or community of the lands which were marked out as arable by that community for such common cultivation.

The following curious extract from Fitzherbert's Surveying, written in 1539 (s), shows how universal the system of common field cultivation then was, and it recommends the substitution of the modern system of separate enclosures.

" Howe to make a township that is worthe xx. marke a yere, worth £20 a yere.

Fitzherbert's proposal for the enclosure of common fields.

" It is undoubted, that to euery townshyppe that standeth in tyllage in the playne countrey, there be errable landes to plowe and sowe, and layse to tye or tedder their horses and mares upon, and common pasture to kepe and pasture theyr catell and shepe upon. And also they have medowe grounde to get theyr hey upon. Than to let it be knowen how many acres of errable lande euery man hath in tyllage, and of the same acres in euery felde to chaunge with his neighbours, and to leye them toguyther, and to make hym one seuerall close in euery fielde for his errable landes, and his leyse in euery felde to leye them togyther in one felde, and to make one seuerall close for them all. And also another seuerall close for his portion of his common pasture, and also his porcion of his medowe in a seuerall close by itselfe, and al kept in

(r) 7 Rep. 5.   (s) Chap. 40.

seueral both in wynter and somer: and euery cottage
shall have his portion assigned hym accordynge to his
rent, and than shall not the rych man overpresse the
poore man with his catell, and every man may eate his
owne close at his pleasure. And vndoubted, that hay
and strawe that will finde one beest in the house will
find two beestes in the close, and better they shall lyke.
For those beastis in the house have short heer and
thynne, and towarde Marche they will pylle and be
bare. And therefore they may nat abyde in the felde
byfore the heerdmen in winter tyme for colde. And
those that lie in a close under a hedge have longe heare
and thyck and they wyll never pylle nor be bare, and by
this reason the husbande maye kepe twyse so many
catell as he did before."

LECTURE VI.

THE communities who cultivate common fields sometimes have special customs of their own. As a rule,
the owner of lands in a common field cannot enclose
them. But a custom may exist for any owner of land Custom to
in a common field to enclose his portion, and so keep enclose common field
out his neighbours, giving up his right of common land.
over the rest of the field. The validity of such a
custom is denied by Chief Baron Comyns in his
valuable Digest (*a*). But he was mistaken. And his
mistake is pointed out and corrected by Mr. Justice Such a cus-
Bayley in his judgment in the case of *Cheeseman* v. tom is valid.
Harding (*b*). The law on the point of a custom to
enclose lands in a common field is thus laid down by
Lord Coke in *Sir Miles Corbet's case* (*c*). " If," he *Sir Miles*
says, " in the town of D. for example " (and mark, he *Corbet's case.*
says in the *town* of D. and not in the manor of D.), " if
in the *town* of D. one who hath purchased divers parcels
together, in which the inhabitants have used to have
shack, and long time since has enclosed it; and notwithstanding always after harvest the inhabitants have
had shack there, by passing into it by bars or gates
with their cattle, there it shall be taken as common
appendant or appurtenant, and the owner cannot
exclude them of common there, notwithstanding he
will not common with them, but hold his own land so
enclosed in severalty; and that is proved by the usage,
for, notwithstanding the ancient enclosure, the inhabitants have always had common there. But if in the
town of S." (mark again the word *town*), " the custom

(*a*) Com. Dig. tit. Common   (*b*) 1 B. & Ald. 712.
(E.).   (*c*) 7 Rep. 5.

and usage hath been that every owner in the same
town hath inclosed their own lands from time to time,
and so hath held it in severalty there, this usage proves
that it was but in the nature of shack originally for
the cause of vicinage, and so it continues; and therefore
there he may enclose and hold in severalty, and exclude
himself to have shack with the others."

Cases of
customs to
inclose lands
in common
fields.
Barker v.
Dixon.

There are two cases in Serjeant Wilson's Reports, in
which a custom for the owners of lands in common
fields to inclose against their neighbours was proved
and acted upon. The first of these is *Barker* v. *Dixon* (d).
In that case there was a great field, containing 110,000
acres, in which the plaintiff had a right of common, and
the defendant inclosed part of the field. The defendant
pleaded the custom that from time out of mind all those
who had any land in the said field might inclose as
much thereof *ad libitum* as they pleased, and that the
defendant by virtue of his possession and of the custom
inclosed. The plaintiff replied and traversed the custom
to inclose. But at the trial of the case in 1742 the
defendant proved his plea very satisfactorily; and it
was held by the court that it was a very good custom,
and that the freeholders under such a custom might
well inclose against one another, as in *Sir Miles Corbet's*

How v.
Strode.

case. The other case is that of *How* v. *Strode* (e).
This was an action of replevin for taking the plaintiff's
cattle in a certain place called Banbury's Furlong, in the
county of Somerset. The defendant avowed that the
place Banbury's Furlong was his own soil and freehold,
and because the plaintiff's cattle were trespassing there,
he took them *damage feasant*. The plaintiff then pleaded
that the land was parcel of a field called Eastfield, in
the parish of Butleigh in the said county, and that she
was seised in her demesne as of fee of ten acres of land
in the same parish; and that she, and all those whose

(d) 1 Wilson, 44.   (e) 2 Wilson, 269.

estate she had, had from time immemorial been accustomed to have common of pasture in Eastfield, whereof
Banbury's Furlong was parcel, her and their own lands
in the same field excepted, for all her and their commonable cattle, levant and couchant on the said ten
acres of land, every year, when the same field had been
sown with any kind of corn or grain, from the time that
the corn or grain in that year growing therein had been
cut down and carried away until the same field or some
part thereof had been re-sown with some kind of corn or
grain, as to the said ten acres of land belonging and
appertaining. The defendant replied that in the parish
of Butleigh there are two common fields, one called
Eastfield and the other called Westfield, in which common fields the lands of divers persons for the time being
now do lie, and from time immemorial have laid dis-
persedly and in several parcels; and also pleaded a
right of inter-commoning, while the lands were not
inclosed, throughout all the uninclosed parts, as alleged
by the plaintiff. But he further said that within the
said parish there was an ancient custom, that ever person, having any lands in the common fields or either of
them, and wishing to inclose the same or any part
thereof from the rest, might do so, and so hold them in
severalty, discharged from any common of pasture of
any other person whatsoever; and that the person so
inclosing thereby discharged all the rest of the uninclosed lands, in the said common fields or either of them,
from all common of pasture in respect of the lands so
inclosed by him. And he pleaded that, in pursuance of
that custom, he inclosed his own lands accordingly. The
plaintiff denied the custom to inclose; and the defendant at the trial produced five very old deeds, and
several other deeds, which proved the custom to inclose.
He also called seven old witnesses; three of the oldest
proved the custom to inclose of their own knowledge,
for a great number of years; and that they had been

told, when they were young, by very old persons then
living, that it was the custom for the landowners in
these fields to inclose, and said that they thought any
man might inclose his land. Some of the witnesses
however swore that if a man left any bit, only an acre,
uninclosed, he used to enjoy his common in regard to
that acre uninclosed just as before, and used to put in
any number of cattle without stint. Upon this the
judge who tried the case thought the defendant had not
proved his custom; but the court granted a new trial on
the ground of misdirection. And the learned judges of
the Court of Common Pleas held that the right of common before inclosure made was for cattle levant and
couchant upon each person's uninclosed lands, and that
what some of the witnesses said of common without
stint is nothing to the purpose; for there is no such
thing as common without stint belonging to land;
common belonging to land can only be for cattle levant
and couchant thereon; that the custom to inclose was
clearly proved; and when the land is inclosed it is freed
and discharged from any person's former right of common thereon; and of this opinion was the whole court.
There may therefore in some cases be a valid custom
that any one owner in a common field may inclose
against the others. And, where such a custom exists,
it is possible that, as Lord Coke says, the right of common may have existed merely by reason of vicinage;
but the general rule is undoubtedly otherwise.

With regard to the mention of common fields in Acts
of Parliament, there is an incidental reference to lands
which on certain days of the year are open for common
of pasture in the Act of 24 Geo. II. c. 23, anno Dom.
1751. This was an Act for regulating the commencement of the year, and for correcting the calendar then
in use. Previously to this Act, the year begun on the
25th of March, and not as now on the 1st of January.

Stat. 24 Geo.
II. c. 23, for
correcting the
calendar.

It was also found that the calendar had gone wrong by eleven days; and what is now called the old style, was altered into the new style. By this Act the year was to commence in future on the 1st of January; and the natural day next immediately following the 2nd of September, 1752, was to be reckoned and accounted as the 14th of September, omitting for that time only the eleven intermediate nominal days of the common calendar. By this means some persons supposed that their lives had been shortened by eleven days. The Act then recites (*f*) that according to divers customs, prescriptions and usages, in certain places within the kingdom, certain lands and grounds were, on particular nominal days and times in the year, to be opened for common of pasture and other purposes; and, at other times, the owners and occupiers of such lands and grounds have a right to inclose or shut up the same for their own private use; and there is in many other instances a temporary and distinct property and right, vested in different persons, in and to many such lands and grounds, according to certain nominal days and times in the year. The Act then recites that the antici- pation or bringing forward the said nominal days and times by the space of eleven days, according to the new method of supputation, might be attended with many inconveniences. And it enacts that nothing in the Act contained shall extend or be construed to extend to accelerate or anticipate the days or times, on which any such temporary or distinct property or right in or to any such lands or grounds as aforesaid, was to com- mence; but that all such lands and grounds as aforesaid should be opened, inclosed or shut up, and such tempo- rary and distinct property and right in and to such lands and grounds as aforesaid, should commence and begin upon the same natural days and times, on which the same should have been so respectively opened, in-

(*f*) Sect. 5.

closed or shut up, or would have commenced or begun, in case the Act had not been made; that is to say, eleven days later than the same would have happened according to the said new account and supputation of time.

The first time in which I can find any express notice by the legislature of lands in common fields is in the statute 13 Geo. III. c. 81, which is intituled "An Act for the better cultivation, improvement and regulation of the common arable fields, wastes and commons of pasture in this kingdom." This Act provides (*g*) to the effect that three-fourths in number and value of the occupiers of such open or common field lands, in each parish or place, cultivating and taking the crops of the same, and having the consent of the owners in manner therein mentioned, and likewise the consent of the tithe owner first had in writing, may, at a meeting to be held and summoned as therein mentioned, direct the ordering, fencing, cultivation and improvement thereof; and that the same shall be continued in such course of husbandry, and be cultivated under such rules, regulations and restrictions as the meeting shall direct. But such rules, regulations and restrictions are not to be in force for any longer term than six years, or two rounds (*h*), according to the ancient and established course of each parish or place respectively (*i*). The Act also empowers (*k*) the appointment of a field reeve, or field reeves, to superintend the ordering, fencing, cultivating and improving of such common fields, and to see that the same are cultivated according to the regulations agreed upon at the general meeting for that

Stat. 13 Geo. III. c. 81. Regulation of common fields.

Field reeves.

(*g*) Stat. 13 Geo. III. c. 81, s. 1. This Act still remains unre-pealed, except so much as relates to double costs, which is repealed by the Statute Law Revision Act, 1861, stat. 24 & 25 Vict. c. 101.

(*h*) See *ante*, p. 67.
(*i*) Sect. 2.
(*k*) Sects. 3, 5, 6.

purpose. The Act contains provisions (*l*) saving the rights of persons who may have rights of common over the common field, without having any land therein. The Act also empowers the ploughing up, under certain conditions, of waste balks, slades or meers, which often lie very inconveniently interspersed amongst the arable lands in common fields (*m*). But the Act contains no provision authorizing any permanent inclosure of land in common fields, saving only this proviso (*n*), that nothing in the Act contained shall prevent or extend to prevent any person or persons from inclosing all or any part or parts of his, her or their land to and for his, her or their own use or benefit, such person or persons having full power or right so to do; evidently referring to such cases as I have just mentioned (*o*), where a custom for any one to inclose his lands may be proved to exist.

Authority for the exchange of lands in common fields was, however, given by the Act 4 & 5 Will. IV. c. 30, intituled "An Act to facilitate the exchange of lands lying in common fields." But this did not in any way interfere with the mode of cultivation; nor did it give any right to the parties exchanging to inclose their lands. The advantage of an exchange was that, whereas in almost all cases the lands were held in very small strips, and generally apart from one another, the owners of several strips might, by means of exchange, consolidate their holdings into larger parcels. Soon after this, however, an Act was passed "for facilitating the inclosure of open and arable fields in England and Wales," statute 6 & 7 Will. IV. c. 115. The power given by this Act was to inclose lands in such fields, so as to extinguish the right of intercommonage which existed, as well over as in respect of such lands; and it enabled

Exchange of lands in common fields.

Stat. 4 & 5 Will. IV. c. 30.

Inclosure of common fields.

Stat. 6 & 7 Will. IV. c. 115.

(*l*) Sects. 8, 9, 10. (*n*) Sect. 27.
(*m*) Sects. 11, 12, 13, 14. (*o*) *Ante*, pp. 71, 72.

such inclosures to be effected by means of commissioners, and made the inclosures binding on persons under disabilities as well as on those able to concur. This Act was afterwards extended by statute 3 & 4 Vict. c. 31, so as to enable the commissioners, not only to determine, but also to straighten the boundaries of parishes, manors, hamlets, or districts in which the lands, which had been inclosed, lay (*p*) ; and the provisions of the Act were also extended to such open and common arable fields as have adjacent thereto, but not separated by any fence therefrom, certain tracts of grass land commonable during part of the year, and holden in severalty, or by lot or apportionment, by or among persons interested therein during other parts of the year (*q*).

There is now, however, a General Inclosure Act, statute 8 & 9 Vict. c. 118, which has been amended and extended by numerous subsequent Acts (*r*). And the 11th section of that Act specifies the lands which are subject to be inclosed under the Act. They are as follows:—"All lands subject to any rights of common whatsoever, and whether such rights may be exercised or enjoyed at all times, or may be exercised or enjoyed only during limited times, seasons, or periods, or be subject to any suspension or restriction whatsoever in respect of the time of the enjoyment thereof; all gated and stinted pastures, in which the property of the soil, or of some part thereof, is in the owners of the cattle-gates, or other gates or stints, or any of them; and also all gated and stinted pastures, in which no part of the property of the soil is in the owners of the cattle-gates, or other gates or stints, or any of them; all land held,

Stat. 3 & 4 Vict. c. 31, extending stat. 6 & 7 Will. IV. c. 115.

General Inclosure Act. Stat. 8 & 9 Vict. c. 118. Sect. 11, lands subject to be inclosed.

(*p*) Stat. 3 & 4 Vict. c. 31, s. 2.
(*q*) Sect. 4.
(*r*) Stats. 9 & 10 Vict. c. 70 ; 10 & 11 Vict. c. 111 ; 11 & 12 Vict. c. 99 ; 12 & 13 Vict. c. 83 ; 15 & 16 Vict. c. 79 ; 17 & 18 Vict. c. 97 ; 20 & 21 Vict. c. 31 ; 22 & 23 Vict. c. 43 ; 31 & 32 Vict. c. 89 ; 36 Vict. c. 19 ; 39 & 40 Vict. c. 56, and 42 & 43 Vict. c. 37.

occupied or used in common, either at all times or during any time or season, or periodically, and either for all purposes, or for any limited purpose, and whether the separate parcels of the several owners of the soil shall or shall not be known by metes or bounds, or otherwise distinguishable; all land in which the property or right of or to the vesture or herbage, or any part thereof, during the whole or any part of the year, or the property or right of or to the wood or underwood growing and to grow thereon, is separated from the property of the soil; and all lot meadows and other lands, the occupation or enjoyment of the separate lots or parcels of which is subject to interchange among the respective owners in any known course of rotation, or otherwise."

And this leads me to mention the fact which has already incidentally appeared that, in addition to the arable lands possessed by each community, and owned in severalty by its several members, were not unfrequently common meadow or pasture lands, originally belonging to the community, and subsequently holden by lot, or apportionment amongst the persons interested, during the whole or part of the year. These *lot meads*, as they are called, are mentioned in the law books; and they are a curious kind of shifting inheritance. Lord Coke, in his Commentary on Littleton (s), has the following passage:—"And albeit land whereof our author here speaketh, be the most firm and fixed inheritance, and therefore it is called *solum quia est solidum*, and fee simple the most highest and absolute estate that a man can have; yet may the same at several times be moveable, sometime in one person and *alternis vicibus* in another; nay sometime in one place and sometime in another. As, for example, if there be eighty acres of meadow, which have been used time out of mind of man to be divided between certain persons,

Common meadows.

Lot meads.

(s) Co. Litt. 4 a.

and that a certain number of acres appertain to every of these persons ; as, for example, to A. thirteen acres, to be yearly assigned and lotted out, so as sometime the thirteen acres lie in one place and sometime in another, and so of the rest; A. hath a moveable fee simple in thirteen acres, and may be parcel of his manor, albeit they have no certain place, but yearly set out in several places, so as the number only is certain and the particular acres or place wherein they lie after the year incertain. And so it was adjudged in the King's Bench upon an especial verdict." And in another place (t), Lord Coke inquires, where livery of seisin shall be made, in a case, where a man has a moveable estate of inheritance, according to the example here put, in thirteen acres. And he says, first, if they be parcel of a manor, they may pass by the name of the manor ; but if they be in gross, then the charter of feoffment must be of thirteen acres lying and being in the meadow of eighty acres, generally, without bounding or describing of the same in certain ; and livery of seisin of any thirteen acres allotted to the feoffee for a year *secundum formam cartæ* is a good livery to pass the contents of thirteen acres, wheresoever the same lie in that meadow. And in another place (u), he remarks that if the owner of those thirteen acres grant a rent-charge out of those thirteen acres generally, lying in the meadow of eighty, without mentioning where they lie particularly, there, as the state of the land removes, the charge shall remove also. Some of the meadows in which limited rights of common exist are thrown open on Lammas Day, which is the 1st of August, and they are accordingly called Lammas meadows. And, by virtue of the Act of Parliament to which I have just referred (x), the time of throwing open the land to the commoners is now

Livery of seisin of lot meads.

Lammas meadows.

(t) Co. Litt. 48 b.　　　　　(x) Stat. 24 Geo. 2, c. 23, *ante*,
(u) Co. Litt. 343 b.　　　　　p. 74.

eleven days later, viz. on the 12th of August in every year.

The Act of 13 Geo. III. c. 81, to which I have already referred (y), contains provisions (z) for postponing the opening of common pastures, and also for fixing the time for shutting up and unstocking the same. And there is a curious provision (a) empowering the major part in number and value of persons having right of common in a common pasture, at a meeting to be called as therein mentioned, by writing under their hands, to alter and change the manner and custom of feeding and depasturing the common pastures, so far as instead of horses, cows and other cattle, to allow the same to be fed and depastured with sheep, at the option of each person respectively having right of common; and to limit and stint the number of sheep each such person, having right of common in such common pastures, shall respectively feed and depasture thereon in due proportion to their respective stints or rights.

Opening and shutting of common pastures.

Power to pasture sheep on common pastures instead of cattle,

and to stint the number of sheep.

You will observe that the Act of 8 & 9 Vict. c. 118, speaks of two distinct kinds of what are there called gated and stinted pastures, viz., those in which the property of the soil, or of some part thereof, is in the owners of the cattle gates or other gates or stints or any of them; and, secondly, those gated and stinted pastures, in which no part of the property of the soil is in the owners of the cattle gates, or other gates or stints, or any of them. And I think that the distinction here taken serves to reconcile, what otherwise appears to be a great contradiction and confusion in the books, with respect to what are commonly called cattle gates or beast gates. In some cases they are said to comprise an interest in the soil,—in other cases they are said to comprise no interest in the soil. I appre-

Cattle or beast gates.

(y) *Ante*, p. 76.   (z) Sects. 17, 18, 19.   (a) Sect. 20.

W.P.   G

hend the true reason for the different decisions is this,—
that in some cases the soil is vested in the different
owners as tenants in common in fee, in undivided shares,
corresponding to their interest in the surface, as measured
by the number of cattle they have a right to put on.
In this case, the mines and minerals would belong to
the persons entitled to rights of pasture; and no person
would have any right to sport over the lands without
their leave. Whereas, if the right of the soil was in
the lord of the manor, he alone would be entitled to the
mines and minerals; he would have the sole right to
sport over the lands; and the persons entitled to rights
of pasture would have nothing but an incorporeal right
to take the grass and herbage by the mouths of their
cattle. An instance of the former class of cases seems
to have occurred in the case of *The King* v. *The Inhabitants of Whixley* (b). In that case the cattle gates in
question are stated to have passed by lease and release;
and the judgment of the Court implies that such an
assurance was necessary to pass them. They were,
therefore, held to be a tenement, sufficient to enable a
pauper to gain a settlement, by the occupation of such
a cattle gate, within the poor law then in force (c).
Here the fact that a lease and release were necessary
for the conveyance of the cattle gates showed that they
must have comprised some interest in the soil; for a
mere incorporeal hereditament then lay in grant only,
and was not required to be conveyed by lease and release, which was the proper assurance of a hereditament
which was corporeal. And there are other authorities
to the effect that an ejectment will lie for a cattle gate
or beast gate (d). But the authorities are far from dis-

(b) 1 T. Rep. 137.

(c) Some hereditaments clearly
of an incorporeal nature have,
however, been held to be tenements within the Poor Law Acts.
See per Lord Ellenborough in

The King v. The Inhabitants of
Hollington, 3 East, 114.

(d) A dictum in *Barnes* v.
Peterson, 2 Strange, 1063; *Ben-
nington* v. *Goodtitle*, 2 Strange,
1084, in which latter case, how-

tinct; and in these cases I think it must be considered
that the phrase *cattle gate* or *beast gate* was a popular
mode of expressing the ownership of an undivided share
in the soil, coupled with an agreed mode of enjoying
the surface, by putting thereon so many cattle, in
common with the cattle of the other owners of the
remaining undivided shares.

On the other hand, I believe that, generally speaking, no part of the property of the soil belongs to the
owner of a cattle gate. It is often a mere right of
common for so many cattle belonging to a farm.
Sometimes it is a right of common in gross for so many
cattle (*e*). Sometimes it is a right to an undivided
share of a several pasture (*f*). There is a case of *Earl
of Lonsdale* v. *Rigg* (*g*), in which the cattle gates there
mentioned were held to confer no interest in the soil,
but to be merely rights of pasture by the cattle gate
owner, the soil remaining in the lord of the manor; so
that the lord might maintain an action of trespass
against a cattle gate owner for sporting over it without
his permission. In this case, each cattle gate gave the
owner thereof a right of depasturing in a tract of
inclosed pasture land, within the manor of Bretherdale
in the county of Westmoreland, called Bretherdale
Bank, a certain number of cattle and sheep, from the
26th of May to the 24th of April; but neither cattle
nor sheep were allowed to pasture there between the
24th of April and the 26th of May. The time of
opening the pasture appeared originally to have been
the 1st of June; for which the 26th of May had been
substituted. There were eighty cattle gates in Bretherdale Bank; and the whole of the cattle and sheep

Where cattle gates comprise no interest in the soil.

Earl of Lonsdale v. Rigg.

---

ever, it is said that *beast gate* in
Suffolk imports *land* and common
for one beast.

(*e*) See *post*, Lecture XII.
(*f*) See *ante*, pp. 21—30.
(*g*) 11 Exch. 654, affirmed on
appeal, 1 Hurls. & Nor. 923.

of the cattle gate owners depastured Bretherdale Bank in common. A frith man, as he was called, was appointed by the cattle gate owners, whose duty it was to take care that Bretherdale Bank was properly stinted; and he was rewarded for his trouble by the cattle gate owners. The cattle gate owner, having a house within the manor, had also a right to cut peat for consumption in his house. The cattle gates were held of the lord of the manor as customary estates of inheritance. They passed by customary deed, followed by admittance at the next Lord's Court, or out of Court by the steward of the manor. The lords of the manor had always searched for, pursued and killed grouse and other game at Bretherdale Bank, no other person having claimed to do so, or having done so, except by their licence. These facts were held to show that the owners of the cattle gates had no interest in this case in the soil. The term *cattle gate* in this case was evidently applied to a mere right of pasturing, and that not during the whole of the year; and such a right of exclusive pasture is, as we have already seen (h), entirely consistent with the ownership and possession of the soil of the land in the lord of the manor, or any other person (i).

The members therefore of the original community or vill, had arable lands, which they cultivated on a common system, pasture lands which they either divided or allotted amongst themselves, or else depastured in common, and also rights of common on the adjacent and uncultivated land, which constituted the mark in its primary sense, out of which the arable and pasture were anciently reclaimed, and from which they were divided. In most cases, from one cause or another, this simple

(h) *Ante*, p. 21.
(i) By stat. 9 & 10 Vict. c. 70, s. 11, provision is made for the exchange of cattle-gates with the sanction of the Inclosure Commissioners.

state of things in time disappeared. The lords of the manors obtained authority over the freeholders, who became their tenants; and the ancient system of common agriculture became converted into the system of manors, consisting of lords and tenants, whose rights are laid down in law books. There is however, or was until the year 1854, a community still existing, having laws of their own and self-government, with respect to whom an attempt was made by the lord of a manor, of which some of the tenements were held, to destroy their custom and to bring the whole within his manorial jurisdiction. But owing to the sturdy manner in which the freeholders disputed his rights, his attempt failed, and the lord himself was fain for some years to become one of the officers of this little community. This community was established in the vill or township of Aston, and the hamlet of Coate, in the parish of Bampton in the county of Oxford; and as many of the facts relating to it are within my own knowledge, I propose to make the little history of this village community the subject of my next Lecture.

LECTURE VII.

In my last Lecture I promised to give an account of a vill or township, which retained its ancient customs until a recent period, and the history of which is an example of the manner in which rights belonging to village communities have been attempted to be destroyed by lords of manors, and often effectually; though it was not so in the present case.

The vill of Aston and hamlet of Coate.

The vill of Aston is situate in the parish of Bampton in the Bush in the county of Oxford; and adjoining to it is the hamlet of Coate, Coat or Cote in the same parish. There are within this township and hamlet sixteen hides of land. A hide is a Saxon term, and is supposed to comprise as much land as would serve for the maintenance of a household. Each of these sixteen hides of land was divided into four yard lands, also a Saxon term; so that there were within Aston and Coate sixty-four yard lands; each of these yard lands had a right of common on a large moor adjoining called Coate Moor. Each yard land had a proportion of arable land, which lay in the common fields belonging to the community; and to each yard land also belonged a certain proportion of meadow or pasture. Of these yard lands forty, or ten hides, belonged to the manor of Aston Boges which remained for a long time in the family of Horde. Other of the yard lands, about eight, or two hides, were formerly parcel of the manor of Shifford, a village adjacent, and were formerly held of that manor by copy of court roll, but had been enfranchised by the lord. Four yard lands, or one hide, belonged to the manor of Bampton Deanery,

A hide.

Yard land.

another manor also adjoining to Aston and which belonged to the Bishop of Exeter. The remaining three hides were ancient freehold, not holden of the manor of Aston Boges, nor paying rent to the lord thereof, nor doing any suit to the Court there. It does not appear clearly of whom these three hides were held, but they were held apparently either of the manor of Bampton next mentioned or directly from the Crown. The hundred and manor of Bampton, which comprised all these three several manors, was a superior lordship. The manor of Aston Boges was held of the manor of Bampton at the rent of a gilt sword and eighteen pence yearly.

The customs of this little community of Aston and Coate have been preserved in writing; and you will find *Customs of the town.* them printed in the Archæologia (a). They existed in writing so long back as the year 1593, the 35th year of the reign of Queen Elizabeth, when they were signed by most of the substantial inhabitants of Aston and Coate. They are as follows:—" 1. The custom is, that, upon our Lady-day eve, every year, all the inhabitants of Aston and Coat shall meet at Aston Cross, about three of the clock in the afternoon, or one of every house, to understand who shall serve for the sixteens for that year coming, and to choose other officers for the same year. 2. The said sixteens being known, the hundred tenants of the same sixteens, do divide themselves some distance from the lord's tenants of the said sixteens. And the hundred tenants do choose one grass steward, and one water hayward; and the lord's tenants do choose two grass stewards and one water hayward. 3. After the said officers are chosen and known, the said inhabitants do refer themselves to such orders and pains for breaking the said orders as shall be set down by the said sixteens or the major part of them

(a) Vol. 35, p. 472.

for that year, as well for the hayneing of the commons, as for the breaking of the commons, or for any other orders, which they conceive beneficial for the said inhabitants of Aston and Coat. 4. The said sixteens hath not any authority to make any orders or to set any amercements touching the commons, except there be do meet at the Cross nine of the said sixteens at the time, and those nine may pin the rest of the sixteens. The custom is that no team shall be in the Inn mead after sunset to fetch away any hay or grass, upon pain of two shillings every team so offending. 5. The custom is, that if any of the inhabitants of Aston and Coat aforesaid do fail to appear upon any Lady-eve, or someone of every house for him, the parties making default to forfeit and pay fourpence. 6. If there be any fault found by any of the inhabitants aforesaid, contrary to the order made by the said sixteens or nine of them, the same inhabitants or those that find the fault may cause the stewards, or any of the said stewards, to warn the sixteens to the Cross, to see some redress; and if the said sixteens upon the same warning do not come at the time appointed, every one making default to forfeit and pay fourpence. And it is also lawful for the stewards and the body of the town to pin the sixteens to pay fourpence for every fault trespassed and approved as aforesaid. 7. The ordinary days for the sixteens to meet without warning are, on the Tuesday in Easter week, the Wednesday in the Rogation week or Cross week, the Wednesday in the Whitsun week, and upon Lammas eve, and every failing to forfeit fourpence. 8. The custom is, that the chief lord of Bampton Hundred shall have every year a draught with a lawful net in the common water of Aston and Coat and no more; and if he draw his net up he is not by the custom to put in his net again that year. 9. Cricklet ham is yearly to pay for coming over Beareheards Bridge sixpence; the Gally Acres in

Bosingay mead twelvepence. And every person that hath meadow and no feeding must rid_ their hay by Lammas eve at noon, or otherwise they cannot after the same time carry away their hay, but it is to be eaten by the cattle of the inhabitants of Aston and Coat aforesaid. And at the laying out of Bosingay mead, the occupiers of the Gally acres are to bring with them into the mead to the layers out, everyone of them one gallon of ale and a loaf of bread. 10. The sixteens are to set and remove their stones in the mead of Aston and Coat as often as need shall require. 11. After our Lady-eve that the whole town have met together, and that they have referred all matters unto the new sixteens' hands for that year, they are not to meddle any further for that year than this; that if they find any fault with the new sixteens, that they do not their office, then they are to tell them of such faults as they find; and if the said sixteens do not mend those faults, then the said inhabitants and stewards may pound them as above said, that is, to pay fourpence for every fault. 12. The custom is and hath been that the said sixteens shall and may distrain for any forfeitures made, if any shall refuse to pay upon demand."

You will observe that as the year then began on the 25th of March, the inhabitants met at Aston Cross on the last day of the year, namely, on Lady-day eve, which I apprehend to be the eve preceding Lady-day, for the purpose of appointing sixteen persons as the officers to manage the commons for the next year. The number of persons, you will also observe, corresponds to the number of hides in the township. There were sixteen hides, and sixteen officers; that is, an officer for every hide. Each of these officers was furnished with a small piece of wood about three inches long with a mark cut thereon, by which to know the Marks. portion of meadow over which he had the superinten-

'dence for the coming year. You will see an account of
these little marks in the Archæologia (*b*). A sketch of
them is given in the accompanying plate.

The mode in which the allotment of the common
meadows took place is thus described by Doctor Giles in
his History of Bampton, as it is set out in the Archæologia (*c*). " The common meadow is laid out by
boundary stones into 16 large divisions technically
called 'layings-out.' These always remain the same,
and each laying-out in like manner is divided into four
pieces called 'sets,' first set, second set, third and fourth
set. Now, as the customs of Aston and Coat are based
upon the principles of justice and equity between all
the commoners, and the common meadow is not equally
fertile for grass in every part, it becomes desirable to
adopt some mode of giving all an equal chance of
obtaining the best cuts for their cattle. To effect this,
recourse is had to the ballot, and the following mode is
practised. From time immemorial there have been
sixteen marks established in the village, each of which
corresponds with four yard lands; and the whole
sixteen consequently represent the 64 yard lands, into
which the common is divided. A certain number of
the tenants consequently have the same mark, which
they always keep, so that every one of them knows his
own. The use of these marks is to enable the tenants
every year to draw lots for their portion of the meadow.
When the grass is fit to cut, which will be at different
times in different years according to the season, the
grass-stewards and sixteens summon the tenants to a
general meeting, and the following ceremony takes·
place. Four of the tenants come forward each bearing
his mark, cut on a piece of wood, as, for example, the
'frying pan,' the 'herns foot,' the 'bow,' the 'two

Allotment of
common
meadows.

(*b*) Vol. 37, pp. 383 et seq.   (*c*) Vol. 33, p. 275, note.
See also vol. 35, p. 471.

ASTON AND COATE.

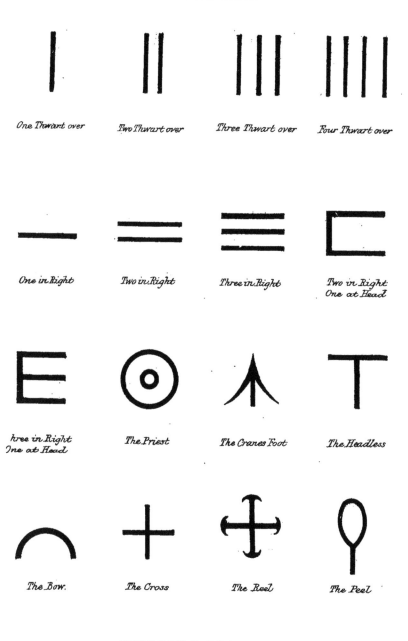

One Thwart over   Two Thwart over   Three Thwart over   Four Thwart over

One in Right   Two in Right   Three in Right   Two in Right
One at Head

hree in Right
One at Head   The Priest   The Cranes Foot   The Headless

The Bow.   The Cross   The Reel   The Peel

MARKS USED BY THE SIXTEENS.

face p. 90.

strokes to the right and one at head,' etc. These four marks are thrown into a hat, and a boy, having shaken up the hat, again draws forth the marks. The first drawn entitles its owner to have his portion of the common meadow in 'set one,' the second drawn in 'set two,' etc., and thus four of the tenants having obtained their allotments, four others come forwards, and the same process is repeated until all the tenants have received allotments. The most singular feature of this very intricate system remains to be told. When the lots are all drawn, each man goes armed with his scythe, and cuts out his mark on the piece of ground which belongs to him, and which in many cases lies in so narrow a strip that he has not width enough to take a full sweep with his scythe, but is obliged to hack down his grass in an inconvenient manner as he is best able."

The "frying pan" spoken of above appears to be the same mark as the peel. The duties of the grass-stewards were to see that the mounds and fences were in good repair, and to secure the meadows from the incursions of cattle, and also to provide at their joint expense four two-year-old bulls every season to run on the common pasture. At the end of the season they sold them for their own benefit, and in the meantime they had the privilege of claiming a fee of eighteen pence for every cow that fed on the common during the summer. Within the meads of Coat and Aston there were two great lot meads, one called Aston in mead, and the other Aston out mead. Within these two meadows were several hams or home closes of meadow, viz., the Bull ham, the Hayward's ham, the Warden's ham, the Wontner's ham, the Grass-steward's ham, the Water Hayward's ham, the Water Steward's ham, the Homage ham, the Smith's ham, the Penny ham, the Herd's ham, the Brander's ham, and the Constable's ham—thirteen in all. These hams together were for-

Duties of the grass-stewards.

Lot meads.

Hams or home closes.

merly of the value of 40*l.* per annum, and were disposed
of at the discretion of the sixteens; some to the officers
whose name they bear, some to the public use of the
town, as for the making of gates, bridges, &c., and some
were sold to make ale for the merry meeting of the
inhabitants. There were also in Aston and Coat several
leys of green sward lying in the common fields, two
years mown and one fed, which were disposed of at the
discretion of the sixteens or officers. You will find an
account of the different officers for whose benefit these
hams were used in the Archæologia (*d*), with the use to
which these hams were appropriated in the year 1850,
shortly preceding the inclosure of these lands in 1854.

The lord's attempt to destroy this custom.

It appears, however, that in the year 1657, Mr. Horde
(the son of Sir Thomas Horde, knight), who was the
then lord of the manor of Aston Boges, under a settlement made by his father, desired to put an end to the
authority of the sixteens, and to reduce the government
of the town to the obedience of the courts of his manor.
And, in order to effectuate his purpose, he took covenant of seven or eight of his tenants, to whom he had
then lately let several of his yard lands in Aston and
Coat, that they would wholly submit to the orders of
his court, and not agree to any of the sixteens' orders.
Mr. Horde, further conceiving that all the hams above
mentioned were parcel of the waste, and that the sixteens had no warrantable custom to create a right in
them to the soil or inheritance of the said hams, and
that the officers chosen by the sixteens could be no
lawful officers, because not chosen or sworn at any lord's
court, did, about the year 1654, carry away the hay
growing on the said hams. And at a court holden by
the said Mr. Horde at Lady-day, 1657, several officers
were chosen and sworn, and the hams were there
granted to them, which they that year enjoyed accord-

(*d*) Vol. 33, p. 276.

ingly. But at Michaelmas, 1657, the sixteens, amongst other officers, chose a hayward, who refused to be sworn at the court held at Lady-day; whereupon the homage, who were the greater number of the sixteens, chose another hayward, who was there sworn into the said office. But the new chosen hayward, being frightened with the threats of Sir Thomas Horde—who does not appear to have been on good terms with his son—refused to execute his office, and the old hayward continued; whereupon Mr. Horde took to himself the ham called the Hayward's ham. The sixteens gave a horse common to the hayward of their own choosing, which had anciently been enjoyed by those that had the same office. This horse common the hayward stocked; whereupon Mr. Horde impounded his horse, which lay in the pound about a fortnight, and then broke out.

In consequence of these attempts on the part of Mr. Horde, a joint case appears to have been submitted on behalf, as well of Mr. Horde as lord, as of the freeholders, copyholders, and leaseholders of Aston and Coat, to Sir Orlando Bridgman and Mr. Jeffrey Palmer on the 30th November, 1657. The first question they put was this:—Who in reason may be thought the lord and owner of the soil of the commons in Aston and Coat, and of the lot meads there? *Case for opinion of Sir O. Bridgman.*

The answer of Sir Orlando Bridgman was:—The soil of the common is the lord's; but of the lot meads, the freeholders and others who have the lots. The opinion of Mr. Palmer does not appear.

Another question was:—Query, whether the custom of the sixteens, though used time out of mind, be a sufficient authority to make orders, choose officers, &c., and whether the officers chosen by them be lawful officers?

Bridgman: I conceive the custom is good, and the officers lawful officers.

Query, whether the custom of the sixteens be not destroyed, if Mr. Horde's-tenants, in pursuance of their covenants, shall refuse to act with them?

Bridgman: Their refusal doth not destroy the custom, but the rest may act without them; and it may be a better way for Mr. Horde to make use of his tenants for elections, so having the majority of voices, rather than invade the custom.

The next query is as follows:—The sixteens, being no corporation, can have legal estate in the said hams of meadow and lays of greensward, to dispose of the same; or, whether the officers, not being chosen at any court, can have any estate therein, or whether they belong not all to the lord of Aston as parcel of his waste, wherein no other person can claim any particular estate; and whether any person whatsoever may maintain an action against Mr. Horde for taking away the hay, and what is the best course for Mr. Horde to take to try his right to them; and, if Mr. Horde should break up and sow the said lays in the fields, whether he may not justify it, and carry away the corn thereof growing, and who can bring any good action against him for it?

Bridgman: I do not conceive that Mr. Horde had any right to the lays in the fields. If the custom be good, as I take it to be, the same custom will give the officers an interest as incident to their offices, and may

Warden of
the Fleet.

belong to an office, as in the case of the warden of the Fleet (e).

Another query: If the custom of the sixteens should

(e) This refers to a passage in the Year Book, 8 Hen. VII. 4 a, where it is said, "It is a common principle that land shall not pass without livery of seisin, and yet in special cases it may well enough, as in exchange between land and town which has land annexed to it, this may be given without livery of seisin. And so of an officer, as the officer of the Fleet with land annexed to him, this will pass by the grant of the office without livery and seisin of the land." See also Co. Litt. 49 a.

be destroyed, what course is there to be taken to bring the town in protection, either to Mr. Horde's courts, or any other power that may tend to the good government and regulation of the town?

Bridgman: I think the custom cannot be destroyed by Mr. Horde alone without the consent of others; nor can he bring the matters to his court, which hath not been used; nor choose officers at his court touching the commons.

Another query: Whether Mr. Horde may not justify the taking away the hayward's ham last year, the first hayward refusing to be sworn, and the other to execute the office? And whether the first hayward, or any under him, can maintain a good action against Mr. Horde for carrying away the hay of the ham?

Bridgman: This is in part answered before; the custom being good, Mr. Horde's justification will be bad.

Another query: Whether Mr. Horde may not bring his action of trespass against the first hayward for stocking the common with a horse, having broken out of the pound, and no suit thereupon?

Bridgman: I think he cannot *causâ quâ supra*.

Another query: Supposing the great mead to be a movable inheritance by lot, cast by the sixteens; if any one do dissent from his lot, query he may not put in his cattle as tenants in common notwithstanding the lots?

Bridgman: He must take his lot according to custom; and as his right is maintained by usage, so is the manner of it.

There were some other questions with respect to other matters which I have not here mentioned. You will find the case and opinion set out at length in the Jurist (*f*). In pursuance of this opinion Mr. Horde, the lord of the manor, wisely took Sir Orlando Bridg-

The lord submits to the custom.

(*f*) Vol. 12, part 2, N. S., p. 103. I have myself seen the original case and opinion. There were 14 questions, and the fee marked thereon was 10*s*. 6*d*.

man's advice, to make use of his tenants for elections, having the majority of voices, rather than to invade the custom. And in the year 1668 he presented the town-ship with a book called the Book of the Sixteens, in the commencement of which the customs were inscribed, the old customary of 1593 being first copied out. And in the same year Mr. Horde, as lord of the manor of Aston and Coat, saving to himself and his heirs all and every the privileges and rights that belonged to them as lords of the manor, did with the sixteens, and the rest of the inhabitants and landholders of Aston and Coat, subscribe their hands iu this book for the further ratifying and confirming of this above said ancient custom. The book then contains an account of the six-teen hides of land, opposite to each of which is placed its peculiar mark, and above is written: " In the manor of Aston and Coat are sixty-four yard of meadow, four yard is a hide, and of every hide or four yard there belongs a mark or lot for every man to find out his mead by." Then follow a list of all the landholders and the number of cattle which they had a right to put upon the common. It appears that, by the custom of the place, every yard land had a right to put on twelve beasts and forty sheep, and so in proportion. There then comes a yearly record of the names of the sixteens, and of the lot or mark appropriated to each. And in the year 1666 we find Thomas Horde, Esq., as a sixteen in respect of two lots, no doubt in consequence of the importance of his position as lord of the manor. In 1668 he appears as a sixteen for one lot only. So in 1669. In 1670 he is sixteen for two lots, and 1671 for three lots. The custom, thus fortified by the opinion of Sir Orlando Bridgman, continued in full operation until the year 1854, when the lands were inclosed under the provisions of an Act for the inclosure of lands in Bampton in Oxfordshire and Shilton in Berks (*g*).

(*g*) Stat. 16 & 17 Vict. c. 3. The reader will find more than one reference to the customs of this little community in the

It may be interesting to compare this account of a village community in England with the accounts given by Sir Henry Maine in his Lectures on Village Communities in the East. He says (*h*), " It does not appear to me a hazardous proposition that the Indian and the ancient European systems of enjoyment and tillage, by men grouped in village communities, are in all essential particulars identical. There are differences of detail between them; and I think you will find the discussion of these differences and of their apparent causes not uninteresting nor barren of instruction to the student of jurisprudence."

Sir H. Maine on Village Communities. Lecture IV.

Again (*i*), " If very general language were employed, the description of the Teutonic òr Scandinavian village communities might actually serve as a description of the same institution in India. There is the arable mark, divided into separate lots, but cultivated according to minute customary rules, binding on all. Wherever the climate admits of the finer grass crops, there are the reserved meadows, lying generally on the verge of the arable mark. There is the waste or common land, out of which the arable mark has been cut, enjoyed as pasture by all the community *pro indiviso*. There is the village, consisting of habitations, each ruled by a despotic paterfamilias. And there is constantly a council of government to determine disputes as to custom. But there are some characteristics of the institution, of which no traces, or very faint traces, remain in Europe, though they probably once existed, and there are some differences between the European and Indian examples. Identity in the main being

valuable essay of Professor E. Nasse of the university of Bonn on the Agricultural Community of the Middle Ages and Inclosures of the Sixteenth Century in England, which has been trans-lated into English by Col. H. A. Ouvry and is published by the Cobden Club.

(*h*) Lecture IV. p. 103.
(*i*) Page 107.

H

assumed, a good deal of instruction may be obtained
from these distinctions of detail. First, as to the arable
mark or cultivated portion of the village domain.
Here you will naturally expect the resemblance to be
general rather than specific. The official publications
on Indian Settlement law, contain evidence that, in
some parts of the country, the division into three
common fields is to be found; but I do not attach any
importance to the fact, which is probably quite acci-
dental. The conditions of agriculture in a tropical
country are so widely different from those which can at
any period be supposed to have determined cultivation
in Northern and Central Europe, as to forbid us to look
for any resemblances in India, at once widely extended
and exact, to the Teutonic three-field system. Indeed,
as the great agent of production in a tropical country is
water, very great dissimilarities in modes of cultivation
are produced within India itself by relative proximity
to running streams and relative exposure to the periodi-
cal rain-fall. The true analogy between the existing
Indian and the ancient European systems of tillage
must be sought in the minute but multifarious rules
governing the proceedings of the cultivators, rules which
in both cases have the same object—to reconcile a
common plan and order of cultivation on the part of
the whole brotherhood with the holding of distinct lots
in the arable land by separate families. The common
life of the group or community has been so far broken
up as to admit of private property in cultivated land,
but not so far as to allow departure from a joint system
of cultivating that land." Further on (*k*), "I now pass
to the village itself, the cluster of homesteads inhabited
by the members of the community. The description
given by Maurer of the Teutonic mark of the township,
as his researches have shown it to him, might here
again pass for an account, so far as it goes, of an Indian

(*k*) Page 113.

village. The separate households, each despotically governed by its family chief, and never trespassed upon by the footstep of any person of different blood, are all to be found there in practice; although the theory of the absolute rights of heads of families has never from the nature of the case been acknowledged by the British government. But the Indian villages have one characteristic which could only have been gathered from observation of a living society. The German writers have been struck with that complete immunity of the Teutonic homestead from all external interference, which in this country found a later expression in the long-descended commonplace, that an Englishman's house is his castle. But a characteristic which in India goes along with this immunity, and to a great extent explains it, is the extraordinary secrecy of family life; a secrecy maintained, I am told, in very humble households, and under difficulties which at first sight would seem insurmountable. There can be no question that if the isolation of households in ancient societies was always accompanied by this secrecy of their interior life, much which is not quite intelligible in early legal history would be explained."

Again (l), "The waste or common land of the village community has still to be considered. One point of difference between the view taken of it in the East and that which seems at all times to have been taken in Europe deserves to be especially noted. The members of the Teutonic community appear to have valued the village waste chiefly as pasture for their cattle, and possibly may have found it so profitable for this purpose as to have deliberately refrained from increasing that cultivated portion of it, which had been turned into the arable mark. These rights of pasture vested in the commoners are those, I need scarcely tell you, which

(l) Page 120.

H 2

have descended but little modified to our own day in
our own country ; and it is only the modern improvements in the methods of agriculture which have disturbed the balance between pasture and tillage, and
have thus tended to multiply Inclosure Acts. But the
vast bulk of the natives of India are a grain and not a
flesh eating people. Cattle are mostly regarded by
them as auxiliary to tillage. The view therefore
generally taken, as I am told, of the common land by
the community is that it is that part of the village domain
which is temporarily uncultivated, but which will some
time or other be cultivated, and merge in the arable
mark. Doubtless it is valued for pasture, but it is more
especially valued as potentially capable of tillage. The
effect is to produce in the community a much stronger
sense of property in common land than at all reflects
the vaguer feeling of common which in England at all
events characterises the commoners."

Again (m), "India has nothing answering to the
assembly of adult males, which is so remarkable a
feature of the ancient Teutonic groups, except the
council of village elders. It is not universally found.
Villages frequently occur in which the affairs of the
community are managed, its customs interpreted, and
the disputes of its members decided by a single headman, whose office is sometimes admittedly hereditary,
but is sometimes described as elective ; the choice being
generally however in the last case confined in practice
to the members of one particular family, with a strong
preference for the eldest male of the kindred, if he be
not specially disqualified. But I have good authority
for saying that in those parts of India in which the
village community is most perfect, and in which there
are the clearest signs of an original proprietary equality,
between all the families composing the group, the

(m) Page 122.

authority exercised elsewhere by the headman is lodged with the village council."

Again (n), "There is yet another feature of the Indian cultivating groups which connects them with primitive western communities of the same kind. I have several times spoken of them as organized and self-acting. They, in fact, include a nearly complete establishment of occupations and trades for enabling them to continue their collective life without assistance from any person or body external to them. Besides the headman or council, exercising quasi-judicial, quasi-legislative power, they contain a village police, now recognized and paid in certain provinces by the British Government. They include several families of hereditary traders,—the blacksmith, the harness maker, the shoemaker. The Brahmin is also found for the performance of ceremonies; and even the dancing girl for attendance at festivities. There is invariably a village accountant, an important personage among an unlettered population; so important indeed, and so conspicuous, that, according to reports current in India, the earliest English functionaries engaged in settlements of land were occasionally led by their assumption that there must be a single proprietor somewhere, to mistake the accountant for the owner of the village, and to record him as such in the official register. But the person practising any one of these hereditary employments is really a servant of the community, as well as one of its component members. He is sometimes paid by an allowance in grain,—more generally by the allotment to his family of a piece of cultivated land in hereditary possession. Whatever else he may demand for the wares he produces, is limited by a customary standard of price very rarely departed from. It is the assignment of a definite lot in the cultivated area to particular trades, which allows us to

(n) Page 125.

suspect that the early Teutonic groups were similarly
self-sufficing. There are several English parishes in
which certain pieces of land in the common field have
from time immemorial been known by the name of a
particular trade; and there is often a popular belief
that nobody not following the trade can legally be
owner of the lot associated with it. And it is possible
that we here have a key to the plentifulness and per-
sistence of certain names of trades as surnames amongst
us."

Customs as to trades.

You will observe the remarkable similarity of the
custom as to particular trades thus described with the
names of the different persons to whom hams, or pieces
of inclosed pasture land, were allotted in the township
of Aston. There is the hayward who looks after the
hedges; the warden, who seems to have been the church-
warden; the wontner, or mole catcher; the grass steward,
who looked after the meadows; the water hayward, who
looked after the meadows near the water; the water
steward, who regulated the fisheries. The homage certainly were not any particular trade, but were the
tenants of the manor. But the smith was a tradesman
of great importance, and had a ham to himself; so was
the cowherd, who looked after the cattle on the common; so also was the constable, who had a ham to himself. Brander, I should think, was probably the person
by whom the cattle turned out were branded with the
name of their owners. However that may be, one sees
the traces of a self-supporting village community, carried
down to a very recent date, and remarkably coinciding
with the state of things existing amongst village communities in India; for a knowledge of whose customs
we are indebted to the valuable Lectures of Sir Henry
Maine.

LECTURE VIII.

WE have now considered both the nature and origin of
the right of common appendant, which belongs of common right to every owner of land which was anciently
arable; and though originally the waste, on which the
right was exercised, was undefined, yet gradually it has
become limited, in ordinary cases, to the waste of the
manor of which the tenement is held; though in some
cases such a right still exists over wastes, which are not
the property of the lord of the manor, of which the
tenement is held. And this appears to me to come out
very plainly, when we consider the two statutes, to
which I am now about to call your attention,—namely,
the Statute of Merton (a), and the statutes by which it
has been explained and its operation enlarged,—namely,
the Statutes of Westminster 2nd (b), and the statute
3 & 4 Edw. VI. c. 3. The Statute of Merton is as Statute of
follows:—"Also because many great men of England Merton.
(which have enfeoffed knights and their freeholders of
small tenements in their great manors) have complained
that they cannot make their profit of the residue of their
manors, as of wastes, woods, and pastures, whereas the
same feoffees have sufficient pasture, as much as be-
longeth to their tenements, it is provided and granted
that whenever such feoffees do bring an assise of novel
disseisin for their common of pasture, and it is know-
ledged before the justices that they have as much pasture as sufficeth to their tenements, and that they have
free egress and regress from their tenement unto the
pasture, then let them be contented therewith; and
they on whom it was complained shall go quit of as

(a) Stat. 20 Hen. III. c. 4.   (b) Stat. 13 Edw. I. c. 46.

much as they have made their profit of their lands,
wastes, woods, and pastures; and if they allege that
they have not sufficient pasture, or sufficient ingress
and egress according to their hold, then let the truth be
inquired by assise; and if it be found by assise that the
same deforceors have disturbed them of their ingress
and egress, or that they had not sufficient pasture (as
before is said), then shall they recover their seisin by
view of the inquest, so that, by their discretion and
oath, the plaintiffs shall have sufficient ingress and
egress in form aforesaid; and the disseisors shall be
amerced, and shall yield damages as they were wont
before this provision. And if it be certified by the
assise that the plaintiffs have sufficient pasture, with
ingress and egress as before is said, let the other make
their profit of the residue, and go quit of that assise."

Coke's statement that the lord could not approve by the common law.

On this statute Lord Coke makes the following com-
ment (c): "Hereby it appeareth that the lord could not
approve by the order of the common law, because the
common issued out of the whole waste and of every
part thereof; and yet see Trinity Term 6 Hen. III.,
where the lord approved two acres, and left sufficient,
the tenant brought an assise, and, the special matter
being found, the plaintiff *retraxit se*." However, in the
notes to the explanatory Statute of Westminster the
2nd, Lord Coke has the following, which does not seem
to agree with his Commentary on the Statute of
Merton. His note is (d): "Note.—It is not said that
the lord could not improve against a neighbour, but
that the lords were letted by the contradiction of the
neighbours; for by the common law the lord might
improve against any that had common appendant, but
not against a commoner by grant." I do not know
that these two remarks involve a real contradiction.

Whether this statement is contradicted by him.

(c) Second Institute, part 1,   (d) Second Institute, part 2,
p. 85.   p. 474.

My impression is that they refer to two different matters. Where a lord in ancient times granted out a freehold tenement to be held of himself, he also granted, as a matter of course, a right for the tenant to depasture his cattle on the wastes of his manor. Having granted such right, he could not afterwards derogate from his own grant, by inclosing any part of the waste, without the consent of his tenant. But, from what I have already said in previous Lectures, you will see that, in many cases, there was a right of common, belonging to a freehold tenement, over wastes which were not the wastes of the lord of the manor of which the tenement was held, but wastes belonging to some neighbouring lord. As against such common as this, I understand Lord Coke to say, in his note to the Statute of Westminster the 2nd, that the owner of the soil might inclose or improve by the common law, so that he left the commoner sufficiency of pasture. It does not appear to me likely that Lord Coke would have directly contradicted himself in his commentaries on these two statutes. And when we come to consider the wording of the Statute of Westminster the 2nd, I think the view which I have just taken will be confirmed by the language of that statute. As between the lord and tenant, Lord Coke distinctly says that, by the order of the common law, the lord could not approve, because the common issued out of the whole waste; and the fact which he mentions, that the tenant who brought an assise against his lord, who approved two acres and left sufficient, discontinued his suit, on it being found that sufficient common was left for him, does not to my mind alter the case; as it is very probable that the tenant, having sufficient common, did not think it worth his while to insist upon a right which could give him no practical benefit.

The statute, you will observe, relates only to lords or

great men, which have enfeoffed knights and their
freeholders—*milites et alios libere tenentes,* which strictly
means knights and others holding freely. For you
must remember that this statute was passed before the
passing of the Statute of *Quia emptores* (e) ; and that
when this statute was passed, the usual method of alienation was by subinfeudation, or a grant to the alienee
and his heirs, to hold freely of the grantor and his
heirs. When, therefore, the Statute of Merton was
passed, there must have been numerous very recent
feoffments made by great lords to their inferior tenants.
This indeed is shown by the words of the statute,
which are "because many great men of England, who
have enfeoffed knights and others holding freely, com-

Those who
complained
were those
who had
made sub-
infeudations.
Bracton.

plained, &c." Those who complained appear, according
to the letter of the statute, to be the very persons who
made the feoffments. The Treatise of Bracton, who
wrote in the reign of Hen. III., after the passing of the
Statute of Merton, and before the passing of the Statute
of Westminster the 2nd. which explained and enlarged
it, throws light upon this matter. Bracton says, speaking of this statute (f), "But if they, that is, the commoners, were his own tenants, then it is to be considered
in what way they were enfeoffed; because neither all
the tenants, nor in all things, are they restrained by
the statute. Therefore, it is to be seen whether they
were enfeoffed generally, namely, over the whole,
everywhere and in all places, and for all manner of
beasts, and without number, and so that common of
this kind belongs to them by reason of a feoffment,
and not on account of user, such persons the aforesaid
statute does not bind; because it does not take away
a feoffment, although it takes away an abuse, chiefly on
account of the voluntary consent of those who granted

(e) Stat. 18 Edw. I. c. 1. See   (f) Bracton, Book 4, ch. 38,
Lectures on the Seisin of the Free-   par. 17, p. 228.
hold, p. 21.

the servitude and the common ; but if the common was stinted with a certain and determinate number of beasts, although the user had been larger and wider than was necessary, such commoners the statute binds; so that they may be restrained to a certain place and within a certain place : provided always that that place should be sufficient and competent, with free and competent ingress and egress, so that it may not be troublesome or difficult ; but the place ought to be competent, so that it should not be a long distance, but should be assigned nearer. So, in the same manner, if any one should be so enfeoffed, without the expression of number or kind of beasts, but with pasture as much as belongs to such a tenement in the same town, such a person the statute binds, as before when the number is expressed, because, when you have arrived at the quantity of the tenement, it may easily be calculated as to the number of the beasts, and also as to the kind, according to the custom of the places." It seems, therefore, according to Bracton, that the statute binds all those who have common by reason of use, a very large class, and also those to whom common was granted for their beasts levant and couchant on their tenements, which you may remember is the measure of the number of cattle the tenement may put on (g), and also those who have common stinted or restricted to a certain number of cattle. But beyond this the statute did not extend. There are contradictory *dicta* in modern times as to whether or not the Statute of Merton was in affirmance of the common law ; and Lord Coke himself is elsewhere stated to have said that such was the case, particularly in a case of *Procter* v. *Mallorie* in the Star Chamber (h). In this case, however, Lord Coke is reported even to have said that it seems, where men have common in gross of a certain number of beasts, the lord may approve leaving sufficient for them. A dictum which

Whether the Statute of Merton was in affirmance or not of the common law.

Procter v. *Mallorie.*

(g) *Ante*, p. 31.　　　　　　(h) 1 Rolle's Rep. 365.

the reporter very properly queries, for, as he remarks, the Statute of Westminster 2nd appears to the contrary, as it certainly is. As far as I can judge, the truth of the matter is this,—that so far as the statute enabled lords, who had granted the usual common appendant over their wastes, to derogate from their grants by inclosing a portion of the waste, so far the statute gave a new authority, which the lord had not before. But so far as the statute extended to common acquired merely by user, and of which, as we have seen, there must have been a large quantity in those days, so far very probably at common law the lord had a power to improve by inclosure, provided he left sufficiency for the commoners.

The lords then complained that, after they had made these feoffments, they could not make their profit of the residue of their manor, as their wastes, woods and pastures, although their feoffees had sufficient pasture. And Lord Coke explains (i) that, when a lord of a manor, wherein was great waste grounds, did enfeoff others of some parcels of arable land, the feoffees had common in the waste of the lord, as incident to the feoffment. Then on the words, that they could not make their profit of the residue of their manors, Lord Coke observes (k), "Now it is to be seen how this approvement must be. And it must be divided by some inclosure or defence, as it may be made several; for it is lawful to the tenant to put on his cattle into the residue of the common; and if they stray into that part whereof the approvement is made, in default of inclosure, he is no trespasser. And if the lord make a feoffment of certain acres, the feoffee may inclose, because the feoffment is an approvement in his nature." On the words, "let them be contented therewith, and

Inclosure of part approved.

(i) Second Institute, part 1, p. 85.

(k) Second Institute, part 1, p. 86.

they on whom it was complained shall go quit of as much as they have made their profit of their lands, wastes, woods and pastures," Lord Coke remarks (*l*), " By the approvement of part, according to this statute, that part by this Act is discharged of the common, insomuch as, if the tenant, which hath the common, purchase that part, his common is not extinguished in the residue. If the lord do make an approvement he may improve again, as often as he will, so he leave sufficient common." And, " If the tenant at the time of the approvement have sufficient common left unto him in the residue, with a competent way thereunto according to this Act, and after the residue becometh not sufficient, yet the approvement remaineth good, for the words of the statute are, that they should have so much pasture as is sufficient to their tenement." And again (*m*), " If the lord doth inclose any part, and leave not sufficient common in the residue, the commoner may break down the whole inclosure, because it standeth upon the ground which is his common."

Approved part is discharged of common rights.

Lord may approve from time to time.

Approvement good though residue afterwards insufficient.

If common insufficient commoner may break down inclosure.

This statute, however, was confined to cases between the lord and tenant, and did not extend to cases in which common, belonging to a tenement held of one lord, was exercised over waste belonging to another lord; as must frequently have been the case, if our view of the origin of common appendant is correct. In order, therefore, to remedy a doubt, which the Statute of Merton appears to have caused, as to whether the owner of a waste might approve or inclose against persons having rights of common there who were not his tenants, the Statute of Westminster the 2nd was passed (*n*). This statute appears to me to contain a very distinct implication that, at that time, it was

Statute of Westminster the 2nd.

(*l*) Second Institute, part 1, p. 87.

(*m*) Second Institute, part 1, p. 88.

(*n*) Stat. 13 Edw. I. c. 46.

considered that a person might have common of pasture
of common right in waste ground, which was not the
soil and freehold of the lord of the manor of whom he
held his tenement. And if this be so, it seems to me
an additional confirmation of the view that common
appendant was not generally of manorial origin. This
statute refers to the Statute of Merton (o), by which
statute, as we have seen, lords of wastes were empowered
to approve or inclose for cultivation part of such wastes,
notwithstanding the contradiction of their tenants, provided that the tenants had sufficient pasture to their
tenements, with free egress and regress to the same.
And the statute then recites, " forasmuch as no mention
was made between neighbours and neighbours, many
lords of wastes, woods and pastures have been hindered
heretofore by the contradiction of neighbours having
sufficient pasture; and, because foreign tenants have no
more right to common in the wastes, woods or pastures
of any lord than the lord's own tenants; it is ordained
that the Statute of Merton provided between the lord
and his tenants, from henceforth shall hold place
between lords of wastes, woods and pastures and their
neighbours, saving sufficient pasture to their tenants
and neighbours, so that the lords of such wastes, woods
and pastures may make approvement of the residue."
"And this," the statute goes on, " shall be observed by
them who claim pasture as belonging to their tenement.
But if any person claim common of pasture by special
feoffment or grant for a certain number of beasts, *or
otherwise than of common right he ought to have*, since
covenant derogates from the law, he shall have his
recovery as he ought to have by form of the grant
made to him" (p).

(o) Stat. 20 Hen. III. c. 4.

(p) " Et hoc observetur de his
qui clamant pasturam tanquam
pertinentem ad tenementum

suum. Sed si quis clamat com-
muniam pasturæ per speciale feof-
famentum vel concessionem ad
certum numerum averiorum, vel

Here you will observe that the statute was passed in Mistransla- order to enable the owner of waste lands to approve or tion of the Statute of inclose part of such land, notwithstanding that his Westminster the 2nd. neighbour had a right of common of pasture thereon. But the statute was not to extend to any one who had a special feoffment or grant, or who claimed common of pasture, *otherwise than of common right he ought to have ;* evidently implying that a neighbour might, of common right, claim common of pasture in the land of his neighbour. I do not remember to have seen. the language of this statute, which always seemed to me to bo remarkable, commented upon before; and you will find that, in the ordinary copies of the statute, and also in Lord Coke's Second Institute (*q*), where the statute and translation of it are set out at length, this part of the statute is mistranslated. The passage there runs in this form, "But if any do claim common by special feoffment or grant for a certain number of beasts, or otherwise, which he ought to have of common right, whereas covenant barreth the law, he shall have such recovery as he ought to have had by form of the grant made unto him." The words of the original are "vel alio modo quam de jure communi habere deberet," which certainly mean " or otherwise than of common right he ought to have." And you will find in a subsequent statute, in which this statute is recited, that portion of it to which I have just referred, is translated in the recital in the way I have translated it. The statute is Stat. 3 & 4 Edw. VI. c. 3, s. 2. the 3 & 4 Edw. VI. c. 3, s. 2, by which the Statute of Merton and this Statute of Westminster the 2nd were confirmed, saving only certain small encroachments which had then already been made, and which were not to be affected by such confirmation. If a man might have, of common right, common appendant to

alio modo quam de jure communi habere deberet, cum conventio legi deroget, habeat suum recu- perare, quale habere deberet per formam concessionis sibi factæ."

(*q*) Part 2, p. 473.

his tenement, in lands not belonging to the lord of
whom his tenement was held, it would be a strong
circumstance to show, that there must have been some
origin of the ordinary right of common appendant to
lands, prior to the time when vills and townships were
granted out to lords of manors.

With regard to neighbours, Bracton, writing after the
passing of the Statute of Merton but before the passing
of the Statute of Westminster the 2nd, has the fol-

Bracton's re-
marks on the
operation of
the Statute of
Merton as to
neighbours.

lowing remarks (*r*), "If the commoner is a stranger, the
statute does not impose any law upon him, because he
has the servitude perhaps by consent and agreement,
everywhere, which cannot be dissolved but by a contrary
will and dissent, also because he has not been enfeoffed
by the lord of the soil, so as to allow his being restrained to a number certain and determinate, according to the quantity of his tenement ; and hence, in
this case, if the lord of the soil and property wishes to
appropriate any part to himself and inclose it, this he
cannot do without the will and license of the aforesaid
commoners ; and if he should do it, they can recover by
assise." Here you will observe that Bracton, speaking
of neighbours, merely says that they are not bound by
the Statute of Merton ; and he says that the right on
another man's land may have been granted by consent
and agreement, and the commoner has not been enfeoffed with the right to put on any certain and determinate number. Bracton leaves unnoticed the case in
which the neighbour's right of common may have been
acquired by user. He was commenting only on the
Statute of Merton, and had no occasion to notice this
case. This case, however, would appear to have frequently occurred, and I take it that it was the frequency
of the occurrence of such cases which gave occasion for
the passing of the Statute of Westminster the 2nd.

(*r*) Bracton, Book 4, ch. 38, par. 17, p. 228.

Lord Coke says (s) that, against common thus acquired by use, and not by grant, the lord might have inclosed at common law. And I see no reason to take any exception to this statement.

There is a case of *Glover* v. *Lane* (t), in which it was held that the owner of a waste, in which his neighbours had common, might approve under the Statute of Westminster the 2nd, although he was not lord of any manor. The act extends to every owner of the soil over which his neighbours have rights of common. And in the case of *Patrick* v. *Stubbs* (u), it was said by Baron Rolfe that "the Statute of Merton says nothing as to the nature or extent of the interest that the lord is to have in the soil; and it must be quite indifferent to the commoner, if enough common of pasture is left to him, whether the lord of the manor inclose in his own right or as the grantee of another."

Glover v. *Lane.* Owner of soil may approve.

The statute is silent as to the extent of the lord's interest.

To proceed with our statute : Lord Coke remarks (x) on the words "this shall be observed by them who claim pasture as belonging to their tenements," that "here it is to be observed that neither this statute nor the Statute of Merton doth extend to any common but to common appendant or appurtenant to his tenement, and not to a common in gross to a certain number." The statutes, however, extend to common appurtenant. This was distinctly decided by the Court of Appeal in the recent case of *Robinson* v. *The Maharajah Duleep Singh* (y). "What follows," says Lord Justice Cotton (z), "is in effect this, that if a man produces his grant which says that he shall have a grant, not only of

Statutes do not extend to common in gross.

Extend to common appurtenant.

(s) Second Institute, part 2, p. 474.

(t) 3 T. Rep. 445.

(u) 9 Mee. & Wels. 838.

(x) Second Institute, part 2, p. 475.

(y) 27 W. R. 21; L. R., 11 Ch. D. 798.

(z) L. R., 11 Ch. D. 822.

sufficient pasture for his cattle—which I suppose would
be the presumed grant — but pasture for a certain
number of cattle over all and every part of certain
waste, then the statute is not to enable a man to derogate from that which has been expressly granted. Here
there is no express grant the terms of which the defendant is violating, but it is said that this is a right
which is prescribed for and depends on a presumed
grant, and therefore the defendant cannot avail himself
of the Statute of Merton, because the Statute of Westminster the Second prevents him from doing so. In my
opinion that is a mis-construction of the statute, which
giving the right, or recognizing the right, as existing as
against such as claim pasturage as appurtenant to their
tenements—that is, by presumed grant—says that it
shall not apply so as to enable a man to derogate from
that which he has expressly and in terms granted.   It
does not say that in no case of express grant shall he be
entitled to do what the defendant is, in the present case,
doing.   If it is not in derogation of the express terms
of his grant, why should the Court prevent him from
doing it ?   In my opinion we cannot but come to the conclusion that, if this is a right of common, it is in the
nature of common appurtenant, and that as against such
a right of common the Statute of Merton applies."

Windmill,
curtilage, &c.
            The statute goes on to enact " that by occasion of a
windmill, sheepcote, dairy, or the necessary augmenta-
tion of a court or curtilage, for the future no man shall
be grieved by assise of novel disseisin for common of
pasture." On this passage Lord Coke observes (a) "there
be five kinds of improvements expressed, that both
between lord and tenant, and neighbour and neighbour,
may be done without leaving sufficient common to them
that have it, anything either herein or in the Statute of

(a) Second Institute, part 2, p. 475.

Merton to the contrary notwithstanding; and these five are put but for examples; for the lord may erect a house for the dwelling of a beast keeper for the safe custody of the beasts as well of the lord as of the commoners depasturing there, in that soil, and yet it is not within the letter of this law." Then, with regard to a necessary curtilage, he observes (b) *necessarii* is to be applied to curtilage, both in congruity and by our books; and *necessary* shall not be taken according to the quantity of the freehold he hath there, but according to his person, estate or degree, and for his necessary dwelling and abode; for if he hath no freehold there in that town but his house only, yet may he make a necessary enlargement of his curtilage."

Necessary curtilage.

Lord Coke, in the margin, refers to a case in the 32nd year of the reign of King Edward III., reported in the Book of Assises (c). The Book of Assises is a book of the assises and pleas of the Crown, moved and depending before the justices, as well in their circuits as elsewhere, in the time of King Edward III. In this case, on an assise of novel disseisin, the plaintiff made his plea of common in an acre of land, from the feast of St. Michael until Candlemas, if the land was not sown, and, if the land was sown before Candlemas, then of common from the feast of St. Michael until the land was sown, with all manner of beasts. Finch, the opposite counsel, said he could not have an assise, because there is in the same town a messuage, and from ancient times there has been a messuage and forty acres of land, and this, which he calls an acre of land, is not, perhaps, but a rod of land, and was adjoining to his messuage; and, because his messuage was too small for his dwelling and for his necessaries, according to his estate, he inclosed this rod of land, and on part of it he

Case in the Book of Assises as to inclosure for enlargement of messuage.

(b) Second Institute, part 2, p. 476. (c) 32 Ass. par. 5.

I 2

built rooms necessary to his estate, namely, two granges and two dove houses, and other rooms, and of the rest he made a curtilage; and he demanded judgment, whether the assise should be. And he was driven to say how much was built upon, and how much was curtilage; wherefore he said that one moiety was built upon, and the other moiety was curtilage. Wichingham, the opposite counsel, said that it was an acre of land, as they had said, and that the plaintiff had over this land a common chase and re-chase of his beasts of the same town; and they denied that the defendant had a house, and that the house was not sufficiently convenient and large for his freehold, which he had in the same town; so that it was inclosed without necessity. Finch replied that the statute spoke nothing of the quantity of land, and only that he might inclose that which is necessary to him for his dwelling; so that a man may inclose and enlarge his house, having regard to his person and his estate, and not to the quantity of land. *Skipwith* (who was a judge): A man may have more advantage from his house than all the rest of his land, so that the quantity of the land is not to the purpose on the words of the statute. *Green* (also a judge): If a man has only one house in a town, still he may enlarge the house by the statute; for the benefit of the statute is only that a man may amend his house for his dwelling, and not for the land. Wherefore the issue shall be, whether it was inclosed by necessity, as he has said, or without necessity. And so it was. You will observe here, that the common was claimed for the beasts in a town or vill. It was not claimed over waste land, but over land which was sometimes cultivated, and it was evidently a claim between neighbour and neighbour, according to the Statute of Westminster the 2nd. And it was also a claim, not for commonable cattle only, but for all manner of beasts, and so was a claim for common appurtenant. And the Court held, that the question to be decided simply was, whether the inclosure made by the defendant was necessary or not for his habitation, according to his estate and degree.

There is a modern case on this branch of the statute, namely, the case of *Patrick* v. *Stubbs (d)*, in which it *Patrick* v. was held that the owner of a waste might lawfully erect *Stubbs.* two cottages thereon, for the habitation of two wood- Cottages for wards to preserve the woods, and as beast keepers for woodwards. the safe custody of the cattle of the plaintiff, and of other persons entitled to rights of common. The Court proceeded on the authority of Lord Coke and his com-mentary, which says, as you have seen, that the in-stances put in the act are put merely by way of example. Indeed, as the Court remarked, the building of a house for a beast keeper was expressly said by Lord Coke to be within the spirit of the act.

The statute goes on as follows: "And where some-time it chanceth that one having right to approve doth then make a dyke or a hedge, and some by night or at another time when they suppose not to be espied, do If the hedge overthrow the hedge or dyke, and it cannot be known, be over-thrown, the by verdict of the assize or jury, who did overthrow the men of the hedge or dyke, and the men of the towns near will not towns to indict such as be guilty of the fact, the towns near ad- make it good. joining shall be distrained to make the hedge or dyke at their own cost, and to yield damages." This part of the statute again, by its reference to adjacent towns, seems to add confirmation to our theory with regard to commons having anciently existed in respect of towns. The men of the towns near ought to have indicted those who wrongfully pulled down the dyke or fence ; if they failed to do so the towns, by this statute, were to be distrained to make the hedge or dyke at their own expense.

(d) 9 Mee. & Wels. 830. See also *Nevill* v. *Hancerton*, 1 Lev. 62.

LECTURE IX.

AN important inroad on the Statutes of Merton (*a*) and
Westminster the Second (*b*) has been made by the
Commons Act, 1876 (*c*), which provides (*d*) that any
person intending to inclose or approve a common, or
part of a common, otherwise than under the provisions

Notice of an
intended in-
closure to be
given.of that act, shall give notice to all persons claiming any
legal right in such common, or part of a common, by
publishing, at least three months beforehand, a statement of his intention to make such inclosure, for three
successive times and in two or more of the principal
local newspapers in the county, town or district in which
the common or part of a common proposed to be inclosed is situate ; but the provisions of this section shall
not apply to any commons or waste lands whereon the
rights of common are vested solely in the lord of the
manor. A production of a newspaper containing such
advertisement as aforesaid shall be evidence of the same
having been issued, and the inclosure shall, until the
contrary is proved, be deemed to have taken place at
the time specified in such advertisement.

When the owner of a waste wishes to improve or
inclose it, under either of the Statutes of Merton or

Onus on lord
to prove suf-
ficiency.Westminster the Second, the onus lies on him to prove
that he has left sufficient common for all the commoners
entitled to common on the waste, together with sufficient egress and regress for their cattle. This doctrine

(*a*) Stat. 20 Hen. III. c. 4 ;   *ante*, p. 110.
ante, p. 103.

(*b*) Stat. 13 Edw. I. c. 46 ;   (*c*) Stat. 39 & 40 Vict. c. 56.
(*d*) Sect. 31.

is thus laid down by Mr. Justice Bayley in the case
of *Arlett* v. *Ellis* (e). " It seems to me that the lord's
right is this : he may approve, provided he leave sufficiency of common of pasturage for all the cattle which
are entitled to feed upon it. The common may originally have been destined for a definite number of
cattle, or for all cattle levant and couchant upon certain
lands. Many of those rights may be extinguished, or
the common itself may produce so much more herbage,
that a smaller portion of that common may be sufficient
for depasturing the cattle of the persons entitled, than
when it was originally destined to that purpose. Now,
whenever that is the case, I think that the lord has a
right to inclose; but in order to justify making the
inclosure, it is incumbent upon him or his grantee, when
the right to inclose is questioned, to show that there is
sufficiency of common left." So Lord Hatherley, in
the case of *Betts* v. *Thompson* (f), says : " As to the
argument that there was still enough waste left, the
onus of the proof was on the lord ; and even in cases
where a very large extent of common has been left, the
lord must prove that he has left enough." This proof Proof of suf-
is not always easy ; for it seems to involve in it a ficiency.
proof of the number of persons entitled to rights of
common, and of the nature and amount of their respective rights, in regard to which it would not always
be easy to obtain sufficient evidence. On this point
there is not a great deal of authority. In the case
of *Lake* v. *Plaxton* (g), it was held that the right of Lake v.
the crown to turn deer on the waste did not form an Plaxton.
element for the consideration of the jury on the question of sufficiency of common, in a case where no deer
had been turned on the waste for upwards of twenty
years. It is clear, however, that the right of the crown

(e) 7 B. & C. 369.   (g) 10 Ex. 196.
(f) L. R., 6 Ch. 723, 741.

to turn on deer would not be affected by twenty years non-user, and this case, which related to Epping Forest, cannot be relied on after the decision of the Master of the Rolls in the Epping Forest case, *The Commissioners of Sewers* v. Glasse (*h*).

Lascelles v. *Lord Onslow.*

In the recent case of *Lascelles* v. *Lord Onslow* (*i*), the Court—JJ. Mellor and Lush—were of opinion that if the lord could prove that he had left sufficiency for all the cattle that had been usually put upon the waste for the last ten years, this was enough. Modern use is, however, I venture to think, a very fallacious guide. Sheep and cattle are often now too valuable to be put upon a common, where they run the risk of catching infectious diseases from the poorer and less cared for cattle and sheep, which other commoners may put on. And yet the owner would be sorry to lose his full right of common, and I think ought not to do so, because perhaps for some years he has not fully exercised it. And in the

Musgrave v. *Inclosure Commissioners.*

recent case of *Musgrave* v. *Inclosure Commissioners* (*k*), the Court came to the conclusion that a right of common of pasture existed, and had been usually enjoyed, in respect of a farm called Main's Farm, over a waste called The Fell, although there had been no user at all from 1828 to 1844, sixteen years. The tenant, in 1828, turned a few horses on The Fell, and also sixteen or eighteen sheep during the summer of that year, and a pony in 1844 or 1845. But he did not keep a flock fit to be turned on The Fell; and sheep were not sent by him to The Fell because there was better pasture on the Main Farm. And yet, because in old deeds rights of common generally had been granted, with rights of way for cattle and sheep to and from The Fell, it was held that there was sufficient evidence of a right of pasturage usually enjoyed in respect of this farm;

(*h*) L. R., 19 Eq. 134. (*k*) L. R., 9 Q. B. 162.
(*i*) L. R., 2 Q. B. Div. 433.

although for considerably more than ten years not a single cow, horse, or sheep had been put upon the waste.

The proceedings under the old *writ of admeasurement of pasture* throw some light upon this subject. They are well described by Blackstone in his Commentaries (*l*). He says, "This writ lies, either when a common appurtenant or in gross is certain as to number, or where a man has common appendant or appurtenant to his land, the quantity of which common has never yet been ascertained. In either of these cases, as well the lord as any of the commoners, is entitled to this writ of admeasurement, which is one of those writs which are called *ricontiel*, being directed to the sheriff (vice comiti), and not to be returned to any superior Court till finally executed by him. It recites a complaint that the defendant hath surcharged, *superoneravit*, the common; and therefore commands the sheriff to admeasure and apportion it; that the defendant may not have more than belongs to him, and that the plaintiff may have his rightful share. And upon this suit all the commoners shall be admeasured, as well those who have not, as those who have surcharged the common, as well the plaintiff as the defendant. The execution of this writ must be by a jury of twelve men, who are upon their oaths to ascertain, under the superintendence of the sheriff, what and how many cattle each commoner is entitled to feed. And the rule for this admeasurement is generally understood to be, that the commoner shall not turn more cattle upon the common than are sufficient to manure and stock the land to which his right of common is annexed; or, as our ancient law expressed it, such cattle only as are *levant* and *couchant* upon his tenement" (*m*). Here you observe that all the com-

Writ of admeasurement of pasture.

(*l*) Vol. 3, p. 238.   (*m*) *Ante*, p. 31.

moners were admeasured, as well those who had not as those who had surcharged the common. And this seems the only sure way of ascertaining whether there is a deficiency or not. In case of deficiency every commoner would be obliged in fairness to abate proportionably, and there would be no means of arriving at each man's due proportion, but by ascertaining how many sheep and cattle each commoner's tenement would carry, as levant and couchant thereon. And I confess that I cannot see how else the question of sufficiency can be fairly determined, whenever a substantial portion of the common is inclosed. In the recent case of *Robinson* v. *Duleep Singh* (n), Mr. Justice Fry came to the conclusion that the increase of an inclosure round a warrener's house on the common from three acres and a-half to seven acres did not interfere with the sufficiency of the common as a common for sheep. The common was eleven miles round. There were not many commoners. Very little feed grew on the part inclosed. There was grass in some places, but most parts of the common produced a kind of moss in great abundance, which, when dry, the sheep would not eat, but which after rain was far more than enough for all the sheep that the commoners had a right to turn on. The writ of admeasurement of pasture was abolished by stat. 3 & 4 Will. IV. c. 27 (o), along with a number of others, and in fact the whole of the ancient writs in real and mixed actions (except proceedings for freebench and dower, quare impedit for presentations to benefices, and ejectment). The usual remedies for surcharging a common are, on the lord's part, by distraining so many of the cattle or sheep as are in excess of the number allowed (p), or by action of trespass. On the part of any commoner the remedy is by action on the case (q).

Robinson v.
Duleep Singh.

Writ now
abolished.

Remedies for
surcharge.
Distress,

trespass,
case.

(n) L. R., 11 Ch. D. 798.

(o) Sect. 36.

(p) *Ellis* v. *Rowles*, Willes, 638.

(q) *Hall* v. *Harding*, 4 Bur. 2426; *Cape* v. *Scott*, L. R., 9 Q. B. 269.

I now come to consider the question whether the Statute of Merton extends to copyholders, who have, by custom, a right of common on the waste. The copyholder, you may remember, is in law but a tenant at will; he cannot, therefore, prescribe, as a prescription must be made in the name of the owner of the fee; and the owner of the fee is the lord of the manor, on whose waste it is that the common is claimed. The law therefore allows him to claim by custom (*r*). I apprehend, however, that in the case of an ordinary copyholder, having common by custom on the waste, the lord may approve under the Statute of Merton (*s*). When this statute was passed, I apprehend that it could hardly have been contended that the lord could not inclose against copyholders, whose position then was of a much more uncertain kind than it is at present. And in the case of *Shakespear* v. *Peppin* (*t*), the point was given up by counsel. The lord, however, in the case of copyholders, equally with freeholders, is bound to show that he has left sufficiency of common for all the commoners. In some manors a right is claimed by the lord of granting any part of the waste as copyhold, to be holden of himself by copyhold tenure. Wherever such a custom as this exists, the presumption is that the whole of the waste is of a demisable quality; and, when the grant is made, the tenant becomes a copyholder by virtue of the custom of the manor, just as much as if he had been a copyholder from time immemorial. A custom of this kind, however, is invalid, unless each grant be accompanied with proof, on the part of the lord, that he has left sufficient common for all the commoners. A custom for the lord to grant at his pleasure any part of the waste, irrespective of sufficiency for the commoners, would evidently be destructive to their rights, and as

Copyholders.

Lord may approve against copyholders having customary rights of common.

Shakespear v. *Peppin.*

Grant of part of waste as copyhold.

Custom to grant at pleasure void.

(*r*) *Ante*, p. 17.

(*s*) Stat. 20 Hen. III. c. 4.

(*t*) 6 T. Rep. p. 741.

such would be void (*u*). This is in analogy to the
Statute of Merton. The inclosure under the Statute
of Merton is an inclosure of freeholds ; but, where
the lord grants as copyhold parcel of the waste to be
holden of the manor, that is not within the letter of
the Statute of Merton. But it is held to be within
its spirit ; and the lord cannot grant part of the

Lord must
prove that he
has left suf-
ficiency of
common.
Arlett v. *Ellis*.

waste to be holden as copyhold, by virtue of the custom of the manor in this respect, unless he proves that
he has left sufficiency of common (*x*). In the case of
Arlett v. *Ellis*, the lord of the manor granted two acres
of land, part of the waste, to hold to the plaintiff, his
heirs and assigns according to the custom of the manor,
at the yearly rent of 2*s*. 6*d*. and all other burdens and
services ; and the plaintiff paid for a fine 8*l*. and was
admitted tenant. This was in October, 1825. In
February, 1826, the plaintiff began to inclose the piece
of ground, and made an embankment ; but, before the
inclosure was completed, the defendants, on the 7th
of March then following, entered upon the land and
threw down the embankment. There was neither turf
fit for fuel, nor pasture, on the land in question ; and
the defendants had no cattle with them, nor any instruments to cut turves. They might have entered
upon the common, and upon the piece of land in question, and turned on their cattle, without throwing down
the embankment (*y*). The plaintiff produced several
entries from the court rolls of various grants of parcels
of the waste, made by the lords of the manor, from the
year 1650 to the time of the trial. It did not appear
on the face of the grants that they were made with the
consent of the homage, or that a sufficiency of common
remained for the commoners. The jury found on the
trial that the defendants did more than was necessary

(*u*) *Badger* v. *Ford*, 3 B. & A.   (*x*) 7 B. & C. 346.
153 ; *Arlett* v. *Ellis*, 7 B. & C.   (*y*) 7 B. & C. 349.
346.

for the purpose of asserting their right of common. The learned judge at the trial then directed a verdict to be entered for the plaintiff for 1s. damages; but reserved liberty to the defendants to move to enter a nonsuit, if the Court should be of opinion that the custom was void. In Easter Term, 1827, a rule nisi for a new trial was obtained, on the ground that the defendant had not done more than he was entitled to do, in the exercise of his right of common, and also on the ground that it ought to have been averred that a sufficiency of common was left. And of this opinion was the Court, who made the rule absolute for a new trial. In this case it was proved that there were 2,000 acres of waste land uninclosed (z); but it appeared that there were a great number of tenants; and it was not shown that the common left was sufficient for them all. This is a very strong case, because it appeared that the ground was only two acres, and that there was neither turf nor pasture upon the land in question.

In some manors there is a custom for the lord to grant part of the waste as copyhold with the consent of the homage; and sometimes also a custom for the lord to inclose as freehold part of the waste with the consent of the homage. The homage in this case means the tenants of the manor, who in ancient times were bound to do homage to their lord (a); and it comprises both the freeholders of the manor and also the copyholders, if any. Where a custom of this kind exists it seems to me that the Statute of Merton cannot apply. That statute authorizes the lord to inclose any part of the waste, leaving a sufficiency of common. But, if there be a custom of the manor that the consent of the homage is to be obtained to the lord's grant or the lord's inclosure, surely it would be an utter destruction

Custom to grant with consent of homage.

The homage.

(z) 7 B. & C. 377.   (a) See Lectures on the Seisin of the Freehold, pp. 9, 12.

to this custom, if the lord could inclose, leaving a sufficiency of common. If the custom is valid, and I apprehend that there is no doubt that it is, then the lord cannot inclose without obtaining the consent of the homage. The case seems to me to fall within the exception contained in the Statute of Westminster the 2nd (b), "That agreement barreth the law." Such a custom must have had its origin in an agreement between the lord and his tenants that he would not inclose any part of the waste without their consent. I am not aware of any authority on this exact point. There is a case, *Duberley* v. *Page* (c), in which there was a custom of the manor which was held to be over-ridden by the right of the lord conferred upon him by the Statute of Merton. But when the case comes to be considered, it will be seen that it was not a custom for the lord to inclose with the consent of the homage, but merely a custom enabling a tenant to inclose any part of the waste to be held as copyhold, *first obtaining the consent of the lord*, and then obtaining the licence of the homage. I have obtained an office copy of the pleas in this case. The manor in question was the Manor of Harrow, otherwise Sudbury, in the County of Middlesex; and the custom is thus set out in the pleadings:

Duberley v. *Page.*

Custom of the manor as set out in the pleadings in *Duberley* v. *Page.*

"Within the said manor there now is, and from time whereof the memory of man is not to the contrary there hath been, a certain ancient and laudable custom, there used and approved of, that is to say, that, if any person or persons during all the time aforesaid have or hath been desirous to improve or inclose any part of the waste of the said manor of Harrow, otherwise Sudbury, with the appurtenances, whereof, &c., such person or persons, so desirous to improve and inclose as aforesaid, during all the time aforesaid, have or hath repaired to the homage of the Court Baron of the said manor, at a

---

(b) Stat. 13 Edw. I. c. 46.　　　　　(c) 2 T. Rep. 391, 392.

General Court of the same Court Baron, holden in and
for the said manor, according to the custom of the said
manor, from time immemorial used and approved of
within the said manor ; and such person or persons have
or hath, during all the time aforesaid, at such General
Court desired that such his, her, or their desire to improve or inclose any part of the wastes of the said
manor (first obtaining the consent and licence of the
lord of the said manor whereof, &c., for the time being
so to improve or inclose) might be presented by the
homage of the said Court Baron of the said manor at
such General Court, holden in and for the said manor ;
and that, if the said homage of the Court Baron of the
said manor, at such General Court so holden as aforesaid, have, during all the time aforesaid, thought in
their consciences that the said intended inclosure was of
no prejudice to any tenant or tenants of the said manor,
but that the same might be granted, that then the said
homage of the said Court Baron of the said manor, at
such General Court so holden as aforesaid, have, during
all the time aforesaid, presented and have used and
been accustomed to present, and of right during all the
time aforesaid ought to have presented, and still of
right ought to present, at the said General Court so
holden as aforesaid, that such person or persons, so
desiring the said inclosure (first obtaining the consent
and licence of the lord of the said manor for the time
being) might and may inclose the same ; and, after
making such presentment as aforesaid, the said presentment so made hath been publickly read in open
Court, at such General Court so holden as aforesaid ;
and, if no tenant or tenants then and there present
at such General Court, have or hath, upon the reading of the said presentment, forbid the inclosing of
the said part of the wastes so intended to be inclosed as
aforesaid, that then the steward for the time being at
the said Court Baron of the said manor, at such General

Court so holden as aforesaid, hath set a fine, and hath used and been accustomed to set a fine and rent upon such person or persons so desiring to inclose the said part of the said wastes as aforesaid, for and in respect of the said part of the wastes so intended to be inclosed as aforesaid; and hath, during the time aforesaid, granted, and hath used and been accustomed to grant the same part of the waste, so intended to be inclosed as aforesaid, to such person or persons, so desiring the same to be inclosed as aforesaid, and to no other person, by a copy according to the custom of the said manor; and it hath not been lawful for and during all the time aforesaid for any tenant or tenants of the said manor, for any time after, to forbid or otherwise to hinder the said inclosure so intended to be made, and made, in pursuance of the said custom as aforesaid, or otherwise to disturb the said person or persons or his or their heirs or assigns, or his or their tenant or tenants thereof, in the quiet enjoying of the said waste ground so inclosed as aforesaid, in pursuance of such custom as aforesaid."

The special custom in *Duberley* v. *Page* did not prevent lord's right to approve.

This custom, you will see, is a very different custom from that which not unfrequently exists, by which the lord is empowered to inclose, or to grant as copyhold, part of the waste, first obtaining the consent of the homage. And, in the present case, the custom was held not to interfere with the right of the lord to inclose under the Statute of Merton. Justice *Ashurst* said (d), " The right of the lord of the manor in this case is a common law right, and not dependant upon any custom; every custom must be construed according to the subject-matter of it. Here it is only applicable to the tenants of the manor. It gives them a right of inclosing under certain restrictions, which they would not

(d) 2 T. Rep. 392, n.

otherwise have been entitled to do at all. But the right here exercised by the lord is superior to the custom, and derived from the common law." *Buller*, Justice, also said, " These customs are in favour of the tenants of the manor, but by no means abridge the common law right of the lord. For, by common law, he alone had a right to inclose, and this privilege has been extended to the tenant under certain restrictions, and in this instance the previous steps necessary to be taken were intended as a benefit to the lord, and not as a restraint on him; for before any person can inclose or take any steps towards it, he must first obtain the consent of the lord. The words are, ' any person being desirous of inclosing may apply to the Court, &c., first obtaining the consent of the lord;' therefore, in no instance, can the tenant inclose without such consent."

It is curious that this is the same manor as that in the case of *Lord Northwick* v. *Stanway* (e). In this case *Lord Northwick* v. *Stanway.* it was said, that within the manor there was a custom for the lord to grant parcels of the waste, whenever he should think proper, to hold by copy of court roll,— that there were many tenements within the manor, which had been holden immemorially by copy of court roll, and many which had been granted in the above manner out of the waste. A general custom, however, for the lord to grant parcels of the waste, to hold by copy, whenever he should think proper, would be void, unless the lord could prove that a sufficiency of common was left (f). There may have been, in addition to the custom detailed in the pleadings of *Duberley* v. *Page*, another custom for the lord himself to grant parcels of the waste, provided he left sufficiency of common. In the case of *Lord Northwick* v. *Stanway*, the defendant refused to pay a fine, which had been assessed on his

(e) 3 Bos. & Pul. 346.   (f) *Ante*, p. 123.

W.P.   K

admission to a copyhold tenement, formerly part of the waste, on the ground that the premises were not strictly copyhold ; because it was the essence of copyhold tenure that the premises should have been demised or demisable by copy of court roll from time immemorial ; whereas it appeared in the present case that the premises had been parcel of the waste within time of memory. But, with respect to this point, the Court observed that, although the premises in question had been newly granted by copy of court roll, yet that, having been granted by virtue of an immemorial custom to demise parcel of the wastes as copyhold, they were to be considered as much copyhold tenements as if they had been immemorially holden by copy of court roll; and that the tenure had its foundation in custom, which had immemorially attached upon the waste, the subject of the grant.

Customs to inclose with consent of homage.
Stepney.

A custom for the lord to make grants or inclosures of part of the waste with the consent of the homage continues in several manors. In the manor of Stepney, in the county of Middlesex, there is a custom for the lords of the manor, upon the presentment of seven of the copyholders thereof, to determine what waste ground was to be set out and inclosed, in order to build on the same ; and such presentment being agreed unto by the major part of the homage at the next court, the same was set out and inclosed accordingly. This custom was

Lady Wentworth v. Clay.

held valid in the case of *Lady Wentworth* v. *Clay and others* (g), and it was held that the lady of the manor had power to grant leases and estates at her pleasure of

Hampstead.

land which had been so set out. The manor of Hampstead is also an instance ; and the custom is mentioned in the case of *Folkard* v. *Hemmett* (h), which was a case relating to this manor. The custom is there stated to be a custom for the lord, with the consent of the homage,

(g) Cases temp. Finch, 263.   (h) 5 T. Rep. 417, n.

to make grants of portions of the wastes for the purpose of building. In this manor the custom appears to be also to grant portions of the waste as copyhold. The case of *Folkard* v. *Hemmett* is reported on another point in Sir Wm. Blackstone's Reports (*i*), from which it appears that the manor in question was the manor of Hampstead. On a case of this sort, Mr. Justice Bayley makes the following remarks in the case of *Arlett* v. *Ellis* (*k*):—"In *Folkard* v. *Hemmett* the grant of the soil was made by the lord with the consent of the homage. Now, the homage are persons associated together at the lord's court (at which all the tenants of the manor may attend) to act as between the lord and his tenants. Being tenants themselves, it is not very likely that they will lean unfairly towards the lord; and if the homage say, therefore, that a grant shall be made, assuming that the lord has a right to grant wherever there is more land than is necessary for the purpose of the commoners, it may be reasonably presumed that the homage have given their consent to the grant, only when it is clear that the land granted may be taken by the grantor, without interfering with the rights of the commoners; and, on the other hand, it may be fairly presumed that the homage would never consent to any part of the common being taken away from the tenants, unless they were satisfied that sufficient remained for the commoners. The case, therefore, is distinguishable from the present: there the grant was made with the consent of the homage, here it is done by the act of the lord himself." Where, therefore, the lord is, by custom, bound to obtain the consent of the homage before he can inclose, I apprehend that the Statute of Merton will not enable him to make an inclosure without such consent.

Where there is a custom for the lord of a manor to inclose or grant any part of the waste with the consent

Homage can only bind tenants of manor.

(*i*) Vol. 2, p. 106.　　　(*k*) 7 B. & C. 368.

K 2

of the homage, it must always be remembered that the homage assembled at the lord's court can only bind those whom they represent, namely, the rest of the tenants of the manor. If any persons, not tenants of the manor, should have rights of common on the waste, the resolution of the homage will not bind them. There is a case *Boulcott* v. *Winmill.* of *Boulcott* v. *Winmill* (*l*), which related to the manor of West Ham, in Epping Forest, in which it was held that a custom for the lord, with the assent of the homage, to grant parcels of the waste, to be held in severalty by copy of court roll, and inclosed, in exclusion of *all persons* having rights of common, was a valid custom. But Overruled in *Commissioners of Sewers* v. *Glasse.* this case was overruled by the present Master of the Rolls, in the case of *The Commissioners of Sewers* v. *Glasse* (*m*). His lordship remarked (*n*) that *Boulcott* v. *Winmill* appears to have been a collusive action. In the *Lascelles* v. *Lord Onslow.* recent case of *Lascelles* v. *Lord Onslow* (*o*), it was held that grants made by the lord of a manor under a custom of portions of the waste to hold as copyhold, with the consent of the homage, all of whom were copyholders, were binding on the freeholders who were summoned to attend, and who might have done so if they pleased.

Whether copyholder grantee of waste is entitled to common. When there is a custom in a manor for the lord to grant a part of the waste as copyhold, either at his own discretion, leaving sufficiency of common, or with the consent of the homage, a question may arise, whether the grantee has or has not a right of common upon the residue of the waste in respect of the land so granted to him. If the lord approves under the Statute of Merton, or approves part of the waste as freehold with the consent of the homage, there is no doubt that the land so approved is not only discharged from all rights of common over it, but cannot entitle its owner to place any Bracton. cattle upon the common. Bracton says, speaking of the

(*l*) 2 Camp. 259.   (*n*) Page 143.
(*m*) L. R., 19 Eq. 134.   (*o*) L. R., 2 Q. B. Div. 433.

defences which may be made to a claim of common, that one defence may be, that no common belongs to such a tenement, because it was formerly forest, wood, and a place and common of vast solitude, and has lately been *assarted*, or newly inclosed or reduced to cultivation; and common ought not to belong to common, and to a place where all in the country were accustomed to have common (*p*). The expression, "where all of the country were accustomed to have common," is remarkable as showing how much ancient rights of common were acquired rather by user than by express grant. If, however, the piece of land, newly inclosed from the common, be granted to hold as copyhold under a custom for that purpose, then it would rather seem that, the custom being from time immemorial, the copyholder would have the same rights and privileges as any other copyholder. He becomes, in fact, an ancient copyholder by virtue of the antiquity of the custom. In the case of *Lord Northwick* v. *Stanway* (*q*), to which I have already referred (*r*), it was said that the tenements granted out of the waste were called *waste hold* copyholds, whilst other tenements were called ancient copyholds, and that the tenants of the former were entitled to some privileges to which the tenants of the latter were not entitled. But the Court held, as we have seen (*s*), that "although the premises in question had been newly granted by copy of court roll, yet that, having been granted by virtue of an immemorial custom to demise parcel of the waste as copyhold, they were to be considered as much copyhold tenements as if they had been immemorially holden by copy of court roll." If so, one would think that the tenement created under such a custom ought to have precisely the same privileges as ancient tenements. There is a

Lord Northwick v. *Stanway.*

(*p*) Bracton, book 4, chap. 38, par. 11, pp. 225, 226.

(*q*) 3 Bos. & Pul. 346.

(*r*) *Ante*, p. 129.

(*s*) *Ante*, p. 130.

Swayne's case. case in Lord Coke's Reports, called *Swayne's case* (t), in which a grant was made by copy of court roll of a house and a yard and a-half of land, according to the custom of the manor, on which land oak and ash trees were growing; and, although all the woods and underwoods had been aliened from the manor, yet it was held that the grantee by copy could have estovers from these woods; on the ground that, although the grant be new, yet the title of the copyholder is ancient, and so ancient that by force of custom, it exceeds the memory of man. In this case, however, the copyholds granted did not form any portion of the waste of the manor; and I am not aware that the point in question has actually been decided.

(t) 8 Rep. 63.

LECTURE X.

Lord Coke, in his Commentary on the Statute of Merton (a), observes (b), " If the lord doth inclose any part, and leave not sufficient common in the residue, the commoner may break down the whole inclosure, because it standeth upon the ground which is his common." And we have seen (c) that in the case of *Arlett* v. *Ellis* (d), it was held, that the commoners might break down the fence, although there was no pasture on the land in question, and although the defendants had not with them any cattle at the time. Mr. Justice Littledale said (e), " It might be a great injury to the commoner to have fences set up on a common in different places; and, although he might bring an action for the obstruction, yet he is in this, as in other analogous cases, entitled to abate the nuisance; and that is much more convenient than that he should bring an action for every obstruction; because, when the fences are thrown down, the question of right may be decided in one action." The most remarkable instance of pulling down of fences in assertion of a common right, which has occurred in modern times, was that which gave rise to the suit of *Smith* v. *Earl Brownlow* (f). In that case, the late Earl Brownlow, who was lord of the manor of Berkhamstead, in the county of Herts, caused 500 acres, part of Berkhamstead Common, to be inclosed. This was effected by the erection of two strong iron fences, each more than half a mile in length, both

Commoner may break down fence if common insufficient.

Arlett v. Ellis.

Smith v. Earl Brownlow.

(a) Stat. 20 Hen. III. c. 4.

(b) Second Institute, part 1, p. 88; *ante*, p. 109.

(c) *Ante*, pp. 124, 125.

(d) 7 B. & C. 346.

(e) 7 B. & C. 378.

(f) L. R., 9 Eq. 241.

of which were carried from one boundary of the common to the other; so that a space in the middle of the common was completely shut in between the fences and the boundaries of the common; while a portion at each end of the common was left uninclosed. On the 6th of March, 1866, Mr. Smith, the plaintiff in equity, who was a tenant of the manor, and claimed a right of common on the ground inclosed, sent down, by an early special train, about 200 men, provided with instruments for nipping the wire of the fence, and digging up the iron standards, and by seven o'clock in the morning, the work, which had been begun about five o'clock, was completely finished. Each several post was laid upon the grass with its appropriate quantity of iron wire carefully folded round it. On the 9th of March, 1866, the late Earl Brownlow commenced an action of trespass against Mr. Smith for breaking up the fence. On the 31st of July in the same year, Mr. Smith filed his bill in Chancery against the late Earl Brownlow, and prayed for a declaration that the freehold and copyhold tenants of the manor were entitled to rights of pasture, and other rights, over the common, and for an injunction to restrain the defendant, the lord of the manor, from inclosing any part of the common and waste, and from disturbing and interfering with any of the rights of the plaintiff, and the other freehold and copyhold tenants of the manor, in and over the common, or interrupting their free ingress thereto or egress therefrom. The late earl died in 1867, and the plaintiff then revived his suit against the present earl. The action at law was not proceeded with. The present earl defended the suit. But the Court made a decree on behalf of the plaintiff in the terms of the prayer of the bill as to the rights of pasture; and a perpetual injunction was also granted in the terms of the prayer of the bill. The costs were ordered to follow the event. So that not only was the fence prostrated, but an injunction was obtained from the Court of Chancery which precluded the defendant from ever setting it up again.

Lord Coke remarks in his Commentary on the Statute of Merton (*g*), that "throughout all this statute, *pastura et communia pasturæ* is named; so as that statute of approvements doth not extend to common of pischary, or turbary, of estovers, or the like." On this subject the case of *Fawcett* v. *Strickland* (*h*) is a leading authority. In that case the defendant Strickland, who was the lord of the manor of Sedbergh, inclosed 700 acres of one of the wastes called Blewcaster Common, leaving sufficient of pasture for all the commonable cattle of the tenants of the manor, and of all other persons who had common of pasture in the wastes or common, together with free ingress and egress into and out of the same. The plaintiff put his cattle into this inclosure, out of which the defendant drove them; and the plaintiff relied on his right of common of pasture, and also on a right of common of turbary in the waste. The Court held that it was certain the common of turbary was not within the Statute of Merton; but here the action was for chasing cattle, put into the waste to use the common of pasture; and that, although the plaintiff had common of turbary, that it would not hinder the lord's approvement; for they were distinct rights. "If, indeed," it was said by the Court (*i*), "by such inclosure their common of piscary or their common of estovers were affected, as they were interrupted in the enjoyment of either of these rights, they might certainly bring their action; and the lord, to be sure, in such case could not justify such inclosure in prejudice of these rights. And so may the plaintiff, in the present case, if he be interrupted in the enjoyment of his common of turbary; but, by his present action, he does not complain of any such interruption,

Statute of Merton extends only to common of pasture.

Fawcett v. Strickland.

(*g*) Second Institute, part 1, p. 86.

(*h*) Willes, 57; 2 Comyns, 578.

(*i*) Willes, p. 61.

nor does he insist upon any such matter in his replication. As, therefore, his only complaint is of an interruption of his common of pasture, and as, by the Statute of Merton, the defendant Strickland might certainly inclose part of the common, notwithstanding the plaintiff's common of pasture, if he has left sufficient common of pasture (which in the present case is admitted by the pleadings), we are of opinion that the right of common of turbary, insisted upon by the plaintiff in his replication, is no answer to the defendant's plea; therefore the replication is bad in substance, and judgment, so far as the demurrer goes, must be for the defendant." This case was followed by that of *Shakespear* v. *Peppin* (*k*), which was also a case in which the plaintiff's cattle were distrained for trespassing upon an inclosure, which had been made by the lord, under the Statute of Merton, leaving sufficient common of pasture. And, in this case, it was held that a right to dig sand and gravel, which the plaintiff set up, was no answer to the lord's right of approval under the Statute of Merton, where the only point raised by the case was, whether the plaintiff had or had not a right to put his cattle into the land inclosed.

Shakespear v. Peppin.

Lord cannot inclose against rights of estovers, turbary, or digging sand or gravel.
Duberley v. Page.

But a right of estovers, or a right of turbary, or a right to dig sand or gravel, if it exists, will prevent the lord from inclosing to the detriment of such a right. Thus in the case of *Duberley* v. *Page* (*l*), to which I have before referred (*m*), the defendants broke and entered into a close, lately part of the waste of a manor, and they pleaded amongst other things a justification under a right of digging sand or gravel upon the waste, which right was traversed by the plaintiff's replication. The case went to trial on the issue thus raised, and the issues relating to the defendants' prescriptive right to dig

(*k*) 6 T. Rep., 741.   (*m*) *Ante*, p. 126.
(*l*) 2 T. Rep. 291.

gravel and sand having been found for them, the jury were discharged from giving any verdict on the other issues, on the ground that the lord could not in- close, under the Statute of Merton, against such a right, or any right of estovers. I have taken an ex- tract from the pleas in this case, in order to show the exact nature of the right of digging sand and gravel which the defendants claimed. Their claim is put in this form; they pleaded that the close mentioned in the declaration was anciently part of Harrow Weald Com- mon in the manor of Harrow, otherwise Sudbury, in the county of Middlesex; and that the defendant Page was seised in his demesne as of fee of divers messuages and land within the manor; and that he and all those whose estate he had, at the time of the alleged trespass, in the same messuages and land, from time whereof the memory of man is not to the contrary, until the time of the inclosure thereinafter mentioned had dug and taken, and had been used and accustomed to dig and take, and during all the time aforesaid hitherto of right ought to have dug and taken, and still of right ought to dig and take, for himself and themselves, his and their farmers and tenants, occupiers of the said last- mentioned messuages and land with the appurtenances, sand and gravel in, upon, and throughout the said waste and common, whereof, &c., for the necessary repairing and amending of the ways, paths, and walks of, and the gardens, orchards, and yards of and belong- ing to, the said last-mentioned messuages, with the appurtenances, and for the necessary repairing and amending of the ways in, upon, and belonging and appertaining to the said last-mentioned land, with the appurtenances, every year, at all times of the year, as often as need or occasion should require, as to the said messuages and land last mentioned, belonging and appertaining. This plea, having been proved, was held a sufficient justification for the defendant in pulling

Plea of right to take gravel in *Duberley* v. *Page*.

down the fence, by which he was prevented from exercising this right, without regard to the question whether there was or was not sufficient gravel or sand left for his use. So the case of *Grant* v. *Gunner and another* (*n*) was an action against the defendants for breaking and entering into a close of the plaintiff, and digging up, prostrating and levelling a mound or fence of the plaintiff there erected which separated the close in question from a certain common called Farnborough Common. The defendants pleaded that the close in question was part of the common, and they further pleaded a grant in fee simple of a certain copyhold messuage and land within the manor, and averred a custom that the tenants thereof had immemorially had common of turbary, (to wit) peat and turf, in and upon Farnborough Common, to be had and consumed in the said messuage every year, and at all times of the year as occasion required, as belonging and appertaining to the said customary tenement with the appurtenances. The plaintiff pleaded the Statute of Merton, alleging that when he inclosed the close in question he had left sufficient common. The Court, however, gave judgment for the defendants. Mr. Justice Lawrence observed that, if there be common of turbary by grant, to issue out of all and every part of the waste, the lord cannot, in derogation of his own grant, approve against the right of turbary. Chief Justice Mansfield said, that "no case, since the Statute of Merton, is to be found in which it has been held that the lord may approve against the right of common of turbary. If the law be not against the approver, all the reasoning in the case of *Fawcett* v. *Strickland* is absurd. Chief Baron Comyns and all the books recognize Lord Coke's doctrine without a doubt. *Shakespear* v. *Peppin* recognizes the authority of *Fawcett* v. *Strickland*, and that case throughout the whole argument takes it for granted that the law is so." "The universally

Grant v. *Gunner*.

Lord cannot approve against common of turbary.

received opinion of the profession, ever since I have been in the law," continued the Chief Justice, "has been that there can be no approver against common of turbary. Again, what Lord Coke says of approving at common law against common appendant is only applicable to common of pasture."

There is a case, *Peardon* v. *Underhill* (*o*), in which it was held that, in order for a right of common of turbary or common of estovers to prevail against an inclosure made by the lord, the land must be such as either does produce, or in its nature may be capable of producing, turf or fuel. In that case, the spot inclosed by the lord was a bare rock; and it appeared from its nature that not only no turf, nor furze, nor anything fit for fuel had ever been found there, or could be expected to be found there. "Of course some convulsion of nature," as Mr. Justice Erle said (*p*), " or some geological change, might convert the spot into a turf bog; but, in the ordinary course of nature, no fuel could ever be expected there." And the Court were of opinion that, even if a grant to take turf on the common, wherever turf was to be found, were produced, it ought not to be construed to extend to a part of the common in which no fuel could, in the ordinary course of nature, be expected at any time to be found.

Peardon v. *Underhill.*

Land must produce or be capable of producing turf or fuel.

But although the lord cannot approve, under the Statute of Merton, as against any right of common but common of pasture, yet there may be a custom of the manor enabling him to do so, as against rights of turbary or estovers, provided he leave sufficiency for the commoners. This was held to be the case in *Arlett* v. *Ellis* (*q*), to which I have already referred (*r*). It was there held, that a custom to inclose, even as against

Lord may by custom approve against turbary or estovers, leaving sufficiency.

(*o*) 16 Q. B. 120.
(*p*) 16 Q. B. 127.
(*q*) 7 B. & C. 346.
(*r*) *Ante*, pp. 124, 135.

common of turbary, parcels of the waste, leaving a sufficiency of common, was good; and that it lay on the lord, or his grantee, to show that a sufficiency of common was left. And a custom of this nature was held to exist on Chobham Common, in the county of Surrey, in the recent case of *Lascelles* v. *Lord Onslow* (s).

Lascelles v. *Lord Onslow.*

Inclosures for growth of timber.

Several statutes have from time to time been passed with a view to the encouragement of the growth of timber, some of which it may be desirable to mention, as by their means inclosures were in old times effected. And the interpretation placed upon these statutes affords a good illustration of the manner in which all statutes ought to be construed. There is an old act of the 22nd of Edward IV. chap. 7, which does not appear to have been repealed, and is intituled " An Act for Inclosing of Woods in Forests, Chases and Purlieus." This act comes rather under the head of forest law, and was intended to benefit those persons who had lands subject to a right in the crown or other persons to sport over the same. The statute enacts that " if any of the king's subjects, having woods of his own growing in his own ground, within any forest, chase or purlieu of the same, should fell the wood, by licence of the king or his heirs, in his forests, chases or purlieus, or without licence in the forest, chase or purlieu of any other person, or make any sale of the same wood, it shall be lawful to the same subjects, owners of the same ground whereupon the wood so felled did grow, and to the persons to whom the wood should happen to be sold, immediately after the wood was felled, to inclose the same ground with sufficient hedges *able to keep out all manner of beasts and cattle from the same*, for the preserving of their young spring ; and the hedges so made, the said subjects may keep them continually by the space of seven years next after the same inclosing, and repair and sustain the

Stat. 22 Edw. IV. c. 7.

(s) 2 Q. B. Div. 433.

same as often as shall need, within the same seven years, without suing of any other licence of the king or his heirs, or other persons, or any of their officers, of the same forest, chases and purlieus." By the forest law, the king, or owner of the chase, had a right to prostrate all fences put up without licence, as such fences prevented the owner of the chase pursuing the deer and other wild animals therein. And this act provided that where wood was felled and sold, the ground might be kept inclosed for seven years, in order to enable the young wood to spring. You will observe the words of the statute, that the inclosure was to be made *with sufficient hedges able to keep out all manner of beasts and cattle from the same ground.* It was, however, held, in *Sir Francis Barrington's case* (*t*), that this enactment did not affect a person who had a right of common on the forest. In that case the plaintiff, one Richard Chalke, was seised in fee of a house and six acres of land in Hatfield, in the county of Essex, to which he had common appurtenant for all cattle levant and couchant in and through the whole forest or chase of Hatfield. It appeared that Lord Rich was seised of the forest or chase of Hatfield in fee ; and by his deed granted to Sir Thomas Barrington and his heirs all trees, as well timber trees, underwoods and thorns, growing and standing, or in future to grow and stand, on certain parts of the forest called Bushend Quarter and Takely Quarter, except the land and soil of the same wood, with liberty to inclose them, and to hold them inclosed for the preservation of the spring of wood, which should be, for such time as by the laws and statutes of the realm is appointed and enacted, without the disturbance of the said Lord Rich, his heirs and assigns, and to exclude the deer and all other cattle out of the wood so inclosed, and to have herbage and feeding thereof as any owner of the wood might do, by the laws and statutes of

Sir Francis Barrington's case.

The statute 22 Edw. IV. c. 7, does not affect commoners in a forest.

(*t*) 8 Rep. 136.

the realm, without interruption of the said Lord Rich, his heirs or assigns. Sir Thomas Barrington died, and the wood descended to Sir Francis Barrington, as his son and heir, who felled the wood and inclosed it for the preservation of the spring. The plaintiff's cattle appeared to have got into the inclosure, and were distrained by the servants of Sir Francis Barrington, upon which the plaintiff brought his action of replevin; and the question was, whether the plaintiff was, by this statute, deprived of his common or not. The provisions of the act of 22 Edward IV. chap. 7, were urged upon the Court, and it was said that there was no saving in the act for the commoners; and therefore, as it was urged, they should be excluded of their common during the seven years; for every one is party and privy to an act of parliament, and the rights and interests of those which are not saved by the act of parliament are bound. But the Court held, first, that Sir Francis Barrington had an inheritance as profit apprender *in alieno solo*, and the soil remains to the Lord Rich. And, secondly, that the statute of 22 Edward IV. extended to Sir Francis Barrington, notwithstanding he had not the soil. But, thirdly, they held that the act doth not extend to the wood of a subject in which any other has common, but only to a several wood; for by the common law, he who has a wood in which another has common, cannot inclose it to exclude the commoner of his common, be it forest or chase, or out of forest and chase. It was said that the act was intended only to extend the time to which the owner of a several wood might inclose, as against the owner of the chase, from three years to seven years. They held, fourthly, that the preamble showed between what persons, and for and against what persons, the act was made; and the parties to this great contract by act of parliament were the subjects having woods, &c., within forests, chases or purlieus of one part, and the king and other owner of forests, chases and purlieus of

the other part; so that the commoners are not any of
the parties between whom this Act was made. They
held, fifthly, that if the Act had extended to wood in
which others had common, yet the conclusion restrains
the generality of the precedent words; for the statute
doth not give an absolute and indefinite power to the
owners of wood to inclose, &c.; but to inclose the ground,
to keep it inclosed, and to repair it, *without suing the
king's licence*, or other persons, or their officers of the
same forests, chases or purlieus, so that this conclusion
limits the precedent words only against the king and
other owners of forests, chases and purlieus; but no
word in the whole Act gives authority to them to inclose against any commoner. This Act, therefore, was
held by the Court not to affect any persons having a
right of common in a forest or chase, or in the purlieus
of the same. There was another statute, 35 Hen. VIII. Stat. 35 Hen.
c. 17, which enabled the owner of any wood in which VIII. c. 17.
others had common to inclose a fourth part of the wood
by agreement with "the tenants and inhabitants being
commoners" (*u*), or by order of two justices of the peace.
This Act was repealed in the reign of George IV. (*x*).

There is another Act, 29 Geo. II. c. 36, amended by Stat. 29 Geo.
statute 31 Geo. II. c. 41, passed for the purpose of II. c. 36.
enabling the inclosure, by the mutual consent of the lords Inclosure for
and tenants, of part of any common, for the purpose of planting trees.
planting and preserving trees fit for timber or underwood.
The former of these Acts contemplates only the case
of the right of common of pasture, on the ground or soil
inclosed, belonging to all the owners or occupiers of
tenements within the parishes or townships wherein the
wastes lie; and it is a remarkable illustration of what I
venture to think was really the fact, that, in by far the
greater number of instances, the commoners were the
owners and occupiers of land in the township as a

(*u*) See *ante*, p. 15. (*x*) By stat. 7 & 8 Geo. 4, c. 27.

W.P. L

township; although perchance the township might, and in fact in most cases did, correspond and be conterminous with some manor. The Act provides (y), that it shall be lawful for all owners of wastes, wherein any persons have right of common of pasture, with the assent of the major part in number and value of the owners and occupiers of tenements, to which the right of common of pasture doth belong, and also for the major part in number and value of the owners and occupiers of such tenements, with the assent of the owners of the wastes, and for any other persons, with the assent of both of them, to inclose and keep in severalty any part of the wastes for the growth and preservation of timber or underwood. And the second section provides, that any recompense which may be agreed to be given to the commoners shall be paid to the overseers of the poor of the parish or township, to be by them applied for the relief of the poor of the parish or township, where such wastes shall lie. The

Stat. 31 Geo. II. c. 41.

amending Act of 31 Geo. II. c. 41, recites that in many cases the right of common of pasture, in the ground or soil inclosed, may not belong to all the owners and occupiers of tenements within the parishes or townships wherein such wastes shall lie, and provides for a recompense being made to the persons interested in the right of common, in proportion to their respective interests therein, instead of being paid to the overseers of the poor as directed by the former Act. These Acts, though still in the main unrepealed, have now become obsolete (z).

Power to lease twelfth part of wastes of

The Act of 13 Geo. III. c. 81, to which I have already referred (a), empowers the lord of any manor, with the

---

(y) Stat. 29 Geo. II. c. 36, s. 1.

   (z) Sects. 6, 7, 8 and 9 of stat.

29 Geo. II. c. 36, were repealed by stat. 7 & 8 Geo. IV. c. 27, s. 1.

   (a) *Ante*, pp. 76, 81.

consent of three-fourths of the persons having right of manor for four years by public auction. common upon the wastes within his manor, at a meeting to be held after fourteen days' notice, to be given as therein directed, to lease for any term not exceeding four years any part of such wastes, not exceeding a twelfth part thereof, for the best and most improved yearly rent that can by public auction be got for the same,—the clear net rents to be applied by the lord and the major part of his tenants in the draining, fencing or otherwise improving the residue of the wastes (*b*). There is in the same Act a power, in every manor where there are stinted commons, in lieu of leasing part of the wastes, for the lord and the major part in number and value of the owners or occupiers of such commons, present at a meeting to be held within the manor, in pursuance of fourteen days' notice, to be given as therein directed, to direct an assessment to be levied upon the lord and the owners or occupiers of the commons, the money to be employed in the improvement of the commons from time to time as need shall require; with power of distress for enforcing the assessment (*c*).

Power to levy assessment for improving wastes.

I now come to mention certain statutes, by which the lord of a manor is authorized to make inclosures for certain purposes. One of these is the old Poor Law Act (statute 43 Eliz. c. 2), which provides to the following effect (*d*):—to the intent that necessary places of habitation may more conveniently be provided for poor impotent people, be it enacted that it shall be lawful for the churchwardens and overseers, or the greater part of them, by the leave of the lord or the lords of the manor, whereof any waste or common within their parish is or shall be parcel, and upon agreement before

Stat. 43 Eliz. c. 2, s. 5. Inclosure for habitations of poor.

(*b*) Stat. 13 Geo. III. c. 81, s. 15. (*c*) Sect. 16.
(*d*) Sect. 5.

with him or them in writing, under the hands and seals
of the said lord or lords, or otherwise according to any
order to be set down by the justices of peace of the said
county at their general quarter sessions, or the greater
part of them, by like leave and agreement of the said
lord or lords, in writing under his or their hands and
seals, to erect, build and set up in fit and convenient
places of habitation in such waste or common, at the
general charges of the parish or otherwise of the
hundred or county as aforesaid, to be taxed, rated and
gathered in manner before expressed, convenient houses
or dwellings for the said impotent poor. And also to
place inmates, or more families than one, in one cottage
or house; which cottages and places for inmates are
only to be used for the impotent and poor of the parish.

Inclosure for church, churchyard or glebe for residence.

There is also an Act of the 51 Geo. III. c. 115, s. 2,
which empowers any person seised in fee, by deed
enrolled to grant as therein mentioned, any parcel of
the waste of a manor, not exceeding five statute acres,
for the purpose of erecting or enlarging a church or
chapel, or for making or enlarging the churchyard, or
burying ground, or for glebe to erect a mansion house,
or make other conveniences, for the residence of the
rector, vicar, curate or other minister, freed and absolutely discharged of and from all rights of common
thereon. There is a recent case upon the construction
of this enactment, in which it was held that rights of
common only being mentioned, the Act did not extend
to enable the lord of a manor to grant part of the waste
under this Act, in a case where the land granted was

Village green.

part of the village green, and was subject to a customary right in the inhabitants, for enjoyment and exercise, amusement and recreation, and for all lawful

Forbes v. Ecclesiastical Commissioners.

village sports, games and pastimes. The case is *Forbes*
v. *The Ecclesiastical Commissioners for England* (e). Al-

(e) L. R., 15 Eq. 51.

though inhabitants of a place cannot, as we have seen (*f*), claim a right of common by custom, yet they may lawfully set up a custom to hold lawful sports on a village green or other piece of land. The leading case on this subject is *Abbot* v. *Weekly* (*g*), which was followed by the Exchequer Division of the High Court in the recent case of *Hall* v. *Nottingham* (*h*). The marginal note of that case is, " A custom for the inhabitants of a parish to enter upon certain land in the parish and erect a maypole thereon, and dance round and about it, and otherwise enjoy on the land any lawful and innocent recreation at any times in the year is good." And in a case of *Magdalen College, Oxford,* v. *Hiatt* in the Court of Exchequer (*i*), in which I was counsel, the right of the college, as lord of the manor, to inclose a village green, on which a custom was proved of carrying on village sports, was given up by Mr. Manisty, now Mr. Justice Manisty, counsel for the college, as a point which he could not argue.

Custom to hold lawful sports.

Hall v. *Nottingham.*

The Act to afford further facilities for the conveyance and endowment of sites for schools (*k*) provides (*l*) for the gift of any quantity not exceeding one acre of land as a site for a school for the education of poor persons, or for the residence of a schoolmaster or schoolmistress; and further provides that where any portion of waste or commonable land shall be gratuitously conveyed by any lord or lady of a manor for any such purpose as aforesaid, the rights and interests of all persons in the said land shall be barred and divested by such conveyance. But the land so granted is to revert on its ceasing to be used for the purposes of the Act.

Gift of site for school.

(*f*) *Ante*, p. 13.
(*g*) 1 Lev. 176.
(*h*) L. R., 1 Ex. D. 1.
(*i*) 25 January, 1875.
(*k*) Stat. 4 & 5 Vict. c. 38.
(*l*) Sect. 2.

LECTURE XI.

THE soil of the waste lands of a manor, you will remember, is always vested in the lord of the manor, notwithstanding the rights which the commoners may have upon it. The lord, therefore, as owner of the soil, has the same rights as other owners, except so far as the existence of the rights of the commoners may prevent him from exercising these rights. One important right which he has is that of putting his own cattle or the cattle of the tenants of his demesne lands, upon the waste. The right of the tenants of his manor is only a right of common; and the word common itself implies a community of right (a). This right of the lord, to put upon the waste the cattle, which plough and manure his own cultivated land, is of great importance in case of the inclosure of the common. His right, of course, is not strictly speaking a right of common, because he puts on the cattle as owner of the soil. And a man cannot have a right of common over his own land. Still it is a *quasi* right of common, and is as valuable to him as if it were a strictly legal right. It has consequently been held that, where commons are by Act of Parliament directed to be inclosed, and divided amongst the several proprietors thereof and persons interested therein, in satisfaction of their lands and grounds, rights of common, and other rights and interests therein, the lord of the manor has a right to an allotment in respect of his right to stock the common from his demesne land. This was decided in the case of *Arundell* v. *Viscount Falmouth* (b), followed by

Lord's right to put cattle on the waste.

In case of inclosure lord has a right to allotment.

Arundell v. *Viscount Falmouth.*

(a) Co. Litt. 122 a.   (b) 2 M. & S. 440.

the case of *Lloyd* v. *Lord Powis* (c), and more recently by the case of *Musgrave* v. *Inclosure Commissioners* (d). In this last case, the lord succeeded in obtaining an allotment in respect of a farm called "The Mains," part of his demesne lands, on the ground that his tenants had usually enjoyed a right of pasturage in respect of this farm over the land inclosed, which was called "The Fell," although between 1828 and 1844 no cattle had actually been turned on. I mentioned this case in a former Lecture (e).

Lloyd v. *Lord Powis.*

Musgrave v. *Inclosure Commissioners.*

In many places the lord exercises, and I apprehend that he always has, a right of *driving the common*, as it is said, that is, the right, once a year or oftener if he thinks fit, of driving all the cattle and sheep upon the common into some corner or inclosed place, for the purpose of ascertaining whose sheep and cattle they are, and whether or not they have been rightfully put upon the common, in exercise of a lawful right of common. This right, which used frequently to be exercised in former times, has now become obsolete in many places, owing to the neglect of the owners of the waste to look after their own interests. The lord has a right to plant trees upon the waste, so that he do not materially injure the grass, which the commoners have a right to eat by the mouths of their cattle (f). He has also a right to make rabbit burrows upon the common, subject in like manner to this limitation, that he does not materially deprive the commoners of their right of pasture (g). Subject to the same limitations, he has also a right to dig for gravel, sand, loam, clay, &c., to quarry for stone, and to mine for coal, iron and other minerals, which may lie under the waste, for his

Driving the common.

Planting trees.

Rabbit burrows.

Gravel, &c.

(c) 4 E. & B. 485.
(d) L. R., 9 Q. B. 162.
(e) Lecture IX., *ante*, p. 120.
(f) *Kirby* v. *Sadgrove*, 1 Bos. & Pul. 13, 17; per Bayley, J., in *Arlott* v. *Ellis*, 7 B. & C. 362.
(g) *Cooper* v. *Marshall*, 1 Bur. 259.

own profit; and the onus lies upon the commoner who objects to any of these proceedings, to show that the enjoyment of his right of common has been injured thereby (h). There is a case of *Bateson* v. *Green* (i), in which it was held that the right of the commoner might, by the custom of the manor, be subservient to the lord's right in the soil; so that the lord might dig clay pits on the common, or empower others to do so, without leaving sufficient herbage for the commoners, if such right were proved to have been always exercised by the lord. This case has been much remarked on (k); but it seems to be still law. The lord is also entitled, as owner of the soil, to sport over the waste; and it is very desirable that he should exercise his rights, as, for want of such exercise, it may happen that he will lose the ownership of the soil altogether. For instance, if a person builds a hovel or cottage upon the waste, then makes a little garden, and then puts up a fence around the whole, and continues in possession of his encroachment formerly for twenty (l), and now for twelve years or upwards (m); the lord being then seised in fee and under no disability; the person who has made the encroachment becomes himself absolutely seised in fee of the piece of land which he has inclosed; and, being seised of the surface, he becomes seised also of the mines and minerals under the surface.

I was counsel the other day in a case of *Seddon* v. *Smith* in the Court of Exchequer, and afterwards in the Court of Appeal (n), in which a long strip of land, parcel of the waste of a manor, had been set out by an inclosure Act as a road or way to a certain tenement.

Margin notes:
Onus on commoner.

Bateson v. *Green.*

Sporting.

Encroachments.

Seddon v. *Smith.*

(h) *Hall* v. *Byron*, L. R., 5 Ch. D. 667, 680; *Robinson* v. *Dulcep Singh*, L. R., 11 Ch. D. 798, 831.

(i) 5 T. Rep. 411.

(k) See L. R., 4 Ch. D. 678, 680.

(l) Stat. 3 & 4 Will. IV. c. 27.

(m) Stat. 37 & 38 Vict. c. 57.

(n) Now reported 36 Law Times, N. S. 168.

The Act set out a road or way of thirty feet in width, which was more than was necessary for the few carts and waggons which had occasion to go to the tenement. The owner of the tenement, to which and to which alone this road led, although there was a public footpath along the side, began by planting a few cabbages over three-quarters of this lane, leaving the other quarter for the footpath and for his carts. And from year to year he went on planting sometimes cabbages, at length wheat and other crops, and so he continued for upwards of twenty years. There were valuable minerals under the waste, which the lord as owner of the soil worked by a tenant. When, however, the tenant began to work the minerals immediately under this piece of land; the tenant of the farm, who or whose predecessors in title had planted the cabbages, brought an action of trespass against him for taking away coal, which he alleged to be his own, by reason of his acquisition of a title to the soil, by twenty years adverse possession under the Statute of Limitations. And the Court, Barons Bramwell and Amphlett, held that an action for trespass lay under the circumstances. And on appeal this judgment was affirmed by the Chief Justice and JJ. Brett and Baggallay. The only point on which the Court above differed from the Court below was this. The Court below held that the plaintiff in trespass, that is, the encroacher, was entitled to the whole thirty-feet road, and to the minerals under it: thus giving him a right to a wall of coal thirty feet wide between the mines of the lord on the one side and on the other. But the Court of Appeal considered that the quarter of the space, or seven feet and a half, which had been left all along for the public footpath, still belonged to the lord; and that, as to that portion, there had been no adverse possession, the encroachment not reaching so far. They, therefore, held the plaintiff to be entitled, not to a wall of coal

thirty feet wide, but to a wall of coal thirty feet, minus
seven and a half, or twenty-two and a half feet, wide.
Cases of this sort show how important it is for the
owners of waste lands to see that no encroachments are
made upon them. A strip of cabbage garden, a few
yards wide, may be of little importance; but a wall of
coal a few yards wide may be of the greatest impor-

Commoners
formerly
barred after
twenty years.
tance, when mines come to be worked. Twenty years
adverse possession not only barred the owner of the
soil, but also all persons having rights of common over
the land encroached on. And if the encroachments
had been gradual, that part which had been inclosed
for twenty years was discharged of all rights of common,
though that which had been inclosed for a less time
was not (o). On the 1st of January, 1879, the new
Statute of Limitations came into operation (p), and the
period of twenty years given by the late Act (q) was

Now barred
after twelve
years.
reduced to twelve years. I cannot help thinking that
it is a pity that in this respect our legislature has not
followed the example of some other countries, and made
a distinction between *bonâ fide* though mistaken acquisitions for valuable consideration, and acquisitions by
purely wrongful acts, which I think our law now rather
tends to encourage.

Tyrwhitt v.
Wynne.
There is a case of *Tyrwhitt* v. *Wynne* (r), in which
the plaintiff brought an action of trespass for breaking
down a wall, and the defendant pleaded that the place
in which the alleged trespass was committed was his
own soil and freehold. The plaintiff had recently purchased a farm in Wales, consisting of about sixty acres
of arable land; and the question was whether he was
entitled to the soil of the *locus in quo*, or only to a right
of common thereon. And the plaintiff produced no

(o) *Tapley* v. *Wainwright*, 5 B.   (q) Stat. 3 & 4 Will. 4, c. 27.
& Adol. 395.   (r) 2 B. & A. 554.
(p) Stat. 37 & 38 Vict. c. 57.

documentary evidence or title deeds, but rested his case on the proof of various acts of ownership on the place in question, by owners of the farm for sixty years, by feeding sheep exclusively thereon, cutting trees, turf, and fern, and granting leave to other persons to do so. The defendant, Sir W. W. Wynne, claimed the soil and freehold of the land as lord of the manor, and proved different acts of enjoyment by shooting repeatedly by himself and gamekeeper, without interference, on the premises in question, and also by collecting and taking estrays, and forbidding the burning of the gorse growing thereon. The jury at the trial found a verdict for the plaintiff, and the Court refused a rule for a new trial. The main question in the case seemed to have been with regard to the rejection of certain evidence put in on behalf of the defendant. But the case is a very strong one to show that if the lord permits other persons to cut trees or turf on the waste without his leave, or to exercise other acts of ownership thereon, he may in time lose his freehold. There is, however, a case of *Attorney-General* v. *Reveley*, in the Exchequer—which is not reported in the usual Reports, but a report of which has been printed, though not published, by Mr. W. W. Karslake, who was counsel for the Crown in the case—in which it was held that the exclusive enjoyment of the pasturage of sheep on a certain piece of uninclosed land for upwards of sixty years, was not of itself evidence of ownership of this piece of land as against the Crown, who was lord of the manor. It was proved that the piece of land in question was anciently part of a waste which belonged to the Crown; and acts of ownership on the part of the Crown were proved on other parts of the waste. It appeared in evidence in that case that it was the custom in Wales for farmers, who had rights of common on a waste, to appropriate the common amongst themselves for the purpose of pasturing their sheep on those parts of the

Freehold in soil proved by acts of ownership.

Att.-Gen. v. *Reveley.*

Appropriation by tenants of parts of common.

common most convenient to their respective homesteads; and it was inferred that the exclusive occupation of the parcel of land in question by the owners and occupiers of an adjoining farm was referable to such a custom.

Hall v. Byron. And in the recent case of *Hall* v. *Byron* (s), before Vice-Chancellor Hall—which related to the commons of the parish of Coulsdon, near Croydon, in the county of Surrey—it appeared in evidence that it was the custom of the farmers, who had rights of common on the waste, to agree amongst themselves to appropriate certain defined portions of the waste for the sheep of certain particular farms; and these limits so marked out between themselves were strictly observed. Upon the strength of these agreements, it was endeavoured, on the part of the lord, to confine the rights of the tenants of the manor to common only on those portions of the waste which were adjacent to their respective tenements. But the Court held that the tenants had the usual right of common appendant in respect of their tenements; and that the circumstance of the shepherds having parcelled out the waste amongst themselves was no evidence of any restricted right in the tenants; but that, on the contrary, their rights of pasture extended over the whole of the wastes within the manor. In that case, as in many others, the manor and parish were conterminous.

Stints. In some cases the right of common is *stinted* or limited to a certain number of cattle and sheep, according sometimes to the extent, and sometimes to the yearly value of each tenement. It does not follow in these cases that the right of common, the exercise of which is thus restricted, is not common appendant. We have seen, on the authority of Lord Coke, that an upland town may make bye-laws for the regulation of its commons (t). And when, as now most frequently

(s) 25 W. R. 317; L. R., 4   (t) Co. Litt. 110 b; *ante*, p. 49. Ch. D. 667.

happens, a common is claimed by the tenants of a
manor, it is clear that such tenants may make bye-laws
touching their commons, which will bind themselves,
and by immemorial custom, will bind all the other
tenants of the manor; but of course this cannot bind
strangers. The law on the subject of bye-laws is collected in *Scriven* on Copyholds (*u*). In the case of
Aston and Coat, to which I drew your attention the
other day (*x*), the right of common on Coat common or
moor was limited to four rother beasts and forty sheep
for every yard land; and so in proportion for any less
quantity. In the case of *Ellard* v. *Hill* (*y*) the prescrip- *Ellard v. Hill.*
tion was that every yard land within the vill should
havé common for twelve cows; and for a quarter yard,
three cows; and for half a quarter a cow and a half, as
I mentioned in a former Lecture (*z*). The case of *Morse* *Morse and*
and *Webb* (*a*) is an example of a stint of four rother *Webb's case.*
beasts, two horse beasts, and sixty sheep in respect of
two yard lands. In that case it was held that if so No common.
small a parcel of the land to which the right of common for very small
belongs be demised, which will not keep one ox nor parcel of land.
a sheep, then the whole common shall remain with the
lessor. And it was said that there is no difference when
the prescription is for cattle levant and couchant, and
when for a certain number of cattle levant and couchant.
In Epping Forest the number of cattle, which the
tenants of the townships or parishes within the forest
might put on, was limited according to the rental of
each tenement. Every tenant had a right to put on one
mare or gelding or two cows in respect of every 80*s.*
annual rent. This stint was proved in the Epping
Forest case (*b*). The stint also appears in the case of

(*u*) Scriv. Cop. part 3, Ch. 20,
s. 4.

(*x*) *Ante*, p. 86.

(*y*) Siderfin, 226.

(*z*) *Ante*, p. 49.

(*a*) 13 Rep. 33.

(*b*) *The Commissioners of Sewers*
v. *Glasse*, L. R., 19 Eq. 134,
161.

Palmer v. *Stone.*

Palmer v. *Stone* (c), which was a question as to a right of common upon the forest. And in *The Commissioners of Sewers* v. *Glasse* the Court held that this right was merely the measure of levancy and couchancy,—in fact, a convenient method of measuring the number of cattle which each tenement had a right to put on. So in the manor of Hackney, Middlesex, called the Lord's Hold, a stint was fixed by a bye-law made by the homage of so many head of cattle according to the rental of each tenant. And portions of the common lands having been taken compulsorily for waterworks and railway and other purposes, the compensation paid for the rights of common was divided amongst the commoners accord-

Fox v. *Amhurst.*

ing to the stint, in the recent case of *Fox* v. *Amhurst* (d). So in the recent case of *Hall* v. *Byron* (e) bye-laws were put in evidence, made at different Courts baron, to the effect that no tenant should put upon the waste more than one sheep per acre. But this again was considered by the Court to be merely a convenient measure of levancy and couchancy. And the Court decreed that the tenants had a right of common of pasture for their cattle levant and couchant upon their respective lands (f).

Presentments by homage.

In some cases presentments are made by the homage with respect to the right of some particular tenement to put cattle upon the waste. These presentments are of little value if a constant user be shown contrary to such presentment. This occurred in the case of *Arundell* v. *Viscount Falmouth* (g), to which I have already referred (h). In that case it was proved that Brimpton Farm, containing about 273 acres, formed part of the demesne of the manor of Brimpton, and that there had been an uninterrupted usage, for a long series of years,

(c) 2 Wils. 96.   (f) L. R., 4 Ch. D. 673, 681.
(d) L. R., 20 Eq. 408.   (g) 2 M. & S. 440.
(e) L. R., 4 Ch. D. 667.   (h) *Ante*, p. 150.

for the occupiers of that farm to turn out the cattle,
which had wintered there, on the marshes in question,
and which were inclosed under the authority of an
Inclosure Act. There was no evidence to oppose this,
but some presentments by the homage restricting the
right to three head of cattle; but these presentments
had never been acted on. The jury found that the
defendant, the lord of the manor, was entitled under
the Act, in right of Brimpton Farm, to an allotment in
respect of the depasturing of cattle upon the marshes,
over and above such allotment as he might be entitled
to in respect of his right as lord of the manor to the soil
of the marshes. The Court held that the presentments
of the homage were entitled to no weight; they were in
their origin decidedly for the interest of those who
made them, and were made against the rights of a
person, who was not entitled to be heard; and they
were not followed up by any act. There is also a case
of *Chapman* v. *Cowlan* (*i*), which was an action on the
case by a copyholder against a freeholder of the manor
of Crowle in Lincolnshire, for the disturbance of the
plaintiff's right of common, by the defendant surcharging the common. An old parchment agreement
was produced by the steward of the manor, dated in
1698, which purported to be signed by many persons,
copyholders, stating an unlimited right of common,
which having been found inconvenient, they had agreed
to stock the common in a certain manner, under which
the plaintiff claimed, in respect of a messuage and thirty
acres of land, common in a part of commonable ground of
the manor called the Stinted Cowpasture, for six cows, six
mares or geldings if above three years old, and for
sucking foals of such mares, levant and couchant upon
the said messuage and lands, upon and from May-day
old style unto and to Michaelmas-day old style. There
was also another parchment writing to the same effect
dated 1717. A nonsuit was directed at the trial, and

Chapman v.
Cowlan.

(*i*) 13 East, 10.

on motion to set aside the nonsuit, the Court held that these instruments were evidence at least of the reputation of the manor, at that time, as to the prescriptive right of common, against the right set up by the plaintiff. Lord Ellenborough, C. J. said, "It destroys the right insisted upon by the plaintiff by showing what the prescriptive rights of the copyholders were before. And, as an agreement, it could have no effect to bind subsequent copyholders, but only those who executed it. It will be better to recur to the original right of common as restricted by levancy and couchancy." And the Court refused a rule to set aside the nonsuit; being of opinion, as you see, that the agreements signed by the copyholders were evidence of an ancient right of common for cattle levant and couchant upon their tenements, which ancient right was not defeated by the agreement for stinting the common to which many of the copyholders had come.

Bill of peace.

When the rights of the commoners are denied by the lord, the most effectual remedy is a bill of peace, or now an action in the nature of a bill of peace, brought by one of the commoners on behalf of himself and the others against the lord, for the purpose of establishing their rights. An early case on this subject is that of *Powell* v. *Earl of Powis and others* (*l*). The plaintiffs in

Powell v.
Earl of Powis.

that case were freehold tenants of the manor of Clun in the county of Salop, and claimed right of common throughout a certain forest or waste parcel of the honor or lordship of *Clun* called the forest of *Clun*. Earl Powis, the lord of the manor, had inclosed certain portions of the forest, and had granted the parts so inclosed to the other defendants, who were in possession of them. The plaintiffs, a short time before the filing of the bill, broke down the fence of the parts so inclosed, for the purpose of exercising their commonable

(*l*) 1 You. & Jerv. 159.

rights. The defendants commenced their action of trespass against them. The bill of the plaintiffs prayed that the rights of common of the plaintiffs, and · the other freehold tenants of the honor or lordship, might be established, and that the plaintiffs and their tenants might be quieted in such rights; that the Earl of Powis might be restrained from inclosing any part of the forest, to the prejudice of the plaintiffs and their tenants, and from obstructing or molesting them in their commonable rights, and for an injunction against the action of trespass brought by the other defendants. To this bill the defendants demurred. Lord Chief Baron Alexander overruled the demurrer, saying, "The cases establish that a bill may be brought by a lord against his tenants, and by tenants against the lord, in respect to rights of common. It is a bill of peace, and to prevent multiplicity of actions. The dicta and cases show that it is no objection to this bill, that the defendants may each have a right to make a separate defence, provided there be only one general question to be settled, which pervades the whole. It would be against all the cases to allow this demurrer: it would put the bill out of Court." This case was followed by Lord Romilly, the late Master of the Rolls, in the case of *Smith* v. *Earl Brownlow* (*m*), to which I have already called your attention (*n*). The bill in that case was filed on behalf both of the freehold and of the copyhold tenants of the manor of Berkhamstead, the manor in which was situate the common there in question. And this was followed by the case of *Warwick* v. *Queen's College, Oxford* (*o*), decided by Lord Romilly, Master of the Rolls, and affirmed on appeal by Lord Hatherley (*p*). This case related to the manor of Plumstead in the county of Kent, of which Queen's College, Oxford, were the lords. And the bill was filed by

Smith v. *Earl Brownlow.*

Warwick v. *Queen's College.*

(*m*) L. R., 9 Eq. 241. (*o*) L. R., 10 Eq. 105.
(*n*) *Ante*, p. 135. (*p*) L. R., 6 Ch. 716.
W.P. M

three persons on behalf of themselves and all other the freehold tenants of the manor of Plumstead against the College as lord of the manor, praying for a declaration of the rights of the freeholders. In this manor there were no copyholders; all the tenants were freehold tenants. And a decree was made in their favour establishing a right of pasture upon all the commons in the manor, and some other rights claimed by them.

Betts v. *Thompson.*

This was followed by the case of *Betts* v. *Thompson* (*q*), in which the bill was filed by a freehold tenant of the manor of Tooting Graveney, in the county of Surrey, on behalf of himself and all other owners of freehold tenements within the ambit or former ambit of the manor, to establish rights of common against the lord. It was proved that the plaintiff and the other freehold tenants within the present ambit of the manor had commonable rights, and that the copyholders of the manor had also commonable rights. But it was not proved that the owners of freehold tenements within the former ambit had such rights. It was held that the joining as plaintiffs the owners of freehold tenements within the former ambit amounted merely to a misjoinder of plaintiffs, and did not prevent the Court from making a decree under the bill. It was also held that though the plaintiff might have sued on behalf of the copyholders also, if they had rights co-extensive with those of the freeholders, he was able to maintain his bill on behalf of the freeholders alone.

Commissioners of Sewers v. *Glasse.*

The case of *The Commissioners of Sewers* v. *Glasse* (*r*), to which I have before referred (*s*), is a similar instance of a representative suit. In that case the bill was filed by the plaintiffs on behalf of themselves and all other the owners and occupiers of lands and tenements lying within the Forest of Essex, other than the waste lands of the forest, except such of them as were defendants,

(*q*) L. R., 6 Ch. 732.   (*s*) *Ante*, p. 54.
(*r*) L. R., 19 Eq. 134.

or were in the bill alleged to be sufficiently represented by the defendants or some of them. Objection was taken to the form of the suit on the ground that the bill was on behalf of owners and occupiers. And a demurrer to the bill was put in accordingly, but the demurrer was overruled by Lord Romilly, then Master of the Rolls, and his order overruling the demurrer was affirmed on appeal by the Lord Justices James and Mellish (t). Lord Justice James observed that the case was in accordance both with precedents and principle. " It is the case," he said (u), " of a bill filed by a person or persons claiming a general right against several persons claiming several rights to have that general right ascertained. To determine whether there is any foundation for this claim, we of course on the present occasion must take the allegations in the bill as being admitted; and if those allegations are well founded, and can be proved by sufficient evidence, it seems to me that it is far better that the whole case should be tried in a Chancery suit, in which all persons interested in disputing the right claimed by the bill can join in making a defence, the costs of which, if they combine, cannot be very oppressive, and where the general right can be tried once for all as between the persons interested on the one side and the persons interested on the other side, than that it should be tried by the only other proceedings I know of. One of such proceedings would be the bringing actions against every one of the trespassers for the disturbance of the rights of common. If it was done in that way, there might be thousands of actions brought; because every one of the occupiers claiming the right of common could bring an action against every one of the persons who has made an encroachment. The only other

(t) *Commissioners of Sewers* v.   (u) Page 464.
Glasse, L. R., 7 Ch. 456.

proceeding would be that, if the inclosures are an encroachment and a nuisance to the forest, a person
entitled to common might, if he could do it without
committing a breach of the peace, sweep away the walls,
hedges and fences, and put the occupiers to bring
actions for trespass. Supposing that course to be resorted to, the commoner, if reasonable, would give
notice that he was going to demolish the fences, and
then the lord or the tenant who was threatened might
file his bill to restrain him from doing so, and no doubt
the destruction of property would be restrained by this
Court; but of course only in such a way as that the
real question should be tried in the suit in which the
injunction was obtained." . . . . "Then it is said that
the allegations are not sufficient; that is to say, that the
allegation of title to the right of common is on behalf of
owners and occupiers. G*ateward's case* (x) and other cases
have been cited for the purpose of showing that no such
right as this can be claimed by custom. Of course it is
settled and clear law that you cannot have any right to
a profit à *prendre in alieno solo* in a shifting body like
the inhabitants of a town, or residents of a particular
district. But construing the allegations here according
to their plain meaning, it appears to me that, if they
were judged most strictly, the allegation here is of a
right of common in the owners and occupiers of lands
in respect of those lands, for it is in express terms
claimed as a right of common either appendant or
appurtenant for their cattle levant and couchant upon
the tenements. That is an allegation of a right of
common not unknown to the law—a right of common
which is alleged as being appurtenant to land, and of
course claimed by persons who are either owners or
occupiers of the land, in respect of which that easement

(x) 6 Rep. 59 b; *ante*, p. 13.

is claimed. It appears to me that the occupiers have a right to join and to be joined in any suit in this Court for that purpose. The occupier alone is entitled, during the continuance of his occupancy; he may be an occupier for a long term of years; and he may be the only person substantially interested in the assertion of the right. Therefore I cannot conceive that there is any objection to joining owners and occupiers in this way in their character of *quasi* co-plaintiffs and as persons on behalf of whom the right is alleged." Lord Justice Mellish was of the same opinion. He considered that the right of common in the forest was one which legally might exist. "The main objection," he said, "which was taken was, that the right was alleged in the occupiers, and that the occupiers could not have such a right. There is no doubt that the occupiers simply as such could not have the right; but looking at the allegations in the bill it appears to me that the right is substantially alleged in the owners on behalf of themselves and the occupiers." "The rights granted to the owner have been enjoyed by the owner and occupier. Of course the occupiers are the persons who *de facto* enjoy the right, although that right is gained to them through its belonging to the owner from whom they get their estates." "When the bill mentions the plaintiffs and their predecessors in title and their respective tenants, and then adds and the other owners and occupiers, I think that clearly means the other owners and their tenants under them. Therefore it appears to me that the right in that respect is quite rightly laid."

Having now spoken of the means by which a right of common appendant may be enforced, I now proceed to the means by which it may be lost. Of course this right, like every other right, may be given up by a release by deed to the owner of the soil; but if not released, the right, when it has once been established, continues until on sufficient evidence it is held that the tenant has abandoned his right.   The question of aban-

donment is eminently a question of fact for the considera-tion of a jury.   Of course non-user for a comparatively short time, if it be coupled with evidence that the non-user was accompanied with a desire or determination to abandon or give up altogether the right of common, would be sufficient evidence of abandonment.   But with regard to mere non-user a long continued ceasing to put on cattle, is not necessarily evidence of an inten-tion to abandon.   There is no doubt that the change, which has taken place in the modes of agriculture in the present day, has rendered common of pasture far less valuable than it was formerly.   The breeds of sheep now in use are many of them far too valuable to be intrusted beyond the bounds of the farm.   And the placing of horses and cows to feed upon a common was more the custom in times gone by than it is now.   Few persons would be so imprudent as to place a valuable hunter or carriage horse on an open common simply for the benefit of the pasture which he might pick up. Generally speaking I think it may be laid down that non-user for less than twenty years would hardly be considered sufficient of itself to prove an abandonment unless accompanied by other circumstances.   And non-user for more than that period may not amount to an abandonment if properly explained (y).

If the commoner purchase the waste his right of common is of course extinguished.   And if he should take a lease of the waste his right of common would be suspended during the lease.   Common appendant does not however become extinguished, if the owner of the

(y) Ward v. Ward, 7 Ex. 838.

tenement, in respect of which the right of common is exercised, should purchase a portion of the waste. He would still have his right of common appendant over the other part. The common appendant will in this case be apportioned, because it is of common right, and will not be totally extinguished; whereas common appurtenant is said not to be of common right, and so, not being favoured by the law, is held to be extinguished altogether by the purchase by the commoner of any part of the waste.

Apportionment of common appendant.

LECTURE XII.

Common appurtenant is against common right.

WE now come to the consideration of common appurtenant. Common appendant is of common right, but common appurtenant is said to be against common right. Common may become appurtenant to lands either by reason of long user, or by grant express or implied. All common of pasture acquired by long user, which is not common appendant, is common appurtenant. Thus although donkeys, goats, swine and geese are not commonable animals, yet a right to put them upon a common or waste may be acquired by long user. With regard to swine, in old times the right of putting them into woods to feed on the acorns and mast of beech trees was a very usual right, and was called the right of pannage or pawnage; but in the present day the right has almost become obsolete. In Manwood's Forest Law there is a whole chapter about pawnage (a). The right of pawnage or pannage of the woods within the king's forests, was under the direction of officers called agistors of the forests ; but such rights are rarely claimed in modern times. Common appurtenant may be created by express grant. A grant to a man and his heirs, owners and occupiers of a certain farm, of a right to depasture on a certain waste so many cattle or sheep, or as many cattle and sheep as are levant and couchant upon the tenement, is a grant of common appurtenant. And from and after the grant the right of common becomes appurtenant to the tenement, and passes from owner to owner by a conveyance of the tenement with the appurtenances, and even without the word " appurtenances ; " for by grant

Donkeys, goats, swine and geese.

Pannage.

Grant.

Appurtenants pass by conveyance of tenement.

(a) Manwood, ch. 12.

of any subject, that which is appendant or appurtenant to it, will by implication pass also. Thus it is laid down by Lord Coke (*b*), "Whatsoever passeth by livery of seisin either in deed or in law, may pass without deed; and not only the rents and services parcell of the manor shall with the demeans as the more principal and worthy pass by livery without deed, but all things regardant, appendant and appurtenant to the manor, as incidents or adjuncts to the same shall, together with the manor, pass without deed; all which, as here it appeareth and elsewhere is said, shall pass without saying *cum pertinentiis*." Now, as you know, every feoffment must be evidenced by deed (*c*); but the law as to appurtenances remains the same.

The question sometimes arises as to what words will be sufficient to create a common appurtenant by grant. If a right of common, though not appendant or appurtenant to a tenement, has been usually enjoyed therewith, then a grant of the tenement, with all commons and commonable rights *therewith used or enjoyed*, will operate as a fresh grant of the right of common. This was decided in the case of *Bradshaw* v. *Eyre* (*d*). A lease was made of a house and twenty acres of land, with all commons, profits and commodities thereto appertaining, or occupied or used with the said messuage. The lease was made by one Nicholas Bradshaw, who was the owner of the common, and prior to the lease he had taken a feoffment of the farm in question, which had previously enjoyed a right of common, so that the common was extinguished by unity of possession. But the Court held, that the words in the lease "with all commons, &c. occupied or used with the messuage," were a good grant of a new common for the time; for, although it was not common

What words sufficient to create common appurtenant by grant.

Bradshaw v. *Eyre.*

(*b*) Co. Litt. 121 b. (*d*) Cro. Eliz. 570.
(*c*) Stat. 8 & 9 Vict. c. 106.

in the hands of the feoffor, yet it was *quasi* common used therewith ; and although it be not the same common as it was before, yet it is the like common. But because there was not a sufficient averment, that this common was used by the lessee at the time of the lease, it passed not (*e*). Again in the case of *Worledg* v. *Kingswel* (*f*), a copyhold of a manor, which had common in part of the demesnes of the manor, escheated to the lord, and the lord by deed granted it to another in tail " with all commons whatsoever to the same belonging or in any way appertaining or with the same messuage used." And it was resolved by all the Court that the donee in tail should have such common as the copyholder had, although the ancient common had determined by unity of possession in the lord. The grant was held to enure as a new grant of the same common. When a copyholder, who has rights of common in respect of his tenement, takes a conveyance of the fee simple thereof from the lord of the manor by way of enfranchisement, the ancient rights of common, which were by custom only, are thenceforth gone at law (*g*), unless revived by the use in the deed of enfranchisement of such words as " together with all commonable rights therewith used or enjoyed " (*h*). But in equity it is said that the common rights remain (*i*), on the ground, I presume, that the intention is that the tenant by enfranchising should lose no right he had before, but should gain the freehold in addition.

Worledg v. *Kingswel.*

Copyholder enfranchising.

Lost grant of right of com'n on.

As common appurtenant may be claimed as well by grant within time of memory as by prescription, and as a grant may be lost, a grant of common as appurtenant

(*e*) See also *Hall* v. *Byron*, L. R., 4 Ch. D. 667, 671, 672.

(*f*) Cro. Eliz. 794.

(*g*) *Marsham* v. *Hunter*, Cro. Jac. 253.

(*h*) *Grymes* v. *Peacock*, 1 Bulst. 19.

(*i*) *Styant* v. *Staker*, 2 Vern. 250.

will in some cases be presumed after long enjoyment. Thus in the case of *Cowlam* v. *Slack* (*k*), the plaintiff declared that he was possessed of a messuage in the parish of Crowle, in the county of Lincoln, and by reason thereof he had common of pasture for all his commonable cattle, levant and couchant upon his said messuage and land, in certain large wastes in the parish, as belonging and appertaining to his said messuage and land; and then alleged a grievance to him by the defendant's surcharging the common and waste grounds. A third count in his declaration, more general, stated the plaintiff's lawful possession, at the time of the grievance, of the messuage and land with the appurtenances, and that by reason thereof he was entitled of right to common of pasture throughout all the commonable waste grounds in the parish of Crowle, for all his commonable cattle levant and couchant upon his last-mentioned messuage and land with the appurtenances, without claiming such right of common as belonging and appertaining to his messuage and land. It appeared that the plaintiff, his father and grandfather had occupied the manor house and farm for about fifty years past, during all which time they had constantly stocked and enjoyed the common. But it appearing also upon cross-examination that the messuage and farm were so held by the plaintiff and his ancestors as tenants to the lord of the manor, the objection was taken that neither the lord nor his tenants could have a right of common upon the lord's own soil; but that the unity of possession extinguished the common; and the learned judge, being of that opinion, nonsuited the plaintiff. A rule however was obtained to set aside the nonsuit; and after much consideration the nonsuit was set aside by the Court, and a new trial granted. Lord Ellenborough said that there did not appear to be any material difference in point of legal effect between the

Cowlam v. *Slack.*

(*k*) 15 East, 108.

claims of common as made in these several counts; in
all the claim is in substance a claim of common appurtenant to the closes in respect of which the common is
claimed. And the only question upon the argument
of which the Court wished further to consider, was
whether common appurtenant, for which, as is said in
the text of Co. Litt. 122, one must prescribe, is, as
suggested in the notes of the learned commentators,
also claimable by grant as well as by prescription.
And, after going through several authorities, the Court
came to the conclusion that, it appearing that common
appurtenant, such as was claimed by the plaintiff's
declaration, may be created by modern grant, it was
proper that the jury should have had the usage in this
case left to them as a foundation, whereupon they might
or might not, according as the evidence of enjoyment
would have warranted them, have presumed such a
grant to have been made by the lord to the plaintiff, or
his father, as would have sustained the right claimed of
common appurtenant in respect of their lands. And as
this was not done, the Court was of opinion that the
nonsuit should be set aside, and a new trial granted.
It would seem therefore that, although the right may
have commenced within legal memory, yet after long
enjoyment, it may be presumed that a grant was made,
which grant has now been lost.

But undoubtedly the usual method of claiming common appurtenant is by prescription from long enjoyment; and when a claim of this kind is made by any
person, not as one of a class, such as the tenants of
a manor, or the tenants of a township, but simply in
consequence of long enjoyment, he must, unless a lost
grant can be presumed, either be prepared to have his
claim negatived by its being shown that it has arisen
within time of legal memory (*l*); or else he must avail

(*l*) See *ante*, p. 5.

himself of the provisions of the Prescription Act, 2 & 3 Will. IV. c. 71, sometimes called Lord Tenterden's Act, to which I now call your attention. The Act is intituled " An Act for shortening the Time of Prescription in certain cases." It begins by reciting that the expression " from time immemorial or time whereof the memory of man runneth not to the contrary," is now by the law of England in many cases considered to include and denote the whole period of time from the reign of King Richard the first, whereby the title to matters that have been long enjoyed is sometimes defeated by showing the commencement of such enjoyment; which is in many cases productive of inconvenience and injustice. And it enacts (*m*) that no claim, which may be lawfully made at the common law by custom, prescription or grant, to any right of common or other profit or benefit, to be taken and enjoyed from or upon any land of the king, his heirs or successors, or any land being parcel of the Duchy of Lancaster, or of the Duchy of Cornwall, or of any ecclesiastical or lay person, or body corporate, except such matters and things as are therein specially provided for; and except tithes, rent and services, shall, where such right, profit or benefit shall have been actually taken and enjoyed by any person claiming right thereto, without interruption, for the full period of *thirty years*, be defeated or destroyed, by showing only that such right, profit or benefit was first taken or enjoyed at any time prior to such period of thirty years; but nevertheless such claim may be defeated in any other way by which the same is now liable to be defeated; and when such right, profit or benefit shall have been so taken and enjoyed as aforesaid for the full period of *sixty years*, the right thereto shall be deemed absolute and indefeasible, unless it shall appear that the same was taken and enjoyed by some consent or agreement expressly made or given for

The Prescription Act, stat. 2 & 3 Will. IV. c. 71.

Thirty years' enjoyment.

Sixty years' enjoyment.

(*m*) Sect. 1.

that purpose by deed or writing. And it enacts (n)
that each of the respective periods of years before men-

Next before some action or suit. tioned shall be deemed and taken to be the period next
before some suit or action, wherein the claim or matter,
to which such period may relate, shall have been or

What is an interruption. shall be brought into question; and that no act or
other matter shall be deemed to be an interruption
within the meaning of this statute, unless the same
shall have been or shall be submitted to or acquiesced
in for one year after the party interested shall have had
or shall have notice thereof, and of the person making
or authorizing the same to be made. It also enacts (o)
that in all actions upon the case and other pleadings
wherein the party claiming may now by law allege his
right generally without averring the existence of such

General allegation, when sufficient. right from time immemorial, such general allegation
shall still be deemed sufficient; and if the same shall be
denied, all and every the matters in this Act mentioned
and provided, which shall be applicable to the case,
shall be admissible in evidence to sustain or rebut such
allegation; and that in all pleadings to actions of
trespass, and in all other pleadings wherein, before the
passing of the Act, it would have been necessary to
allege the right to have existed from time immemorial,
it shall be sufficient to allege the enjoyment thereof as

Allegation of enjoyment by occupiers. of right by the occupiers of the tenement, in respect
whereof the same is claimed, for and during such of the
periods mentioned in the Act as may be applicable to
the case, and without claiming in the name or right of
the owner of the fee, as is now usually done; and if the
other party shall intend to rely on any proviso, exception, incapacity, disability, contract, agreement or other
matter before mentioned, or on any cause or matter of
fact or of law, not inconsistent with the simple fact of
enjoyment, the same shall be specially alleged and set
forth in answer to the allegation of the party claiming,

(n) Sect. 4.   (o) Sect. 5.

and shall not be received in evidence on any general traverse or denial of such allegation. And the Act further provides (*p*) that in the several cases mentioned in and provided for by the Act, no presumption shall be allowed or made in favour or support of any claim, upon proof of the exercise or enjoyment of the right or matter claimed, for any less period of time or number of years, than for such period or number, mentioned in the Act, as may be applicable to the case and to the nature of the claim. And, further (*q*), that the time during which any person, otherwise capable of resisting any claim to any of the matters before mentioned, shall have been or shall be an infant, idiot, *non compos mentis*, feme covert or tenant for life, or during which any action or suit shall have been pending and which shall have been diligently prosecuted, until abated by the death of any party or parties thereto, shall be excluded in the computation of the periods before mentioned, except only in cases where the right or claim is thereby declared to be absolute and indefeasible. So that in case of an enjoyment for thirty years only, the fact that the owner of the servient tenement has been, during part of that time, under disability or tenant for life, or that an action or suit has been pending and diligently prosecuted during part of the time, will prevent the thirty years' time being sufficient to establish the claim. There must have been thirty years' enjoyment, irrespective of any disability, or of any pending action or suit, on the part of the party entitled to resist the claim. But the fourth and the seventh sections of the Act are to be read together, so that the thirty years "next before some suit or action," mentioned in the fourth section, may be made up of two periods, comprising together thirty years, one commencing more than thirty years before the suit or action, and ending with the commencement of a tenancy for life of the

Exceptions of infancy, &c.

The fourth and seventh sections to be read together.

(*p*) Sect. 6.   (*q*) Sect. 7.

servient tenement, and the other commencing at the expiration of the tenancy for life, and ending at the

After sixty years' enjoyment no allowance for any disability.

commencement of the suit or action (*r*). Where, however, an enjoyment as of right for sixty years can be shown, there, by the 1st section the right is to be deemed absolute and indefeasible ; and, by the 7th section, in that case no allowance is made either for any disability or tenancy for life, or for the time during which an action or suit may have been pending and diligently prosecuted.

Claim must be lawful.

The claim under this statute must be one which may be lawfully made at the common law, by custom, prescription or grant. If, therefore, the claim is an unlawful one, actual enjoyment for thirty or even sixty years will not avail under this statute. Thus, in the

Mill v. *Commissioners of New Forest.*

case of *Mill* v. *The Commissioners of the New Forest* (*s*), it appeared that by statute 9 & 10 Will. III. c. 36, an Act relating to the New Forest, it was enacted (*t*), that, in case any person or persons whatsoever should presume to take, or should obtain, any gift, grant, estate or interest of and in the inclosure or wastes of the New Forest, or any woods or trees growing thereon, every such gift, grant or interest should *ipso facto* be null and void. And by a subsequent statute of 1st Anne, st. 1, c. 7, s. 5, the Crown was restricted from making leases, beyond thirty-one years or three lives, of any of the lands belonging to the Crown. The forest belonged to the Crown. An allotment of waste land had been made to the plaintiff, under an Inclosure Act passed in 1810, and in respect of this allotment the plaintiff claimed a right of common of pasture in the waste lands of the forest, and a right of pannage in the open woods of the forest ; and he proved an enjoyment of the right claimed for the full period of

(*r*) *Clayton* v. *Corby*, 2 Q. B. 813.

(*s*) 18 C. B. 60.

(*t*) Sect. 10.

thirty years, as of right and without interruption, as provided by the statute 2 & 3 Will. IV. c. 71, s. 1. But the Court held that the claim could not be supported; because there could not be any grant to the plaintiff from the Crown of any right of common; seeing that the Crown was by statute incapacitated from making any such grant. It was impossible that any legal grant of the right could have existed; the user therefore for thirty years was of no avail. So in the case of *The Attorney-General* v. *Mathias* (*u*), the Court was of opinion that no user however long could establish a right which was unlawful in itself. The right claimed in that case was a right for the defendants, as woodwards or foresters of the Crown, to grant to certain free miners, gales or licences for making stone quarries in inclosed land, part of the Forest of Dean, the soil whereof was in the Crown, and to exact gale fees or rents in respect thereof, and to apply the same to their own use, without accounting to the Crown. The Court held that no length of user could establish such a right.

Att.-Gen. v. *Mathias.*

Again, the user must be by a person claiming right thereto. It must not be by leave or licence granted at any time during the period. And, as a person cannot claim a right against himself, if it be shown that, during any part of the prescribed period, the claimant himself has been owner of the waste or other servient tenement upon which the right of profit *à prendre* is claimed, such time must be excluded from the period of thirty years, or sixty years, as the case may be. In the case of *Warburton* v. *Parke* (*x*), there was a claim of the enjoyment of a right of common for thirty years under the statute, and also for sixty years. But, as it appeared that the claimant had been owner in fee of the farm, in respect of which his right of common was

User must be by persons claiming right.

A person cannot claim right against himself.

Warburton v. *Parke.*

(*u*) 4 Kay & J. 579.   (*x*) 2 Hurl. & Norm. 64.

claimed, and had been also tenant for life and occupier of the common, over which the right was claimed, during a large portion of these periods, it was held that the statute could not assist him; and it was also held that, as he could not have an enjoyment as of right against himself, within the meaning of the statute, so neither could his tenants of the farm in question.

The right must have been actually taken and enjoyed, by a person claiming right thereto, without interruption, for the full period of thirty years. It is not necessary, and obviously would often be impossible, to prove the exercise of a right of common over the whole of a waste. "Where the spot in question is parcel of a larger tract, it is sufficient to show user over that larger tract. But the evidence must be that the right has been so used over the larger tract, that, taking into account all the circumstances, the contiguity of the spot to those on which the right has been exercised, its hability for the exercise of the right, and all the other circumstances, the jury may reasonably infer that the right extended over the whole of the larger tract, including the spot in question." The law on this subject is thus laid down by Mr. Justice Patteson in the case of *Peardon* v. *Underhill* (y); and I have simply quoted his language. In the case of a right of common, it does not appear to be absolutely necessary that evidence should be given of the exercise of the right every year; provided the cesser of exercise can be accounted for, as by the fact that, for a year or two, the owner or his tenants had no commonable cattle to put upon the waste. This was decided in the case of *Carr* v. *Foster* (z). In that case the plaintiff claimed a right of common in respect of a farm called Mealingscales, of which he was tenant; and he proved a continued user of such right by the tenants of Mealingscales for nearly forty years next before the commence-

User of right of common over part of waste.

Cesser of user for a time.

Carr v. *Foster.*

(y) 16 Q. B. 120, 123.   (z) 3 Q. B. 581.

ment of the action; except that, about eighteen years back, the owner of the farm had it for two years in his own hands, and, having no commonable cattle, made no use of the common during that period. The Lord Chief Justice Denman left it to the jury to say, whether the tenants of Mealingscales had substantially enjoyed the right of common for thirty years next before the commencement of the action. A verdict was given for the plaintiff. And a rule for a nonsuit or for a new trial, upon the ground that the verdict was against the weight of evidence, was discharged by the Court of Queen's Bench. Lord Denman, Chief Justice, observed, that " the words of section 1 are ' without interruption,' not without intermission. And the intermission must be a matter open in every case to explanation. Sect. 6 enacts, that no presumption shall be made in favour of any claim, on proof of the right having been exercised for a less period than that prescribed by the Act in the particular case. But that provision is meant only to encounter presumptions, from an exercise of the right during such an imperfect period, that it was exercised in older times. The effect of the clause is, that a claimant, proving enjoyment for less than the specified time, shall not, on that ground, carry back his right to a period before that which his proof extends to. But this does not affect the mode of proof: and, where actual enjoyment is shown before and after the period of intermission, it may be inferred from that evidence that the right continued during the whole time." Mr. Justice Patteson observed, " It is suggested that the argument for the plaintiff might apply equally if there were a cesser for seven years. I am not prepared to say that it would not. It might be that, under the circumstances, the party had no occasion to use the right. The question would always be for the jury. So long an intermission would be a strong piece of evidence against the continued right; but it would be for them to determine. The Act makes no provision for such a case, sect. 6 relating only to the non-presumption of right, at a period antecedent to that over which the proof extends." Mr. Justice Williams was of the same opinion: "Interruption," he said, "means an obstruction not a cesser or intermission or anything denoting a mere breach in time. There must be an overt act, indicating that the right is disputed. Before the statute, in cases relating to common, it was very usual to explain the ceasing to turn on cattle by the fact that there were not at the time commonable cattle to turn on. No necessary inference arises from a cesser during two, three or seven years. In this particular case enjoyment for the requisite period was abundantly made out." In

Lowe v. *Carpenter*.

the case of *Lowe* v. *Carpenter* (*a*), which was a case of a right of way under other sections of the statute, which require twenty or forty years' user, the Court held, that some user must be shown to have been exercised in the year in which the action was brought. Baron Parke expressed an opinion that some act of user ought to be shown to have been exercised at least once a year. However that was a case, not of a right of common, but of a right of way. And on this case, Lord St.

Lord St. Leonards on *Lowe* v. *Carpenter*.

Leonards has the following remarks in his Essay on the Real Property Acts (*b*). "The point decided in this important case was, that there must have been an user sometime in the year next before the commencement of the action. This is a strict construction of the statute, where, after long enjoyment, although there has been no actual user within the last year, which might be accounted for, there has been no interruption, that is, in such a case, no attempt to prevent the user,—for example, putting a lock on a gate. But it would be found difficult to support the proposition that there must be proved to have been an actual user every year during the twenty or forty years. This case shows the necessity, where time

(*a*) 6 Ex. 825.   (*b*) Page 177, 2nd ed.

constitutes the title under the statute, not to omit the exercise of the right in any one year, for every neglect will expose the claimant to the loss of the easement." In the case of *Bailey* v. *Appleyard* (c), a right of com- *Bailey* v. mon of pasture was set up by the plaintiff by reason *Appleyard.* of thirty years' enjoyment under the statute. But, it having been proved that in the year 1809, which was twenty-eight years only before the commencement of the action, a rail had been erected which prevented access of cattle from the plaintiff's land to the common in question (which rail had been removed in conse- qnence of an agreement), it was held that the proof of enjoyment before that time could not be brought in aid to make up the period of thirty years. It was left to the jury to say whether there had been substantially an enjoyment for thirty years, or for twenty-eight only. And a verdict having been found for the defendant, a rule for a new trial on the ground of misdirection was refused by the Court.

The enjoyment must, according to the fourth section Thirty or of the statute, have been for thirty or sixty years *next* sixty years next before *before some action or suit* wherein the claim or matter some action shall have been or shall be brought into question. or suit. Accordingly in the case of *Richards* v. *Fry* (d), which *Richards* v. was an action of trespass, it was held that the right *Fry.* ought to have been claimed by the defendant to have been used by him for thirty years next before the com- mencement of the suit, instead of for thirty years next before the time when the alleged trespass was com- mitted. A special demurrer was taken to a plea, which thus set out the claim as a defence to the action. And on argument judgment was given for the plaintiff. This is an apparent absurdity, and has been more than once so characterised by the Courts. As was remarked

(c) 8 Ad. & Ell. 161.   (d) 7 Ad. & Ell. 698.

Ward v.
Robins.
by Baron Parke in the case of *Ward* v. *Robins* (*d*), with
reference to the period of twenty years provided in
other cases, "An enjoyment for twenty years or more
before the act complained of gives only what may be
termed an inchoate title, which may become complete or
not by an enjoyment subsequent, according as that
enjoyment is or is not continued to the commencement
of the suit."

The interruption must have been submitted to or
acquiesced in for one year, after the party interrupted
shall have had notice thereof, and of the person making
or authorizing the same to be made. In the case of
Flight v.
Thomas.
Acquiescence
in interrup-
tion for a
year.
Flight v. *Thomas,* in the House of Lords (*e*), which was
a case on the section of the Act which relates to window
lights, it was held that an interruption of the enjoyment, in whatever period of the twenty years it may
happen, cannot be deemed an interruption within the
meaning of the Act, unless it is acquiesced in for a
Bennison v.
Cartwright.
whole year. And in the case of *Bennison* v. *Cartwright* (*f*), the Court of Queen's Bench held that an
interruption is not necessarily acquiesced in because no
action or suit is brought in respect of it. Non-acquies-
cence may be shown by other acts, as by correspondence
between the solicitors of the parties, the question of
acquiescence being a question of fact to be determined
by a jury.

Extinguish-
ment of com-
mon appur-
tenant.
Common appurtenant being, as I said (*g*), against
common right, is extinguished if the ownership of the
land, in respect of which the right of common is
claimed, becomes united with the ownership of any part
of land, over which the right of common is exercised.
Tyrringham's
case.
This was the point decided in *Tyrringham's* case (*h*).

(*d*) 15 M. & W. 237, 242.   (*g*) *Ante,* p. 168.
(*e*) 8 Cl. & Fin. 231.   (*h*) 4 Rep. 38.
(*f*) 5 Best & Smith, 1.

The right of pasture was unluckily claimed in that case as belonging to a meadow or pasture. And it was held that, as common appendant is in respect of land anciently arable, although it might afterwards have become meadow or pasture, this common, being claimed only in respect of a meadow or pasture, must be common appurtenant ; and, being common appurtenant, it was totally extinguished by reason of the owner of part of the common having purchased the tenement to which the right of common belonged. Common appurtenant, however, as well as common appendant may be apportioned, in case part of the dominant tenement, in respect of which the right is claimed, come into the hands of one person, and another part into the hands of another person. Each person shall, in such case, exercise his right of common, in respect of the land belonging to himself, according to the number of beasts and sheep or other cattle levant and couchant upon his part of the tenement.

Apportionment of common appurtenant.

It is often said there are four kinds of common. Common appendant, common appurtenant, common by reason of vicinage and common in gross. Common by reason of vicinage was in its origin merely an excuse for trespass, in a case where two wastes, on which two distinct classes of persons have common of pasture adjoin one another without any boundary fence existing between them ; so that the cattle of one class of commoners stray upon the waste which belongs to the other class. The nature of this right is a good deal gone into by the present Master of the Rolls in his judgment in the Epping Forest case, *Commissioners of Sewers* v. *Glasse* (i). Commons by reason of vicinage can only exist between two classes of commoners. It cannot

Common by reason of vicinage.

Commissioners of Sewers v. *Glasse.*

(i) L. R., 19 Eq. 134, 159—162. See also *Cape* v. *Scott*, L. R., 9 Q. B. 269.

exist between two private estates (*k*). Each class must turn out upon their own common, and cannot turn out upon the common of their neighbours. Each class must put on so many cattle as their own common will maintain, and no more ; and if the one class inclose their common against the others, the others' right to common by vicinage is extinct. There must, however, be an actual inclosure ; otherwise the neighbours' cattle will still be excused from trespassing on the waste.

Common in gross.

Common in gross, is common which a man has, irrespective of the ownership or occupation of any tenement. It may be created by the owner of a common appurtenant, for a fixed number of cattle, alienating his common appurtenant, without the tenement to which it belongs. It is held to be immaterial to the owner of the waste, when the right is fixed and stinted to a certain given number of cattle, whether those cattle are put on in respect of a tenement, or by a person who owns no land (*l*). Common appendant, however, for cattle levant and couchant upon a tenement and common appurtenant in like manner for cattle levant and couchant upon a tenement, cannot be severed from the tenement, and aliened so as to become common in gross (*m*). Common in gross, as you have already seen (*n*), is not within the statutes of Merton and Westminster the Second, by which the lord is enabled to inclose, leaving a sufficiency of common. Common in gross may also be created by express grant to a man and his heirs of a right to put on so many cattle on the lands of the grantor, either at all times of the year, or

(*k*) *Jones* v. *Robin*, 10 Q. B. 581, 620.

(*l*) *Drury* v. *Kent*, Cro. Jac. 15 ; *Spooner* v. *Day*, Cro. Car. 432 ; Vin. Abr. tit. Common (O.) ;

Daniel v. *Hanslip*, 2 Lev. 67.

(*m*) *Drury* v. *Kent*, *Daniel* v. *Hanslip*, *ubi sup.*

(*n*) *Ante*, p. 113.

at certain times. It is said also that a grantor may grant to his grantee a right to put an unlimited number of cattle into the lands of the grantor. Common in gross may also be claimed by prescription from long user by a man and his ancestors, whose heir he is, in the same manner as we have seen in former Lectures (*o*), that a right of exclusive pasture may be so claimed. The right of common in gross is not within the Prescription Act (*p*), as that relates only to cases in which there is a dominant as well as a servient tenement (*q*); but, when created, it is an incorporeal hereditament, grantable by deed.

(*o*) *Ante*, pp. 9, 10.

(*p*) Stat. 2 & 3 Will. IV. c. 71; *ante*, p. 173.

(*q*) *Shuttleworth* v. *Le Fleming*, 19 C. B., N. S. 687.

LECTURE XIII.

Common of other matters than pasture.

First, things renewable.

Secondly, things not renewable.

WE now come to the consideration of common in respect of other matters than pasture. These may be classed generally under two heads:—first, the right of taking such matters as, in the course of nature, may be renewed; such as wood or peat for fuel, or fern and gorse, either for fuel, or for fodder for cattle, for the foundation of haystacks, and other agricultural purposes; and secondly, the right of taking such things as, in the course of nature, are not renewable; such as sand, gravel, clay, loam, coals and other minerals.

Common of estovers.

Ancient house.

Luttrel's case.

First with respect to common of estovers, turbary and the like. Common of estovers, as I mentioned in a former Lecture (a), is the right of cutting timber, underwood, gorse or furze, and such like, for fuel to burn in the house, or for the repairs of the house and farm buildings, hedges and fences, and instruments of husbandry. This right to take fuel to burn in a house, if claimed by prescription, must be claimed in respect of an ancient house; for prescription is a title acquired by user, from time whereof the memory of man runneth not to the contrary. And it is evident that no such user can possibly take place except in an ancient house. The law on this point is laid down in *Luttrel's case* (b), where it is said, "If a man has estovers, either by grant or prescription, to his house, although he alters the rooms and chambers of this house, as to make a parlour where it was the hall, or the hall where the parlour was, and the like alteration of the qualities, and

(a) *Ante*, p. 18.   (b) 4 Rep. 86, 87.

not of the house itself, and without making new chimneys, by which no prejudice accrues to the owner of the wood, it is not any destruction of the prescription ; for then many prescriptions will be destroyed; and, although he builds new chimneys, or makes a new addition to his old house, by that he shall not lose his prescription; but he cannot employ or spend any of his estovers in the new chimneys, or in the part newly added." And in *Coster and Wingfield's case* (c), the Court all agreed "that he who set up again a new chimney, where an old one was before, should have estovers to the said new chimney; and so if he build a new house upon the foundation of an old house, that he should have common to his said house newly erected ; so, if a house falleth down, and the tenant or inhabitant sets up a new house in the same place." Common of turbary is a species of common of estovers, being the right to take peat or turf, which has become by course of time fit for burning, and not green turf, for the purpose of using the same for fuel in a messuage ; and, when claimed by prescription, it must be claimed also in respect of an ancient messuage, for the reason I have just stated. It is not, however, necessary in the pleadings to mention the messuage as an ancient messuage, as that would be intended if the contrary were not shown (d). In the case of *Clarkson* v. *Woodhouse* (e), a custom was pleaded, showing that divers ancient messuages within the manor of Stalmine, in the county of Lancaster, had common of turbary upon the waste or common called Stalmine Moss, to dig and take turves in and upon the said waste or common, except such parts as had been inclosed or approved, as after mentioned, for their necessary fuel to be burned and consumed in their respective messuages every year at all time of the year as occasion required, and also common of pasture throughout the waste

Coster and Wingfield's case.

Common of turbary.

House intends ancient.

Clarkson v. *Woodhouse.*

(c) 2 Leon. 44, 45.   Jac. 256.
(d) *Dowglass* v. *Kindal*, Cro.   (e) 5 T. Rep. 412, n.

(except such parts as had been approved and inclosed) for all their commonable cattle levant and couchant upon the said respective messuages and lands. And a custom was pleaded for the owners of the waste by themselves or their superintendent of the waste, called the moss reeve, from time immemorial, to assign to the several owners and occupiers of such ancient messuages and lands, upon their reasonable request in that behalf, certain reasonable parts and proportions of the said

Moss dales. waste or common commonly called moss dales, to be by them respectively held in severalty, exclusive of all others, for digging and getting turves thereon for their necessary fuel to be burned and consumed in such their respective messuages every year and at all times of the year, as to such their respective messuages belonging and appertaining, and that the respective owners and occupiers of such ancient messuages got such turves in their respective moss dales, and in no other part of the waste, so long as any turbary remained in the moss dales so set out; and when and so often as the turbary of such moss dales so assigned had been got and cleared therefrom, the owners of the waste had inclosed and approved to themselves all such moss dales or parts of the common or waste called Stalmine Moss, as had been cleared as aforesaid, commonly called the following ground thereof, and to hold the same in severalty for ever afterwards, freed and discharged from all common of turbary and pasture thereon. This was held to be a reasonable custom. The fuel was to be used in the messuage. The grant was advantageous to both lord and tenant. And the judgment was affirmed in the Exchequer Chamber (*f*).

In addition to the right of taking wood, peat and other matters for fuel, and to the right of taking timber for repairs, may be the right of taking furze,

(*f*) 5 T. Rep. 415, n.

fern, and other matters for fodder and litter for cattle Fodder, litter, &c. and other purposes. There may also be the right which I mentioned in a former Lecture (*g*) of *pawnage* or *pannage;* that is, a right of taking acorns and mast of beech trees by the mouths of swine turned out into the woods to feed there. This, however, is a species of common of pasture. In the recent case of *Smith* v. *Smith* v. *Earl Earl Brownlow* (*h*), the following rights were established *Brownlow.* by the decree. The words of the decree are not set out in the report, but I· have been furnished with a copy of it. It is dated the 14th January, 1870, and it is as follows, so far as regards the declaratory part : "His Lordship doth declare that the plaintiff, and the other freehold and copyhold tenants of the manor of Berkhamstead in the amended bill mentioned, except any tenants whose rights have been purchased by the present or late defendant, are entitled, as to the right of pasture for commonable cattle as appendant, and, as to all other rights of pasture and commonable rights, as appurtenant, to their respective freehold and copyhold tenements, held of the said manor, to the following common rights, viz. a right of common of pasture upon Common of Berkhamstead Common in the amended bill mentioned, pasture. and so much of the four pieces of waste in the amended bill mentioned as now remains uninclosed, for all commonable cattle levant and couchant on their tenements, and to a right of *pannage*, and to a right to cut so much Pannage. furze, gorse, fern and underwood upon the said com- To cut furze, mon, and so much of the said four pieces of waste as &c. now remains uninclosed, as may be required for the purpose of fodder and litter for all commonable cattle and swine, levant and couchant on their tenements, and for fuel, and other purposes of agriculture and husbandry, necessary for the beneficial and profitable enjoyment and use of their said tenements." A similar To cut right of cutting and taking away brackens, or ferns, to brackens.

(*g*) *Ante*, p. 168.   (*h*) L. R., 9 Eq. 241.

be used and consumed on the estate, from the commons within the town and hamlet of Ulverstone, also occurs in the case of *Hollinshead* v. *Walton* (*i*). And in the recent case of *Warrick* v. *Queen's College, Oxford* (*k*), similar rights were established. The decree runs as follows : " His Lordship doth declare that the plaintiff John Warrick and the other freehold tenants of the manor of Plumstead in the county of Kent are entitled, as to the right of pasture for commonable cattle to a right of common as appendant, and as to all other rights of pasture and other common rights to a right of common as appurtenant to their freehold hereditaments, held of the said manor, and that such rights extend to a right of pasture upon the commons called respectively Plumstead Common and Bostal Heath for all sorts of cattle levant and couchant, as well commonable as others, and that they are also entitled to cut turf for use as fuel in their dwelling-houses, and to cut such furze, gorse and fern upon the said commons as may be required for fuel to be consumed on the said hereditaments so held by them, and for the purpose of fodder and litter for cattle levant and couchant on the said hereditaments, and doth order and declare the same accordingly."

Warrick v. *Queen's College.*

Common of pasture for all cattle.

To cut turf for fuel.

To cut furze, &c.

Claims of this sort, when made in respect of a messuage or tenement, must be reasonable ; and the things which are claimed to be taken must be spent or used upon the tenement in respect of which they are claimed. The claim must be reasonable. Thus in the case of *Wilson* v. *Willes* (*l*), the tenants of the manor of Hampstead claimed a customary right for all the customary tenants, having a garden or gardens, parcel of their tenements, to dig and carry away from the heath, by themselves and their farmers and tenants

Claims must be reasonable.

Wilson v. *Willes.*

(*i*) 7 East, 485.   (*l*) 7 East, 121.
(*k*) L. R., 6 Ch. 716.

respectively, occupiers of such customary tenements with the appurtenances, to be used and spent in and upon their said customary tenements for the purpose of making and repairing grass plats in the gardens, parcels of the same respectively, for the improvement thereof, such turf covered with grass fit for the pasture of cattle, as hath been fit and proper to be so used and spent, every year at all times in the year as often and in such quantity as occasion hath required, as to their said customary tenements with the appurtenances respectively belonging and appertaining. Another plea alleged more generally the same right in the customary tenants, the turf to be used and spent in and upon their customary tenements, in and for the improvement of the gardens, parcels of the same respectively, without confining the improvements to the making and repairing of grass plats. The third plea alleged a similar right in the customary tenants to dig, take and carry away turf, to be used and spent in and upon their customary tenements, for the purpose of making and repairing the banks and mounds in, of, and for the hedges and fences thereof. A fourth plea laid the custom still more generally to be, for the customary tenants to take the turf from the *locus in quo*, as often and in such quantity as the occasion required, to be used and spent upon their customary tenements respectively for the improvement thereof. To all these special pleas there was a general demurrer and joinder on the part of the plaintiff. And the Court gave judgment for the plaintiff, thereby allowing the demurrer to all the pleas. Lord Ellenborough, Chief Justice, said, " A custom however ancient must not be indefinite and uncertain ; and here - it is not defined what sort of improvement the custom extends to : it is not stated to be in the way of agriculture or horticulture : it may mean all sorts of fanciful improvements : every part of the garden may be converted into grass plats, and even mounds of earth raised and

covered with turf from the common : there is nothing
to restrain the tenants from taking the whole of the
turbary of the common and destroying the pasture
altogether. A custom of this description ought to have
some limit; but here there is no limitation to the
custom as laid but caprice and fancy. Then this privilege is claimed to be exercised when occasion requires.
What description can be more loose than that? It is
not even confined to the occasions of the garden. It
resolves itself, therefore, into the mere will and pleasure
of the tenant, which is inconsistent with the rights of
all the other commoners as well as of the lord. The
third special plea also is vastly too indefinite : it goes
to establish a right to take as much of the turf of the
common as any tenant pleases, for making banks and
mounds on his estate : it is not even confined to purposes of agriculture. All the customs laid therefore
are bad, as being too indefinite and uncertain."

Must be spent upon the tenement. Not only must the right claimed be reasonable and
definite, but it must also be claimed for the purpose
of being spent or used upon the tenement, in respect
Valentine v. Penny. of which it is claimed. Thus in the case of *Valentine*
v. *Penny* (m), in an action of trespass the defendant
justified that he and all those whose estate he had in a
cottage, have used to have common of turbary, to dig
and sell *ad libitum*, as belonging to the house. And it
was adjudged that it was an ill plea; for a common
appertaining to a house ought to be spent in the house
Hayward v. Cannington. and not sold abroad. So in the case of *Hayward* v.
Cannington (which is perhaps best reported in the second
volume of Keble's Reports (n)) in an action of trespass,
the defendant justified by a prescription for as much
turf as two men can dig in fourteen days, by reason of
an ancient messuage; and did not say to be spent in the
messuage; to which the plaintiff demurred; and the
demurrer was allowed by the Court, judgment being

(m) Noy, 145.   (n) Pages 290, 311.

given for the plaintiff. The Court all agreed that in the case at bar it must be alleged to be spent in the messuage. It was argued that the claim was sufficiently certain, being as much as two men can dig in fourteen days; but, in addition to the certainty, the Court also required that, as the claim was made in respect of a messuage, the matter claimed should be spent in the house. In the report of the same case in Siderfin (o), Siderfin's report. the claim is stated to be a claim on the part of the defendant that he is seised of an ancient messuage, and that he and all those whose estate he has, &c. have had fourteen days' digging of turf in the place where, &c. as to the said messuage pertaining. And in the report of the same case in Levinz (p), the plea is stated to be Levinz's report. a plea on the part of the defendant that he is seised of an ancient house, and prescribes to have so many turves every year as two men could dig in a day, as belonging to his messuage. But all the reports agree that judgment was given for the plaintiff. So the case of *Bailey* Bailey v. Stephens. v. *Stephens* (q) was an action of trespass for breaking and entering into a close of land of the plaintiff's, called Short Cliff Wood, and cutting down two trees of the plaintiff then and there standing and growing, and converting the same to the defendant's use. The defendant pleaded several pleas; amongst others that, at the time of the alleged trespass, William York was seised in his demesne as of fee, of and in a certain close called Bloody Field, immediately adjoining the said close of the plaintiff, and that the said William York, and all those whose estate he had, and his and their tenants, had from time whereof the memory of man runneth not to the contrary, enjoyed the right, at their free will and pleasure, to enter, by themselves and their servants, upon a part or strip, to wit, a lug fall (or perch) of the said close of the plaintiff, adjoining the said close of the

(o) Page 354.
(p) 1 Lev. 231.

(q) 12 C. B., N. S. 91.

said William York, for the purpose of cutting down
and carrying away, and to cut down and carry away,
and convert to his and their own use, the trees and
wood growing and being on the said strip or lug fall, as
to the said close of the said William York appertaining;
and that the alleged trespass was committed by the
defendant as the servant and by the authority of one
James Emery, who was lessee of the close called Bloody
Field from William York. Other pleas stated a user
for sixty years, for thirty years, and also a grant by
deed of the same right, but which grant was alleged to
be lost. To all these pleas the plaintiff demurred, on
the ground that the plea showed no defence to the
action, and claimed too large a right; and of this
opinion was the Court. The claim, you will observe,
was a claim, by the owners and occupiers of the defeu-
dant's close, to cut down the trees on the plaintiff's
land, and to sell and dispose of them at pleasure,
wholly irrespective of any use to be made of them on
the land of the defendant. If the claim had been to
cut the wood for the purpose of repairing the fences of
the close called Bloody Field, or for any reasonable
purpose of agriculture connected with that field, it
would have been good. But this was simply a claim
for the owners and occupiers of one close, always to cut
wood growing upon another close, for any purpose
whatsoever; and such a claim is too wide, and therefore
bad in law.

I have already mentioned (*r*) that, except in the case
of a copyholder, which of necessity forms an exception
to the general rule (*s*), no claim of a *profit à prendre in
alieno solo* can be made by custom, nor can it be claimed
by a fluctuating body such as the inhabitants of a place.
Thus in the case of *Selby* v. *Robinson* (*t*), which was an

Claim of
profit à
prendre can-
not be made
by custom.
Selby v.
Robinson.

(*r*) *Ante,* p. 13.   (*t*) 2 T. Rep. 758.   See also
(*s*) *Ante,* p. 17.   *Chilton* v. *Corporation of London,*

action of trespass for entering the plaintiff's close and cutting down wood, the defendant pleaded a custom, that all and every the poor, necessitous and indigent householder and householders, residing and abiding within the township of Whaddon, in the parish of Whaddon in the county of Bucks, from time immemorial had used and been accustomed at his and their free will and pleasure, standing upon the ground within the chase of Whaddon, as well with their hands as with wood hooks, to break off, gather, pick up, take and carry away, from and out of Whaddon chase aforesaid, as well the rotten wood of and belonging to the boughs and branches of the trees standing and growing on the said chase, as the rotten wood broken and fallen off from the boughs and branches of the said trees, there standing and growing, and found upon the ground within the said chase, for necessary fuel, to be used, burned and consumed in his and their respective dwelling-houses, in the township of Whaddon aforesaid. The Court thought that it was impossible to support the custom as thus set out, and that the question was too clear for discussion. It might perhaps have been otherwise if the defendant could have stated on the record that he was seised of a certain ancient tenement, and so prescribed in a *que estate;* because that would be limiting the benefit claimed to the house, to which the prescription would apply. But there is no limitation at all in this case; and it is impossible to ascertain who is entitled to this right, under the custom as stated on this record; for the description of poor householders is too vague and uncertain.

There may, however, be exceptions to this rule. Thus, in the case of *Weekly* v. *Wildman* (*u*), it is said by

L. R., 7 Ch. D. 735; *Lord Rivers* v. *Adams*, L. R., 3 Ex. D. 361.

(*u*) 1 Lord Raymond, 405.

Special
custom.

Dean of Ely
v. Warren.

Royal forest.

Hainault
Forest.

Willingale v.
Maitland.

Chief Justice Treby that in ancient times such grants
to the inhabitants were allowed to be good, which would
not be good at this day. "So, in this case, a grant of
common to the inhabitants for encouragement of habitation in the fen country may be supposed, which ought
to be adjudged good, if there had been constant enjoyment under such grant." And in the case of *The Dean
and Chapter of Ely* v. *Warren* (*x*), there appears to have
been very strong evidence of a custom in manors in the
fen country for the tenants *and occupants* of tenements
within the manor to dig up the lord's soil for turves,
a custom which Lord Hardwicke denounced as a very
great absurdity; at the same time, the evidence being
very strong, he directed an issue to try it. So an
exception to the rule has been allowed in the case of a
royal forest. Thus it appears from the statute 14 & 15
Vict. c. 43, by which Hainault Forest was disafforested,
that every poor widow in those parts of the parishes of
Barking and Dagenham, which lay within the Forest
of Hainault, who did not receive parochial relief, and
whose husband had been dead a year, had been usually
allowed to have one load of wood yearly on Easter
Monday, from and out of the king's forest or king's
woods, or in lieu of it eight shillings in money, to those
who could not procure a team to carry the wood on
that day. And compensation was made to the widows
accordingly.

So in the case of *Willingale* v. *Maitland* (*y*), the
plaintiff alleged a grant by the Crown, to the inhabitants of Loughton, in the county of Essex (which was
a Crown manor and parish within the royal forest of
Epping), that the labouring or poor people inhabiting

(*x*) 2 Atk. 189.
(*y*) L. R., 3 Eq. 103. But see
as to this case, *Chilton* v. *Corpo-*
ration of London, L. R., 7 Ch. D.
735; and *Lord Rivers* v. *Adams*,
L. R., 3 Ex. D. 361.

the parish and having families might, during a certain period of every year, cut or lop the boughs and branches, above seven feet from the ground, on the trees growing on the waste lands of the manor or parish of Loughton for their own use and consumption, and for sale for their own relief to all or any of the inhabitants, for their consumption within the parish as fuel. This grant was held upon demurrer to be a valid grant. The Court relied on its being a grant by the Crown in derogation of its forestal rights, and entirely assented to the statement of counsel that grants by the Crown in derogation of its forestal rights are to be considered and treated in a different manner from other grants. The forestal rights were excessively oppressive upon the inhabitants, and accordingly the Crown frequently made, to the inhabitants in the neighbourhood of a forest, certain grants in derogation of those rights; which grants, though they might not be good in every other respect, were good so far as they were in derogation of those forestal rights. This is in accordance with the law laid down by Lord Coke (z), where it is said, " And concerning claims, it is especially to be observed that, by the forest law, a grant made of a privilege within the forest to all the inhabitants being freeholders within the forest, or such other commonalties not incorporated, is good."

We have already seen (a) that where there is a right of this kind, namely, of estovers or turbary and so forth, the lord cannot approve under the Statute of Merton (b), or the Statute of Westminster the Second (c), as against such right; although he may approve or inclose any part of the waste in which, according to the usual course of nature, there is no possibility for any turves, furze or ferns to grow (d). So there may be a

Lord cannot approve against these rights.

(z) 4 Inst. 297.

(a) *Ante*, p. 138.

(b) Stat. 20 Hen. III. c. 4.

(c) Stat. 13 Edw. I. c. 46.

(d) *Peardon* v. *Underhill*, 16 Q. B. 120; *ante*, p. 141.

Custom to
approve,
leaving suffi-
ciency.

custom of the manor in which the waste is situate for the lord to make grants by way of approval of portions of the waste, even as against these rights ; provided that he leave a sufficiency of estovers or turbary to be taken from the rest of the waste, with as beneficial egress and regress to and from the same as the commoners had before (e).

(e) *Arlett* v. *Ellis*, 7 B. & C. 346; *ante*, p. 141.

LECTURE XIV.

RIGHTS of the kind which I mentioned in my last Lecture, namely, to cut timber for fuel or repairs, or to get peat or brushwood for fuel, may be created by grant, either as appurtenant to a certain messuage, or as a right in gross; and such right in gross may, I apprehend, be granted either to an individual, or to a corporation. It was laid down in *Sym's case* (a) that " there is a difference between advantages in gross, and advantages which by the grant are made appurtenant or incident to another thing. As if a man be seised of a house in the right of his wife, and another grants to the husband and his heirs to have sufficient estovers to burn in the same house; in that case the estovers are appurtenant to the house, and shall descend to the issue of the husband and wife. So if one hath a house of the part of his mother, and one grants to him that he and his heirs shall have competent house bote to be burned in the same house, this is appurtenant to the house, and although it be a new purchase, yet it shall go with the house to the heir of the part of the mother."

Grant.

Sym's case.

Grant of estovers to be appurtenant to a house.

I apprehend that a right to take wood, turf, furze, fern, &c., may also be granted in gross, irrespective of its use in any tenement. Thus, a man may grant to another and his heirs so many loads of wood per annum to be taken out of his woods. So it was said by Wyndham, Justice, in the case of *Hayward* v. *Cannington* (b), that a man may prescribe to have two loads of wood out of another man's land as in gross, but not as appendant

Grant in gross.

(a) 8 Rep. 54.   (b) 2 Keble, 311.

without application :—that is to say, not as belonging to any messuage without its being applied to the use of that messuage. So in *Lord Mountjoy's case* (c), Lord Mountjoy, being seised of two parts of the manor of Sanford, by deed indented and enrolled, bargained and sold these two parts to John Brown and Charles Brown and the heirs of the said John Brown, in which indenture divers covenants were contained, and amongst them the following :—" Provided always and it is covenanted, granted, concluded and agreed between the said parties to these indentures, and the said John Brown and Charles and their heirs covenant and grant to and with the said Lord Mountjoy, his heirs and assigns by these presents in form following : that is to say, that it shall be lawful to and for the said Lord Mountjoy, his heirs and assigns, at all times hereafter, to have, take and dig, in and upon the heath ground of the premises, from time to time sufficient ores, *heath, turves and other necessaries* for the making, &c. of alum or copperas ; and to build houses there, pull down and alter, without let or interruption of the said John and Charles, their heirs or assigns, or either or any of them." And afterwards Lord Mountjoy, by deed indented, authorized one Richard Leycolt, for thirty-one years, to dig for mines and minerals in the manor, and to convert the same to his own use for thirty-one years, yielding to Lord Mountjoy, &c. one-half of the clear gains and profits to arise by reason of the grant. And the judges certified their opinion to be, that Lord Mountjoy, by this assurance, had sufficient interests and right in fee to dig such turves, ore and other things, for making of alum and copperas, &c., as he should think good. And that all the interest that Lord Mountjoy had to dig or make alum was granted to Leycolt during the term mentioned in the indenture. Lord Coke

---

(c) Co. Litt. 164 b ; 1 Anderson, 307.

says (*d*), that it was held that, though Lord Mountjoy might assign his whole interest to one, two or more, then if there be two or more, they could make no division of it, but work together with one stock; neither could Lord Mountjoy assign his interest in any part of the waste to one or more; for that might work a prejudice and a surcharge to the tenant of the land. They held also that, notwithstanding the grant, Brown, his heirs and assigns, might dig also as owner of the soil. It appears from the report of the same case in Godbolt (*e*) that Lord Coke was counsel for Lord Mountjoy in the case. An instance of the grant of such a right to a corporation occurs in the case of *The Queen* v. *The Chamberlains of Alnwick* (*f*). In that case, so long ago as the year 1290, William de Vesci granted to the burgesses of Alnwick, amongst other things, common in Haydon with all the privileges in Haydon Moor (a large tract of uninclosed land adjoining the town) in the marshes feeding and pasture grounds; with liberty to get peats, turves and brushwoods, and with all the other their free appurtenances and privileges which they were wont to have and to use in the times of the grantor's ancestors, as well as in the forbidden month as in others. Haydon Moor was not only a piece of waste ground but also a forest. The forbidden month is called the fence month, being the time during which the deer are breeding; and during which therefore they ought not to be disturbed. It begins fifteen days before Midsummer and ends fifteen days after midsummer. For these privileges of common during the fence month it appears that the freemen and burgesses paid 2*s*. per annum, pursuant to the following proviso in their charter :—" And it must known that the same burgesses and their heirs, for the privileges which they are

Queen v. *Chamberlains of Alnwick.*

(*d*) Co. Litt. 165 a.
(*e*) Page 18.

(*f*) 9 A. & E. 444.

to have in Haydon in the forbidden month with their
liberties, shall give me and my heirs 2s. annually,
namely, one-half at the feast of St. Martin, and the
other half at Pentecost for ever." The point decided
in this case was that, the interest of the freemen being

Right of
common not
rateable to
the poor.

that of commoners only, the corporation was not
rateable to the poor in respect thereof. A right of
common, as such, is not rateable to the poor; but, if it
is appendant or appurtenant to a tenement, and so
increases the value of the tenement, the tenement to
which it belongs is subject to a higher rate accordingly (g).

As in the case of pasture (h), so in the case of the
right to take brushwood and other matters of the same

Right may be
exclusive.

kind, the right claimed may be exclusive, either by
virtue of a prescription, or by virtue of a grant. Thus

Dowglass v.
Kendal.

in the case of *Dowglass* v. *Kendal* (i), an action of trespass was brought for taking and carrying away thirty
loads of thorns of the plaintiff's, by him cut down, and
lying upon his land at Chippingwarden in a place called
the common waste. The defendant justifies because the
place where, &c. is an acre, and that he is seised in fee
of a messuage, and three acres of land in Chippingwarden aforesaid, and that he and all whose estate it
was, from time immemorial, have used from time to
time to cut down and take *all the thorns* growing upon
the said place to expend in the said house, or about the
said lands, as pertaining to the said house and lands:
and so justifies. The plaintiffs showed that one Sir
Richard Saltington was seised in fee of the manor of
Chippingwarden, whereof the place where the trespass
was committed is parcel, and granted licence to him to
take the thorns; whereupon he cut them down, and the
defendant afterwards took them. Upon this plea it was
demurred; and after argument at the bar adjudged for

(g) *Rex* v. *Churchill*, 4 B. & C.   (h) *Ante*, pp. 9, 21.
750, 755.   (i) Cro. Jac. 256.

the defendant; for, as this case is, the lord may not cut
down any thorns, nor license any other to cut them
down; for the defendant prescribeth to have all the
thorns growing upon that place, and this prescription
excludes the lord to take any thorns there; but, if he
had claimed *common of estovers* only, then, if the lord
had first cut down the thorns, the commoner might not
take them; and if he had cut down all the thorns, the
commoner might have had an assize; but here he prescribes to have all, which is admitted by the replication,
and is well enough.

I now come to the consideration of rights of digging
for sand, gravel, coal, and other matters which, when
taken away, are not in the course of nature renewable.
And with regard to these, a right may be established
either by prescription, as appurtenant to a tenement for
the repair thereof or to be used thereon for any reasonable purposes, or by grant to be appurtenant to a tenement for any such purposes; or, I apprehend, either by
prescription or grant, as a right in gross, independent
of the enjoyment of any tenement. When a right of
this kind is claimed as belonging to any particular tenement, it must, like the claim of estovers or turbary, be
of a reasonable kind, and it must be for materials
which, when taken, are to be used or consumed upon
the tenement in respect of which they are claimed.
An instance of a claim annexed to a tenement, which
was considered unreasonable and therefore void, occurs
in the case of *Clayton* v. *Corby* (*k*). This was an action
of trespass for breaking into a close, and taking away
clay and other things. And in justification the defendant pleaded that, before and at the several times when
the alleged trespasses were committed, the defendant
had been and was the occupier of a certain tenement
and premises, to wit, a brick kiln; and that the defen-

Things not renewable.

Claim must be reasonable.

Clayton v. *Corby.*

(*k*) 5 Q. B. 415.

dant, whilst he was such occupier as aforesaid, and all
the occupiers for the time being of the tenement with
the appurtenances, for the full period of thirty years
next before the commencement of the suit, had respectively had and enjoyed, as of right and without interruption, and the defendant still as of right ought to
have and enjoy, a right to dig, take and carry away, in,
out of and from the said close, in which the alleged
trespasses were committed, so much of the clay of the
said close as was at any time required by him and them,
his and their servants, for the purpose of making bricks
in and at the said last-mentioned brick kiln, in every
year and at all times of the year. This, you see, was a
plea under the first section of the Prescription Act, 2 &
3 Will. IV. c. 71 (m), of thirty years' enjoyment without
interruption; and, under the fifth section (n), enjoyment was alleged as of right by the occupiers of the
tenements, in respect whereof the right was claimed,
without claiming in the name or right of the owner of
the fee. And it was also alleged, in pursuance of the
fourth section (n), that the enjoyment was for thirty
years next before the commencement of that suit. The
Court, however, held the plea to be bad as unreasonable.
Lord Denman, in delivering the judgment of the Court,
observed (o), "The nature of the tenement, so called a
brick kiln, leads to no conclusion, one way or the other,
as to the extent of the claim and demand upon the soil
of the plaintiff. It may have been at the time of the
trespass of any dimensions and capacity. It may have
been, during the thirty years of alleged enjoyment,
continually varying, and consequently the quantity of
clay required for the purpose of making bricks thereat
may have varied also. There is no limit. No amount
of clay, measured by cartloads or otherwise, required,—no
number of bricks, estimated by hundreds or thousands,

(m) Ante, p. 173.   (o) 5 Q. B. 422.
(n) Ante, p. 174.

claimed to be made,—is given or attempted. What is it, therefore, but an indefinite claim to take all the clay out of and from the said close in which, &c., or in other words to take from the plaintiff, the owner, the whole close? We are of opinion, therefore, that the plea cannot be sustained."

So, the materials claimed must not only be reasonably claimed, but must also be claimed for the purpose of being spent upon the premises. Thus, in the case of *Peppin* v. *Shakespear* (*p*), a plea was put in that the tenants of a customary tenement had immemorially been accustomed to have, and still of right ought to have, the liberty and privilege of digging for and carrying away sand, loam and gravel in and from the common, *for their necessary repairs;* and that the defendant Shakespear, in his own right, and the other defendants as his servants, entered in the place in question, being parcel of the said common, for the purpose of digging for and carrying away sand, loam and gravel, *for the necessary repairs of the said Shakespear* the defendant. The Court gave judgment for the plaintiff on account of defects in the pleas, which stated that the defendant entered for the purpose of digging for and carrying away sand, &c., *for the necessary repairs of the said defendant.* In one of the pleas the tenement was stated to be a messuage; and with respect to that they said, "It ought to have been expressly alleged that the house was in want of repair, and that the defendants entered for the purpose of digging for and carrying away sand, &c., for the necessary repairs of that house, and that they used the sand, &c. for that purpose, in order that the plaintiff might have traversed those facts." In the case of *Duberley* v. *Page* (*q*), a right of taking sand and gravel was sustained, and was held sufficient to defeat a claim

Must be spent upon the premises.

Peppin v. Shakespear.

Duberley v. Page.

(*p*) 6 T. Rep. 748.   (*q*) 2 T. Rep. 391.

of the lord to inclose under the Statute of Merton (*r*).
I mentioned this case in a former Lecture (*s*). The
right claimed was, as appears from the pleadings in the
case, to dig and take sand and gravel throughout the
waste for the necessary repairing and amending of the
ways, paths and walks of, and the gardens, orchards
and yards of and belonging to, the messuages, and for
the necessary repairing and amending of the ways
belonging to the lands, as often as need should require.

Marquis of Salisbury v. *Gladstone.*

Custom for copyholder to dig clay out of his own tenement for sale.

There is a case of *The Marquis of Salisbury* v. *Gladstone* (*t*), which relates to copyholds, but which has some
bearing upon cases of this nature. The custom there
set up was a custom for a copyholder, without the
licence of the lord, to break the surface and dig and get
clay without limit, *out of his own copyhold tenement*, with
the object of its being made into bricks, and to be
afterwards sold by him off the manor, for purposes not
connected with the manor. It was found that such a
custom did in fact exist; and the question was, whether
it was a lawful custom or not. The Court held that
the custom was lawful. It was held that there could
be no doubt that the lord, upon the original grant of
the copyhold tenements in question, might have reserved to himself the right to dig and carry away the
brick earth found upon them, and that, if a custom of
this kind existed in the manor, it would be reasonable
and valid. But if the lord might have reserved such a
right to himself, why might he not confer it upon his
tenants ? and, if it is not unreasonable to suppose that
such a right might have been originally conferred, then
the custom which had been proved by the immemorial
exercise of the right was good in law. Here you see
the right claimed was a right to dig and sell the clay
under the copyholder's own tenement only. If the

(*r*) Stat. 20 Hen. III. c. 4;   (*s*) *Ante*, pp. 138, 139.
ante, p. 103.   (*t*) 9 H. of L. 692.

claim had been to dig and sell clay without limit out of the waste lands of the manor, I apprehend that a different conclusion would have been arrived at. Thus in the case of *The Duke of Portland* v. *Hill* (*u*), a custom for the customary tenants of a manor to dig for coal on the waste for their own use was held to be confined to digging coal for their own consumption.

Duke of Portland v. *Hill*.

With regard to a right of estovers (*x*), as well as with regard to a right of common of pasture (*y*), it has been held, as we have seen, that there may be a custom in the manor for the lord to inclose any part of the waste, leaving a sufficiency of common for the commoners. But where a right is proved on the part of the tenants, cr any other class, to take away sand, gravel, or any other substance which cannot be renewed, the question arises whether it is possible for the lord to leave a sufficiency of common for the commoners. Pasture and wood may be renewed, and in the course of nature will be renewed by regrowth. But sand and gravel and substances of that kind cannot be renewed. It seems, therefore, difficult to say, having regard to the length of time during which the rights of the tenants may continue, that it is possible, in such a case as this, to leave a sufficiency for the tenants. I am not aware, however, of any decision on this point.

Whether there may be a custom for the lord to approve leaving sufficiency of sand, &c.

Rights of this kind may be created, as I have said (*z*), not only by prescription, but also by grant. And a grant may be either as appurtenant to some tenement or in gross. An instance of a grant of a right to a man, his heirs and assigns, irrespective of any tenement, to dig for ore in common with the grantor and his heirs, occurred in *Lord Mountjoy's case* (*a*), to which I have just referred.

Grant.

Lord Mountjoy's case.

(*u*) L. R., 2 Eq. 765.
(*x*) *Ante*, pp. 141, 198.
(*y*) *Ante*, p. 123.

(*z*) *Ante*, p. 203.
(*a*) Co. Litt. 164 b; 1 Anderson, 307; *ante*, p. 200.

The Queen v. Chamberlains of Alnwick.

And in the case of *The Queen* v. *The Chamberlains of Alnwick* (b), to which I have also referred, a grant was made to the freemen of Alnwick of liberty at all times to get limestone, slate and freestone in any of the quarries for their own use, and to dig clay, burn bricks, and to dig and take away sand, gravel, clay and marle, for the use of themselves and other freemen, &c., in such parts of the forest or moor as the lord's bailiffs of the borough and the chamberlains should think fit. This was held to be a grant of a right of common for the corporation. And, in the previous case of *Rex* v. *Warkworth* (c), the interest of each individual freeman of Alnwick, who did not himself exercise any of the rights, was held to be a mere personal liberty, and not a hereditament vested in him, sufficient to give him, under the old poor laws, a settlement in the place.

Rex v. Warkworth.

Owner may get unless licence exclusive.

It must always be borne in mind that a licence to get stone, gravel, &c., or to work mines, is not an exclusive licence, unless so expressed. It does not prevent the owner of the land from himself working the minerals, or from granting to other persons the same right. This, you will remember, was one of the resolutions in *Lord Mountjoy's case* (d). The case of *Carr* v. *Benson* (e), is an instance of a grant of a licence to work coal and minerals, including fire-clay, for a certain term, which was held not to be an exclusive licence. The grant was dated the 29th of September, 1854. It was made by Lord Rokeby, the lessor, to two persons of whom the plaintiff was one; and it gave them power to dig, work and burn the fire-clay, and convert or manufacture the same into fire-bricks and other things made of fire-clay, for sale, and also to work the ironstone and coal to be found in connection with such fire-clay for the purpose of the manufactory. Afterwards by an indenture dated

Carr v. Benson.

(b) 9 A. & E. 444, *ante*, p. 201.   (d) Co. Litt. 164 b; *ante*, p. 201.
(c) 1 M. & S. 473.   (e) L. R., 3 Ch. 524.

the 31st August, 1862, and made between Lord Rokeby of the one part, and the defendant Benson of the other part, Lord Rokeby demised to Benson all and every the collieries, coal mines and seams of coal, and also all mines, seams, veins or beds of ironstone and fire-clay, found in connection with such coal seams as were workable as coal seams, within and under, or which should be dug and got from, the lands in question. And it was held by the Court of Appeal that the first deed, having been merely a licence, and not an exclusive licence, the coal and fire-clay remained in the lessor; and that he had full liberty to demise it to Benson, subject to the right of the former licensees to get fire-clay and work the coal. The plaintiff asked for an injunction to restrain the defendant from working the fire-clay; and this injunction was granted by the Court below. But on appeal the decree was reversed, and the bill dismissed with costs. The case, you will see, is like that of common of estovers (f), where both the commoners and the lord have a right to cut down furze or brushwood for their own use. If the lord cuts down brushwood for his own use, the tenant cannot prevent him; and if the tenant cuts down brushwood for his own use, the lord cannot prevent him. In the case of a common right of this kind the rule always is first come first served. An exclusive right of digging for coal, called a mining licence, is a mode not unfrequently adopted for the working of mines. If the grant is in terms the grant of an exclusive right, the grantor cannot himself dig for the minerals included in the licence, or authorize any other person to do so; whereas a licence not exclusive amounts merely to a grant of a right of common.

An exclusive licence.

A licence to take coal and other minerals does not

Licence gives no estate in the land.

(f) *Ante*, p. 203.

W.P.   P

Chetham v. *Williamson.*

convey any legal estate in the substratum of the lands themselves. Thus in the case of *Chetham* v. *William-son* (*g*), one Richard Nettleton was mortgagee of certain lands, and Edward Hyde was the mortgagor thereof. And they, by lease and release, granted the premises to one Hobson in fee. And Hobson granted, for himself his heirs and assigns to Hyde, his heirs and assigns, that it should be lawful for Hyde, his heirs and assigns, at all times thereafter to enter into all or any part of the premises to search for and dig for coal or stone, or any other mine or mineral whatsoever, and the same to take off and carry away for their own use. The Court held that this liberty reserved of digging coals could not give to Hyde the exclusive right in them. They held that the covenant could only operate as a grant, and did not convey any interest in the soil. A grant would not, in those days, pass the land itself without livery of seisin. So in

Doe d. *Hanley* v. *Wood.*

the case of *Doe* d. *Hanley* v. *Wood* (*h*), a grant was made to certain persons, their executors, administrators and assigns, of free liberty, licence, power and authority to dig, work, mine and search for tin, ore, &c. in certain places, and the tin ore so found to bring to grass, pick, dress, &c., and dispose of to their own use, subject to certain reservations. It was held that this did not amount to a lease of the tin ore, but contained a mere licence to dig and search for minerals, and that the grantee could not maintain an ejectment for mines lying within the limits of the set, but not connected with the working of the grantee. This case came before the

Norway v. *Rowe.*

Court of Chancery in the case of *Norway* v. *Rowe* (*i*), and the Lord Chancellor, Lord Eldon, said, "This is nothing like a demise of mines. I do not say that similar principles will not apply to it. These leases, as they are called, are not demises of the mines, but simple

(*g*) 4 East, 469.　　　　　　　　(*i*) 19 Ves. 143, 158.
(*h*) 2 B. & A. 724.

grants of liberties and licences to work, to some persons named and others not named, but described under the character of fellow-adventurers, &c. It is necessary to see not only one of the original leases, but also one of the titles under which the sharers became interested, and the form of the mortgages; for if there is nothing more than a licence to work, there is no estate whatever." If, however, a grant be made of an exclusive right of mining, and the licensee enter upon the mine, and commence working it, he acquires the possession of the mine, and may bring an action of trespass against any person who may intrude upon such possession. This was decided in the case of *Harker* v. *Birkbeck* (k). And you will remember that, in the similar case of a grant of the exclusive right of the herbage of land, the grantee, whilst in possession of the herbage, has a sufficient possession to enable him to bring an action of trespass against any person who may tread down the grass; although the right to bring an action of trespass for meddling with the subsoil does not belong to him, but belongs to the owner of such subsoil. This was decided in the case of *Cox* v. *Glue* (l), to which I called attention in a former Lecture (m). It has been held that, if the licensee digs holes for the purpose of ascertaining the nature of the property, and the minerals to be found therein, and then shuts up the holes again, this is not to be considered as a taking of possession, which will make him liable for use and occupation (n).

Exclusive licensee may maintain trespass.

Harker v. Birkbeck.

Cox v. Glue.

What is taking possession by licensee.

The right to dig for sand, gravel, &c., claimed by one person in the soil of another, must be carefully distinguished from the right of the lord of a manor to dig

Rights of lord of manor to dig sand, &c.

(k) 1 Sir W. Black. 481, more fully reported, 3 Burrows, 1556.
(l) 5 C. B. 533.
(m) *Ante*, pp. 26, 27.
(n) *Jones* v. *Reynolds*, 7 Car. & Payne, 335.

for the same materials in the waste lands of the manor, over which his tenants have rights of common of pasture. The lord's right to dig is by virtue of his ownership of the soil; and his ownership of the soil carries with it the usual rights of all owners, so long as the rights of the commoners are not infringed on (*o*).

(*o*) *Ante*, p. 151.

LECTURE XV.

I now come to consider the general law with regard to mines and minerals, in respect of which incorporeal rights of a prescriptive nature not unfrequently arise. And first with regard to manors. The lord of a manor is seised in fee of the demesne lands of the manor, which comprise his own lands and the wastes which are subject to the rights of common of his tenants, and the copyholds which are parcel of the manor. As to free-hold lands held of the manor, the lord has no right to the minerals under them. They belong to the free-holder as part of the soil of which he is seised. As to the wastes, the mines belong to the lord as part of the soil of which he is seised. And, as we have seen (a), he may work the minerals, so that he do not unduly inter-fere with the common rights of his tenants. With regard to the copyhold lands, a copyholder, as you are doubtless aware, is, in construction of law, simply a tenant at will, but long-continued enjoyment has created a custom, by virtue of which, though legally tenant at will, he is practically the owner of the lands which he holds. Being in possession of the land, he is in posses-sion also of the mines and minerals under the surface of the land; although the property in them, as in the rest of the land, remains in the lord. The law upon this subject is well laid down by the present Master of the Rolls in the case of *Eardley* v. *Granville* (b). "The law," he said, "seems to stand in this way. The estate of a copyholder in an ordinary copyhold (for it is an estate) is an estate in the soil throughout, except as regards for this purpose timber-trees and minerals.

Mines and minerals.

Manors.

Rights of lord.

Copyholds.

Rights of copyholder in mines and minerals.

Eardley v. *Granville.*

(a) *Ante*, p. 151.   (b) L. R., 3 Ch. D. 826, 832.

As regards the trees and minerals, the property remains in the lord, but, in the absence of custom, he cannot get either the one or the other, so that the minerals must remain unworked, and the trees must remain uncut. The possession is in the copyholder; the property is in the lord. If a stranger cuts down the trees, the copyholder can maintain trespass against the stranger, and the lord can maintain trover for the trees. If the lord cuts down the trees, the copyholder can maintain trespass against the lord; but if the copyholder cuts down the trees, irrespective of the question of forfeiture, the lord can bring his action against the copyholder. So in the case of minerals. If a stranger takes the minerals, the copyholder can bring trespass against the stranger for interfering with his possession, and the lord may bring trover, or whatever the form of action may be now, against the stranger to recover the minerals. The same rule applies to minerals as to trees. If you once cut down the tree, the lord cannot compel the copyholder to plant another. The latter has a right to the soil of the copyhold where the tree stood, including the stratum of air which is now left vacant by reason of the removal of the tree. So, if the lord takes away the minerals, the copyholder becomes entitled to the possession of the space where the minerals formerly were, and he is entitled to use it at his will and pleasure. If you have a shaft made for working the mines, the copyholder may descend in the shaft, and either walk about in the space below, or use it for any other rational purpose. That is the position of the copyholder." In the case of *Eardley* v. *Granville*, the plaintiffs were copyholders of part of the manor of Newcastle-under-Lyne; and the crown, in right of the Duchy of Lancaster, was seised in fee of the manor. The defendant, Earl Granville, was lessee under the crown of the collieries, mines and minerals within the manor. By the custom of the manor, the crown and

its lessees were entitled to enter upon the land for the
purpose of working the mines and minerals. Lord
Granville was not only lessee from the crown of the
mines within the manor, but he was also the lessee of
the mines under an adjoining tract of freehold land
belonging to one Sneyd; and he claimed a right to use
a crut, or underground way, beneath the land of the
plaintiffs, for the purpose of conveying minerals from
Sneyd's mine to the deep pit by which the manorial
mines were worked, and thence by a branch railway
constructed by the defendant over part of the same
copyhold, to the main line. It was held that this user
was a trespass, and that the plaintiffs were entitled to
an injunction to restrain the defendant from carrying
the Sneyd minerals over or under their copyhold land.
His lordship observed, that, there being no minerals in
this crut, "the earl as crown lessee cannot have a greater
right than the crown, that is, the lord or lady of the
manor. He has, therefore, no right now to trespass
on the copyhold for any purpose whatever, because I
assume he does not want it for the purpose of working
the manorial minerals: for that purpose he has a right
to use it; but assuming that he does not want it for
that purpose, but only wants it for the purpose of
carrying the coal from under Sneyd's estate—that is,
foreign coal—he has no right to use it at all. Of
course the injunction to be granted will only restrain
him from using it for that purpose; it will not affect the
other right. It is not trespass while he carries crown
minerals. It is trespass when he uses it for any other
purpose." Thus you see that, the possession being in
the copyholder, he can prevent the lord of the manor,
or any person authorized by him, from coming into the
underground vacant spaces, left after the minerals have
been got, except only for such purposes as the custom of
the manor may expressly warrant. If, however, as the

Grant of lands excepting mines.

Master of the Rolls says (c), a freeholder grants lands excepting mines, he grants out his estate in parallel horizontal layers; and the grantee only gets the parallel layer granted to him, and does not get any underlying mineral layer or stratum. That underlying stratum remains in the grantor. The freeholder retains the mineral stratum as part of his ownership ; and whether or not he takes the minerals or subsoil out of the stratum, the stratum still belongs to him. But in the case of a copyholder, that is not so, because the copyholder, though he has no property in the stratum in the sense of being entitled to take the minerals, has property and possession in this sense, that the moment the minerals are taken away, the space is in his possession, and he only can interfere with it, the lord having no right to do so.

The strata of coal, &c. cannot be claimed by prescription.

If a person claim the whole stratum or strata of coal, or other mines and minerals, under the surface of any land, as his corporeal property, and not merely a right, whether in common with others or exclusively, to take coal or other minerals, he cannot make a title thereto by prescription. Prescription is only for an incorporeal right. The land itself, of which the coal, stone or other minerals is part, is a very different thing. There

Wilkinson v. *Proud*.

is a case of *Wilkinson* v. *Proud* (d), which shows this distinction. That was an action on the case for injury to the plaintiff's reversion in certain closes or parcels of land, in the occupation of one Gill as tenant thereof to the plaintiff ; and the damage alleged was, that the defendants, without the leave or licence of the plaintiff, dug and excavated divers holes and pits, and erected and fixed divers engines, gins, buildings and posts on the land, and dug and worked the coal, and carried away and converted the same. The second plea of the defendant was to the effect that John Proud deceased,

(c) L. R., 3 Ch. D. 834.   (d) 11 M. & W. 33.

and all his ancestors whose heir he was, from time whereof the memory of man is not to the contrary, until the time of making the indenture thereinafter mentioned, had been used and accustomed to have, and of right ought to have, all the coals and veins of coal in and under the close, with liberty to enter the close for the purpose of working the mines. The plea then alleged that by deeds of lease and release dated the 2nd and 3rd of September, 1841, the said John Proud bargained and sold to one William Richardson; and the defendants then justified the trespasses as the servants of Richardson. The third plea was framed upon the Prescription Act (e), and it alleged that, for the full period of thirty years next before the commencement of the suit, the said John Proud deceased and his ancestors whose heir he was, and the said William Richardson, that is to say, the said John Proud and his ancestors whose heir he was, before and up to the time of making the indenture before mentioned, and the said William Richardson from the time of making the said indenture, had actually taken and enjoyed, as of right and without interruption, all the coals and veins of coal under the closes, and had, during all that time, as of right and without interruption, at all times of the year, entered into the closes, and cut, dug into and excavated the same, for the purpose of searching for, mining and winning the coals under the same, and so on. A special demurrer was put in to each of these pleas; and the Court, after argument, allowed the demurrers. The Court held that this was clearly a prescription to land. A vein of coal is land. Baron Parke observed, "This is not a claim of a prescriptive right to take coal in the plaintiff's close, but a prescription for all the strata and seams of coal lying under it; that is, for a part of the soil itself, and not for a right to get the coal, which would be the

(e) Stat. 2 & 3 Will. IV. c. 71, s. 1; *ante*, p. 173.

subject of a grant. Possibly the defendants may be able to amend by pleading a seisin in fee in the strata of coal, or by prescribing for the right to take coals in the plaintiff's close." Leave was given to the defendants to amend on payment of costs, otherwise judgment was to be for the plaintiff.

Conveyance of land reserving minerals.

If a man, having land with coals and other minerals under it, conveys the land to another, but reserves to himself the coal and minerals, the coal and minerals remain in him, as I have said (*f*), as part of that corporeal inheritance of which he was previously seised.

When mines are reserved, acts of ownership of surface immaterial.

Where, therefore, the mines are reserved out of a conveyance, there is no necessity for the owner of the mines to keep his title alive by any act of ownership. In that case, whatever acts of ownership may be committed with respect to the surface, have no bearing whatever upon the mines below, which have been severed from the surface. It may therefore be that, for forty or fifty years or more, the mines remain unworked; and yet the ownership will continue the same; for the Statutes of Limitations (*g*) have no effect in this case.

Smith v. Lloyd.

Thus, in the case of *Smith* v. *Lloyd* (*h*), it appeared that, so long ago as the year 1725, one Richard Parkes was seised in his demesne as of fee of the close in question and the coals and minerals under the same. And by an indenture, made on the 5th of May in that year, he conveyed to John Rowley and his heirs the said close, excepting all mines of coals, stone and other mines whatsoever, with powers of working. The plaintiff was entitled under John Rowley to the close and surface; and the defendants were entitled under Richard Parkes to the excepted minerals. And the question was whether, where, more than a century ago, the owner of the fee simple of a close with a

(*f*) *Ante*, p. 216.
(*g*) Stats. 3 & 4 Will. IV. c.
27; 37 & 38 Vict. c. 57.
(*h*) 9 Ex. 562.

stratum of coal and other minerals under it, conveyed
the surface to one, under whom the plaintiff claims,
reserving the minerals, and a right of entry to get
them, to himself, under whom the defendants claim,
that right of entry is barred by simple non-user for
more than forty years, no other person having worked
or been in possession of the mines. And the Court had
not the slightest doubt that the title of the grantees
of the mines was not barred, in that case, under the
Statute of Limitations; for they were clearly of opinion
that that statute applies, not to cases of want of actual
possession by the plaintiff, but to cases where he has
been out of, and another in, possession for the prescribed time. " There must be," they said, " both
absence of possession by the person who has the right,
and actual possession by another, whether adverse or
not, to be protected, to bring the case within the
statute."

If however a person conveys lands, with the mines Otherwise
and minerals under it, reserving to himself, not the when a right
to get mines
mines and minerals, but a right to dig them, either in only is
common with the owners of the closes, or exclusively of reserved.
such owner, a different state of circumstances arises.
The grantor, if he wishes to retain his right, must do
some act in the exercise of it within a reasonable period,
certainly, I should say, within twenty years; otherwise
he runs the risk of losing his right under the doctrine
of abandonment (i). He is then in the same position as Abandon-
a person to whom has been granted a right of common, ment.
but who ceases to exercise that right of common for
upwards of twenty years. The mere cesser of use for
that period is not necessarily an abandonment; for it
may be explained; and the question of abandonment is
one of fact to be submitted to a jury. But the difference
between the two cases is this,—when the coals or other

(i) *Ante*, p. 166.

minerals are retained by the vendor, under an exception of the same from his conveyance of the surface, he continues in the possession which he before enjoyed, notwithstanding that now the surface has been severed from the mines; but he, to whom a right to work coal or other mines has been granted, gets no possession until he actually begins to work, and if, having a right to work, he does not use it for a length of time, there is evidence to go to the jury that he has abandoned it altogether.

Meaning of the word "minerals."

Bell v. *Wilson*.

A good deal of difficulty has sometimes arisen as to the meaning of the word minerals. There is a case of *Bell* v. *Wilson* (*k*), in which that question was much discussed. In that case a conveyance was made of land in Northumberland, and a reservation was made to the grantor, of all mines or seams of coal and other mines, metals, or minerals under the land granted, with liberty to dig, bore, work, lead and carry away the same and to make pits, &c. It was held by the Lords Justices Turner and Knight Bruce, varying the decree of Vice-Chancellor Kindersley, that the term "*minerals*" included freestone; but that the grantor had liberty only to get the freestone by underground mining, and not by working in an open quarry. So in the case of *Hext* v. *Gill* (*l*), a reservation of all mines and minerals within and under a copyhold tenement, with powers of working, was held to comprise china clay; but at the same time the owner of the clay under the reservation was restrained from getting it in such a way as to destroy or seriously injure the surface. These cases suggest the remark that in case stone, clay or other things, which can only be gotten by open quarry working or digging, should be intended to be excepted, they should be specifically

Hext v. *Gill*.

(*k*) L. R., 1 Ch. 303.
(*l*) L. R., 7 Ch. 699. See also *Whidborne* v. *Ecclesiastical Com-* *missioners*, L. R., 7 Ch. D. 375, 379, 381.

mentioned; for, though in strictness of law they are undoubtedly minerals, yet the terms in which they are reserved may indicate an intention on the part of the parties to the deed, that they should not be obtained, otherwise than by underground mining; and, if so, of course it comes in many cases to this, that they cannot be obtained at all.

The possession of coal or other minerals under the surface of land carries with it, as incidental to such possession, the right to work the mines and all such liberties and privileges as are necessary for the purpose of such working, but not more. In the case of *The Earl of Cardigan* v. *Armitage* (*m*), it is laid down by Mr. Justice Bailey, in delivering the judgment of the Court of King's Bench, that the incidental power would warrant nothing beyond what was strictly necessary for the convenient working of the coals; it would allow no use of the surface, no deposit upon it to a greater extent or for a longer duration than should be necessary, no attendance upon the land of unnecessary persons. It would be questionable at least whether it will authorize a deposit upon the land for the purpose of sale, and whether it would justify the introduction of purchasers to view the coals. In consequence of the incidental rights of the owner of mines and minerals being so strictly limited, it is usual, when mines are reserved or granted either in fee or for a term of years, to give in express terms powers of working them, including liberties of using the surface for works connected with the mines, such as the deposit of rubbish, the erection of engines and other works, of cottages for workpeople, tramways, railroads, and such other matters as may be considered useful or expedient for the purpose of working the mines intended to be granted or reserved. But when it is wished to work one mine, by means of a

Incidental right to work.

Earl of Cardigan v. Armitage.

(*m*) 2 B. & C. 197, 211.

shaft in another mine, so as to involve the carrying of the coal from one mine across another, it must always be borne in mind that a right for this purpose requires to be specially granted. Rights of this kind are usually called *way leaves;* and the working of mines, by passing through underground passages in other mines, is called working by *in stroke* and *out stroke*. If a person is a grantee either in fee or for years of the corporeal mine and mineral under the surface, that is, of a horizontal layer of the land itself, then, when the minerals have been taken out, he has a right to use the vacant space, which is his own, for any purpose he pleases; and he may accordingly make a profit of it by granting the use of this vacant space as a way or passage to the owner of any mine adjoining. But a person who has merely an exclusive right to take mines or minerals under certain land, has no right to authorize any other person to carry mines or minerals through any vacant space which may be left after the mines or minerals are taken away. And whether a man be a grantee of the mines and minerals themselves, or has only a right to take them, he cannot, as against the owner of the surface, use any pit or shaft by which the mine is worked for the purpose of bringing up foreign coal got by him from under other lands. For a right of way for one purpose by no means necessarily implies a right of way for any other purpose. Thus in the case of *Cowling* v. *Higginson* (n), a right of way was shown to have existed for many years; and it was held that a proof of user of the way for horses, carts, waggons and carriages for agricultural purposes, would not support a claim to a right to use the way for carrying coal obtained from a coal mine, lying under the tenement in respect of which the right was claimed. But in the case of *Senhouse* v. *Christian* (o), under the grant of a free and convenient way for the purpose of carrying coal and

Way leaves.

In stroke and out stroke.

Grantee of mines may use vacant space.

Way for one purpose gives no right for another purpose.
Cowling v. *Higginson.*

Senhouse v. *Christian.*

(n) 4 M. & W. 245.   (o) 1 T. Rep. 560.

other articles, it was held that the grantee had a right
to lay a framed waggon way. It was, however, held
that, under the grant, he had no right to make a trans-
verse road across the parcel or slip of land, in, through
and along which a free and convenient way had been
granted to him.

When mines are reserved, the owner of the mines is *Support to*
bound to leave sufficient support to the surface, so as to *surface.*
keep it at its ancient and natural level. But this right
may be given up by the owner of the surface; and
the mine-owner may then do as much damage to the
surface as he pleases. There is a case of *Rowbotham* v. *Rowbotham* v.
Wilson (*p*), in the House of Lords, where, on the *Wilson.*
construction of a clause in an Inclosure Act, the owner
of the mines was held entitled to disturb the surface.
But although an express grant may be made by the
owner of the surface of the right to let it down by
working the mines underneath, it has been held that a
prescriptive right for the lord of a manor to work mines
under the copyhold messuages or tenements parcel of
the manor, without making compensation for any
damage occasioned to any messuages or other buildings
by such working, is void as an unreasonable prescrip-
tion. This was decided in the case of *Hilton* v. *Earl* *Hilton* v. *Earl*
Granville (*q*). The authority of this case has, however, *Granville.*
been doubted, on the ground, apparently, that, as
prescription implies a grant, that which may properly
be granted may, with equal propriety, be claimed by
prescription which implies a grant (*r*). There is another *Duke of*
case in the House of Lords (*s*), which related to an *Buccleugh* v.
Wakefield.

(*p*) 8 H. of L. 348. See also
Aspden v. *Seddon*, L. R., 10 Ch.
394.

(*q*) 5 Q. B. 701.

(*r*) See the judgment of Lord
Hatherley, L. C., in *Duke of*
Buccleugh v. *Wakefield*, L. R., 4

H. of L. 399; and of Lord
Chelmsford in the same case,
p. 410; and the remarks of Hill,
V.-C., in *Hall* v. *Byron*, L. R.,
4 Ch. Div. 678.

(*s*) *Duke of Buccleugh* v. *Wake-*
field, L. R., 4 H. of L. 377.

inclosure of waste land belonging to a manor, under an Act of Parliament. The parcel of land in question had been sold under a provision of the Act to the defendant for the purpose of defraying the expenses of the Act. The Act, however, reserved to the lord of the manor all mines, beds, seams and veins of coals, lead, copper, tin and iron, and other mines and minerals whatsoever found or thereafter to be found upon, with (which I suppose meant within) or under the said lands or grounds thereby directed to be divided and inclosed or any part or parts thereof, with full power to enter to search, bore and dig for coal and mines, and to sink shafts and so forth, and to make pits and other necessary works within or upon the land, in as full and ample a manner to all intents and purposes as could have been done if the lands had remained open and uninclosed, or the Act had not been passed; yet nevertheless making reasonable compensation for damages done by such works as aforesaid to the person sustaining such damage. The Court held that, under this reservation, the lord might mine without any limit or stint whatever, and might do that, which, if the soil existed as common before, must have entirely destroyed the soil for commonable purposes, namely, the stacking of minerals upon the ground, and still more, the building of permanent houses for workmen, and the erecting of houses for smelting the ore, and the like, which must have destroyed the surface for any purpose whatever of common. The case, you see, depends entirely on the wording of a section contained in an Act of Parliament. It is important, however, as containing in the discussion of the case a great deal of the law upon this subject.

Right of support as between adjacent landowners.

A few words may not be here out of place with respect to the right of support of lands and buildings as between neighbouring owners. The right of the owner of land to have his surface soil supported not only by the soil immediately below it, but also by the soil of land adjacent to his own, is a right of property which naturally exists. But if the owner builds upon his land, he has no right to any further support for his building; and the adjoining owner may excavate his land so as to let down the building, provided that the excavation so made would not have been sufficient to let down his neighbour's soil, if it had remained unbuilt on. But the adjoining owner may by grant, express or implied (*t*), subject his land to the additional servitude of supporting buildings erected by his neighbour on land adjacent. A servitude of this kind is not within the Prescription Act (*u*). But after twenty years uninterrupted enjoyment of such an easement—for easement it is—a title will be acquired under the doctrine of the presumption of a lost grant (*x*),—a presumption which, it seems, will not be rebutted by the clearest evidence that no such grant was in fact made (*y*). ·

Easement for support of building.

By the Act of the reign of Queen Elizabeth for the Relief of the Poor (*z*), the first Act passed in England for making any provision for the poor, and which is still in force, though largely amended, it is provided that every occupier of, amongst other things, coal mines, should be taxed or rated for the relief of the poor. Coal mines alone being mentioned in the Act, it was considered that no other mines were liable to be rated for the relief of the poor; and in order to amend the law in this respect an Act was lately passed, called the Rating Act, 1874 (*a*). By this Act it is pro-

Coal mines rateable to the poor.

The Rating Act, 1874.

(*t*) *Elliot* v. *North Eastern Railway*, 10 H. of L. Cas. 333.

(*u*) Stat. 2 & 3 Will. IV. c. 71; *ante*, p. 173.

(*x*) *Ante*, p. 170; *post*, Lecture XXI.

(*y*) *Angus* v. *Dalton*, L. R., 4 Q. B. D. 162.

(*z*) Stat. 43 Eliz. c. 2.

(*a*) Stat. 37 & 38 Vict. c. 54.

W.P.   Q

vided (*b*) that, after its commencement, the Poor Rate Acts shall extend, amongst other hereditaments, to mines of every kind not mentioned in the Act of Elizabeth as if they had been mentioned in that Act. Special provisions are made for ascertaining the rateable value of tin, lead and copper mines (*c*), and under the provisions of this section the term " lease " includes a lease or sett or licence to work, or agreement for a lease or sett or licence to work. And it is provided (*d*) that the hereditaments to which the Poor Rate Acts are thereby extended shall be rateable to all local rates in like manner as if the Poor Rate Acts had always extended to such hereditaments. But (*e*) nothing in the Act shall apply to a mine of which the royalty or dues are for the time being wholly reserved in kind or to the owner or occupier thereof.

Local customs.

Cornwall and Devon.

Stannary Court.

Mendipp.

There are in several parts of the country local customs as to mining, to which I cannot do more than advert. Such are the customs of Cornwall and Devon with respect to tin mines, over which a Court, called the Stannary Court, has jurisdiction, the amended laws with respect to which will be found in the Stannaries Act, 1869 (*f*). The custom of tin-bounding, or inclosing a portion of a wastrel or waste land for the purpose of mining tin, is of great antiquity. And the working of the mines is usually carried on on a system called the cost book system, to which reference is made in the Stannaries Act, 1869, to which I have just referred. New orders, rules and forms of procedure in the Stannary Court were issued by authority to take effect upon and after the 14th of March, 1876. So the Forest of Mendipp, in the county of Somerset, was once famous for its lead mines, which were worked under

---

(*b*) Stat. 37 & 38 Vict. c. 54, s. 3.

(*c*) Sect. 7.

(*d*) Sect. 10.

(*e*) Sect. 13.

(*f*) Stat. 32 & 33 Vict. c. 19.

peculiar local customs. Again, the mining customs of the Forest of Dean and Hundred of St. Briavels, in the county of Gloucester, are very peculiar, and have been regulated by divers acts of parliament, particularly by stat. 1 & 2 Will. IV. c. 12, by which commissioners were appointed to examine and report on the customs. In pursuance of their report, the statutes 1 & 2 Vict. cc. 42 and 43, were passed for dealing with encroachments made on the forest, and for regulating the opening and working of mines and quarries within the district. This Act has been followed by statutes 24 & 25 Vict. c. 40, and 34 & 35 Vict. c. 85, which make further provision for the management of the forest and the opening and working of mines and quarries therein. So in the county of Derby there are several peculiar customs confined within certain districts. Thus certain parts of the hundred of the High Peak in that county have customs which have been defined and amended by stat. 14 & 15 Vict. c. 94. The mineral customs within the Soke and Wapentake of Wirksworth and sundry manors in the same county have been defined and amended by a local Act, stat. 15 & 16 Vict. c. 163. And there are other manors in the same county having mineral customs not defined by any Act of Parliament. The mineral customs in the county of Derby appear to be confined to lead mines. The regulation and inspection of coal and other mines, and the persons who may be employed therein, are provided for by the Coal Mines Regulation Act, 1872 (*g*), and the Metalliferous Mines Regulation Act, 1872 (*h*).

Forest of Dean.

Derbyshire.

Mines Regulation Acts.

(*g*) Stat. 35 & 36 Vict. c. 76.   (*h*) Stat. 35 & 36 Vict. c. 77.

LECTURE XVI.

We now come to the consideration of those rights of sporting which are incorporeal in their nature, and which range themselves under the head of *franchises*.

A franchise. A franchise is a royal privilege belonging either to the Crown, or to a subject by virtue of a grant from the Crown, either express or implied by long enjoyment. And I intend to consider in order the following franchises :—a forest, a chase, a park, and a free warren; and afterwards to consider the right of hunting and killing game on a manor, or on other lands which do not constitute a manor. These incorporeal hereditaments come within the description of prescriptive rights. Thus it is laid down by Lord Coke (*a*), that to have a park, warren and the like, a man may make a title by usage and prescription only, without any matter of record.

A forest. And, first, of a forest. There were in ancient times large tracts of land called the king's forests. It by no means necessarily followed that the whole of the lands within the king's forests belonged to the king. It often happened that a large portion of the lands in the forests belonged to private persons, such as lords of manors and others, who, living in the forest, were subject to many oppressive restrictions laid upon them for the purpose of preserving the game. The principal treatise on the Law of Forests is that of Manwood.

Manwood's Forest Law. Manwood (*b*) defines a forest as follows, "A forest is a certain territory of woody grounds and fruitful pastures, privileged for wild beasts and fowles of forest, chase and

(*a*) Co. Litt. 114 b.   (*b*) Manwood, chap. 1, sect. 1.

warren, to rest and abide in, in the safe protection of
the king, for his princely delight and pleasure; which
territory of ground so privileged is meered and bounded
with unremoveable markes, meeres and boundaries,
either known by matter of record or else by prescription,
and also replenished with wild beasts of venery or chase,
and with great coverts of vert, for the succour of the
said wild beasts, to have their abode in. For the preservation and continuance of which said place, together
with the vert and venison, there are certain particular
lawes, privileges and officers belonging to the same,
meet for that purpose, that are only proper unto a
forest, and not to any other place. Therefore a forest doth
chiefly consist of these four things, that is to say, of vert,
venison, particular lawes and privileges, and of certain
meet officers appointed for that purpose, to the end that
the same may the better be preserved and kept for a
place of recreation and pastime, meet for the royal
dignity of a prince." A forest, however, notwithstanding
this definition, certainly may belong to a private person
by grant from the Crown. In former times large tracts
of land were turned into forests, for the recreation of
the Norman kings; "We may read," says Manwood (c),
"of some kings of this land that when they made
forests they did pull down both houses and churches
that were within the same and so thereby caused an
utter depopulation of that place for the quiet of the
wild beasts." Manwood seems rather to have approved
of these proceedings, for he draws from them the following argument. "Then much more, if by the laws of
this realm, kings and princes may pull down houses and
churches that are already builded to make forests in
such places where they please to have forests, they may,
by the same laws, restrain and forbid all inhabitants
and all those that have lands or woods within forests
(that have been ancient forests a long time) to new

(c) Chap. 10, sect. 1.

erect or build any more houses or buildings than are already builded there, without especial licence of the king or his justice in eyre." The people of England, however, took a different view, and several acts of parliament were passed at different times for the purpose of remedying the mischief thus occasioned. I may mention particularly the Charta de Foresta (d), which contained several enactments for the regulation of the forests. The first of these was (e), that all forests which King Henry our grandfather afforested, should be viewed by good and lawful men; and if he had afforested any other wood than his own demesne, to the damage to him whose wood it was, it should be disafforested; and if he afforested his own wood, it should remain forest, saving the common of herbage and of other things in the same forests to them which before were accustomed to have the same.

Charta de Foresta.

Beasts of forest are the hart, the hind, the hare, the boar and the wolf; but all beasts of venery are equally protected in a forest, because a forest comprehends within it a chase, a park and a free warren. The forest laws were very oppressive. Amongst other things it was forbidden for any person living within the forest to keep any kind of dog, except a mastiff and certain little dogs which were supposed to be harmless. A mastiff was thought necessary for the protection of a person's dwelling. And even a mastiff had to be lawed or expeditated according to the forest law, that is, the three claws of the forefoot had to be cut off, in order to prevent him from seizing the deer. The exact manner of doing this is thus explained by Manwood (f). "The mastiff being brought to set one of his forefeet upon a piece of wood of eight inches thick, and a foot square, then one with a mallet, setting a chissell of two inches broad

Beasts of forest.

Forest laws.

Lawing of dogs.

(d) Stat. 9 Hen. III.   (f) Chap. 16, sect. 8.
(e) Chap. 1.

upon the three claws of his forefoot, at one blow doth smite them clean off; and this is the manner of expeditating of mastiffs."

No person having lands within a forest could plough up any part of his lands which had not been ploughed up before; and to do so was considered a grievous offence, and was called an *assart*. Manwood treats of Assart. assarts in the 9th chapter of his work; he says (*g*) that an assart by the laws of the forest is accounted one of the greatest offences or trespasses that can be done to the vert of the forest. "For whereas a waste of the forest is but the felling or cutting down of the coverts, which may grow again and become coverts in time, an assart is the plucking up of those woods by the roots that are thickets or coverts of the forest, to make the same a plain or arable land; so that where woods or thickets or any other land is assarted, that land cannot grow again to become coverts. And therefore the same, being more than a waste of the forest, is called an assart." And the punishment for an assart was, that the whole piece of ground that is assarted, be it in woods, meadow, or pasture, or any other assart of the forest, shall be seised into the king's hands; and so it shall remain in his hands, until such time that the owner of the same replevied it and made his fine to the king for that offence. Another offence was what was called *purpresture* within the forest; that was where Purpresture. any man made any manner of encroachment upon the forest, either by building or inclosure, or by using of any liberty or privilege without lawful warrant so to do. No fence within a forest was allowed to exist to Fences all any greater height than four feet; the intention being under four that the deer should have the full run over the whole of the forest, whether the lands were cultivated or not; and it was supposed that, whilst the deer could leap

(*g*) Chap. 9, sect. 1.

No fence
without
licence.

over a fence four feet high, the erection of any higher fence would prevent them from getting over. And not only that, but no new fence at all, of any height whatever, could be erected within any part of the forest, without the licence of the Crown or other owner

Buildings.

of the forest. Every building erected within the forest without the licence of the Crown, or other owner of the forest, was liable to be pulled down, or else to pay yearly a certain rent to the king, for suffering the same to remain, at the choice and discretion of the lord chief justice in eyre of the forest.

Common of
pasture in
forests.

As some compensation for the annoyance which the inhabitants within the forest experienced from the deer and other game therein, they were allowed rights of common of pasture on the waste lands within the

Horses and
cattle only.

forests. But these rights were only for horses and cattle, and not for sheep, swine, or goats; because they were considered unpleasant to the wild animals within the forest, and, as it was said, they caused their exile

The fence
month.

from the forest. There was one month called the *fence month*, when the deer were breeding, during which it was not lawful for the inhabitants to exercise their rights of common of pasture. And that was a fortnight before Midsummer-day, and a fortnight after that time. There were certain officers appointed, called

Agistors.

agistors, whose duty it was to make profit of the king's woods within the forest, by letting them out for the feeding of hogs or swine, with the mast of the woods,

Pannage.

which was called *pawnage* or *pannage* (*h*). For although no man might put these disagreeable animals into the waste lands of the forest to feed there, there was no objection to his doing so when the mast and acorns were ripe in the woods, provided he paid to the Crown the necessary pawnage. The time of pawnage in the king's demesne woods began on Holy Rood-day, which

(*h*) *Ante*, pp. 168, 189.

was fifteen days before the feast of St. Michael or Michaelmas, and ended forty days after the feast of St. Michael, that is, about the feast of St. Martin, when the agistors were required to meet together to receive the pawnage. Freeholders and others, who had woods and lands within the forest, might agist them for the mast thereof, at such times as were most convenient, when the mast was ripe and ready to be agisted. This agistment of mast during the autumn is a different thing from putting swine to feed upon the waste lands at other times within the forest.

Not only the forest itself, but also certain lands surrounding it were subject to special regulations. The *purlieus* of the forest were grounds adjoining to the Purlieus. forest, meered and bounded, as mentioned by Manwood (*i*), with immoveable marks, meeres and boundaries known by matter of record only; which territory of ground was also once forest, and afterwards disafforested again. Those who had woods and land within the purlieu were said to be *without the regard of the forest;* and therefore they were absolutely free from the bondage of the forest, in respect of felling their woods, and converting of their meadows and pastures into arable land and tillage, and otherwise improving the same at their own pleasure, to their best advantage and profit (*k*). A purlieu man was allowed Hunting by to hunt in his own grounds, within the purlieus, subject purlieu man. to strange regulations; one of which was, that he was not to hunt oftener than three days a week; lest, by often hunting, he should cause the disquiet of the wild beasts of the forest; nor with any more company than his own servants; nor within forty days after the king's general hunting in the forest; because then the wild beasts were scared out of the forest, and did not go out of themselves. Nor within forty days before the king's

(*i*) Chap. 20, sect. 1.   (*k*) Manwood, chap. 20, sect. 6.

general hunting; because then the wild beasts must not be disquieted; to the end that the king may have a full view of them. Nor was he to forestall or take the deer with gun or cross-bow, but only by chasing with his dogs.

Courts and officers of a forest.

There were certain Courts attached to the forest for the government thereof, and officers, the principal of whom were the verderers of the forest; and under them foresters, regarders, keepers, woodwards and other servants. The principal Courts were, first, the Court of attachments or the woodmote Court, which was held before the verderers every forty days, and was therefore called the Forty Day Court. This Court could only inquire as to offences against the forest law, but could not convict. Secondly, the Court of regard or survey of dogs, which was holden every third year for the expeditating or lawing of dogs. Thirdly, the *Court of Swainmote*, of which the verderers were judges. This Court was holden three times in the year; and all freeholders within the forest were bound to attend; and also the reeve and four men of every vill or town within the forest. And, lastly, the Court of the Justice Seat, holden before the chief justice of the forest, called the justice in eyre. This Court could not be held oftener than every third year; and it was required to be summoned forty days at least before its sitting. This Court had jurisdiction over all offences against the forest laws, and also determined on all franchises and liberties claimed by any persons within the forest. A report of the proceedings of one of these Courts with respect to Windsor Forest will be found in Sir W. Jones's Reports (*l*). An appeal lay from the Court of Justice Seat to the Court of King's Bench (*m*).

Forty day court.
Court of regard of dogs.

Court of Swainmote.

Court of Justice Seat.

(*l*) Pp. 266 *et seq.*　　　　　　(*m*) See Coke's Fourth Institute, 293.

The mischief occasioned by such a state of things could hardly be exaggerated. It put an end to all improvements and reclamation of waste lands, holding the cultivation of such lands, which would otherwise have been a profit, to be a most serious offence. It subjected all the crops, that were raised by the inhabitants, to be eaten by the deer at their own pleasure; and it prevented a single house or building of any kind from being erected in the forest, without the licence of the Crown or other owner of the forest. It is not to be wondered at, therefore, that complaints were frequently made. And in the reign of King Charles I. an Act of Parliament was passed for ascertaining with certainty the limits of the different forests then existing. This Act was the 16th of Charles I. chap. 16; and it pro- vided (n) that no place in England or Wales, where no justice seat, swainmote, or Court of attachment had been held or kept, or where no verderers had been chosen, or regard made, within the space of sixty years next before the first year of his then majesty's reign, should at any time thereafter be adjudged or taken to be forest, or within the bounds or metes of the forest; but the same should be, from thenceforth for ever thereafter, disafforested and freed and exempted from the forest laws. Provision was made (o) for the ap- pointment of commissioners to ascertain the bounds of the different forests. And it was provided (p) that all the places that should be without the bounds, to be returned and certified by the commissioners, should be from thenceforth free, to all intents and purposes, as if the same had never been forest or so reputed. But the Act provided (q) that the tenants, owners and occupiers of lands and tenements, which should be excluded from the bounds of the forest, to be returned and certified by virtue of any of the said commissions, should use and

(n) Sect. 5.   (p) Sect. 7.
(o) Sect. 6.   (q) Sect. 9.

enjoy such common and other profits and easements within the forests as anciently or accustomably they had used and enjoyed. Since that time most of the forests have been disafforested, though a few still remain. Amongst them is the New Forest in Hampshire, which is regulated by special enactments passed for the purpose. And another is the notable one of Epping Forest, in which the rights of common, which were granted as compensation for the forestal rights of the Crown, have been used as a means for keeping open the waste lands of the forest for the recreation of the public. The decision of the present Master of the Rolls in the case of *The Commissioners of Sewers* v. *Glasse* (r), was, as we have seen, to the effect that all the owners and occupiers of lands within the forest, had a right of common of pasture for cattle commonable within the forest levant and couchant on their respective tenements, over all the waste lands of the forest, and not merely over the waste lands of the different manors, of which their tenements were held. In some cases the forestal rights of the Crown over portions of Epping Forest had been sold to the different lords of manors; but such sale was evidently of no avail against the rights of common of pasture of the owners of tenements within the forest.

A chase is the next subject for our consideration. A chase is in many respects similar to a forest. The main difference between them is, that a chase is not subject to any of those peculiar laws, which are administered by the officers of a forest. Beasts of chase are said to be the buck, the doe, the fox, the martin, and the roe. If the Crown should grant to a subject a royal forest, without any words enabling him to hold Courts, the grantee would become seised of a chase and not of a

The New Forest.

Epping Forest.

Commissioners of Sewers v. *Glasse*.

A chase.

Beasts of chase.

(r) L. R., 19 Eq. 134; *ante*, pp. 54, 55.

forest (s). King Henry VIII. made a chase in the neighbourhood of Hampton Court Palace, called Hampton Court Chase; but, in order to do this, he was obliged to obtain the consent of the freeholders and copyholders, in the towns and villages over which the chase extended. The agreement which he made with them was contained in an indenture, which was confirmed by an Act of Parliament, of the 31st of Hen. VIII. chap. 5. The freeholders and copyholders stipulated for licences to fell and take their woods, groves and coppices at their will and pleasure, without any view of the Crown officers, and to make hedges and fences about their corn, and to keep out the deer; and, not only that, but a third part of the free rent of every freeholder was deducted; and the moiety of the fine of the heir of every copyholder was also deducted. On this Lord Coke remarks (t), "It hereby plainly appeareth, both by the king's said indenture and by the judgment of the whole Parliament, that the king could neither erect any chase or forest over any man's grounds, without their consent and agreement. And yet King Henry VIII. did stand as much on his prerogative as any king of England ever did." Any person who had woods within a chase might cut down timber or woods growing thereon, without view of any officer, or licence of any person; but if he cut down so much as not to leave sufficient covert for the game, he was to be punished at the king's suit, if the chase was a royal chase. And so, if a common person had liberty of chase in another man's wood, the owners of the wood could not cut down all the woods, but were obliged to leave sufficient for covert, as had been accustomed; no more, as Lord Coke says (u), than the owners of woods, in which others have common of estovers, can destroy the whole woods, but must leave sufficient for the estovers (x).

Hampton Court chase.

Stat. 31 Hen. VIII. c. 5.

(s) Coke's Fourth Institute, p. 314.

(t) Fourth Institute, 301.

(u) Fourth Institute, 298.

(x) See *ante*, pp. 18, 186.

A park.

We next come to a park. A park is an inclosed chase, extending over a person's own grounds, and privileged for beasts of forest and chase, either by the king's grant or by prescription. To a park it is said three things are necessary—1st, a grant from the Crown. This, however, may be implied by long usage under a title of prescription (y). 2ndly, inclosure by pale, wall or hedge. 3rdly, beasts of park, such as buck, doe, &c. When all the deer are destroyed, it shall be no more accounted a park, which consists of vert, venison, and inclosure; but if it be determined in any of these, it is a total disparking. The law on this subject is well laid down in Cruise's Digest (z).

Free warren.

A free warren is a franchise to have and keep certain wild beasts and fowls, called game, within the precincts of a manor, or other known place; in which animals the owner of the warren has a property, and consequently a right to exclude all other persons from hunting and taking them. This franchise, like that of chase or park, must be derived from a royal grant, or from prescription, which supposes such a grant. It is

The Case of Monopolies.

laid down in the Case of Monopolies (a), that none can make a park, chase or warren, without the king's licence; for that is *quodam modo* to appropriate those creatures, which are truly *feræ naturæ et nullius in bonis*, and to restrain them of their natural liberty, which he cannot do without the king's licence; but for hawking, hunting, &c., which are matters of pastime, pleasure and recreation, there needs no licence; but every one may, in his own land, use them at his pleasure, without any restraint to be made, unless by parliament. Grants of free warren were frequently made by the Norman

Forms of grant of free warren.

kings; and the following is the usual form in which these grants were made. "That he and his heirs for ever should have free warren, in all his demesne lands

(y) *Ante,* p. 228.
(z) Vol. 3, p. 247, tit. Fran-

chise, sects. 15—18.
(a) 11 Rep. 87 b.

of such a place in such a county, provided that those lands be not within the bounds of our forests, so that no one should enter such lands to hunt in them, or to take any thing which belongs to warren, without the licence and consent of the said grantee or his heirs, under forfeiture of ten pounds." Beasts of warren are hares Beasts of warren. and rabbits; and fowls of warren are pheasants and partridges (b); and the effect of a grant of free warren Fowls of warren. is to vest in the grantee a qualified property in these beasts and fowls of the above description, that are on the lands comprised in the grant, as long as they remain there, and even after they are hunted out of the warren, but not after they have strayed of their own accord. The grantee of a free warren has a right to appoint a person to watch over and preserve the game, called a warrener. Rights of free warren, when granted Warrener. by the Crown, were always rights extending only over the lands of the grantee, and not over the lands of any other person. But, in course of time, the land might belong to one person, and the free warren over the land to another. Thus a person, having free warren over certain lands of his own, may alien them, reserving the warren. The warren would then be a warren in Warren in gross (c). If he aliens the lands, without reserving the gross. right of warren to himself, it is determined and gone; for the alienor has parted with his right to the lands, discharged of all things; so that he cannot have it; and the alienee cannot have it, because it is not granted to him, but only the land. An action of trespass will lie Trespass on by the owner of a free warren against any person who warren. enters the warren and takes or drives away the beasts or fowls of warren (d). Rights of free warren still exist in many places, and are very important in case of the inclosure of the waste lands of a manor under an

(b) Not grouse; *Duke of Devonshire* v. *Lodge*, 7 B. & C. 36.

(c) See *Earl Beauchamp* v.

Winn, L. R., 6 H. of L. 223.

(d) Com. Dig. tit. Trespass (A. 2).

Inclosure Act.   The lord's right of free warren remains
in him, unless he be expressly deprived of it.   But if
there be no right of free warren, the right which the
lord has of sporting over the wastes, simply by reason
of his ownership of the soil, is destroyed as soon as the
soil is taken away from him, and allotted to other
persons under the provisions of an Inclosure Act.

Right of
sporting on a
man's own
lands.

Blackstone's
contention.

Professor
Christian's
view.

Robinson v.
Wray.

With regard to the right of sporting on a man's own
lands, irrespective of any grant of free warren, there
has been much learned controversy.   Blackstone con-
tends that the sole property of all game in England,
and consequently the exclusive right of taking and
destroying it, is vested in the Crown.   He holds (e) that
no man but he who has a chase or free warren, by grant
from the Crown, or prescription which supposes one,
can justify hunting or sporting on another man's soil,
nor indeed, in thorough strictness of common law, either
hunting or sporting at all.   But Professor Christian, in
his notes on Blackstone's Commentaries, opposes this
doctrine; and certainly the general opinion now seems
to be in accordance with Lord Coke's view (f), that
every owner of land has, by virtue of his ownership, the
right to kill game upon his own land.   The right, however, which exists in game *ratione soli* would be subservient to the franchise of free warren over the same land,
if any such franchise were proved to exist.   Questions
with regard to sporting not unfrequently arise on the
language of Inclosure Acts.   Thus in the case of *Robinson* v. *Wray* (g), there was a reservation in an Inclosure
Act to the lord of the manor of a right to enjoy, search
for and work all mines, minerals, and *other rights and
privileges* in the said waste (*except the right to the soil
thereof,* for which a compensation was thereby directed
to be made) in as full, ample and beneficial a manner,

(e) 2 Black. Com. 417.   (g) L. R., 1 C. P. 490.
(f) *Ante*, p. 238.

as if the Act had not been made. It was held that the effect of the Act was to take from the lord his right to the soil of the waste, and with it the exclusive right of sporting thereon. On the other hand, in the case of *Lord Leconfield* v. *Dixon* (*h*), it was held by the Court of Exchequer Chamber, reversing the judgment of the Court of Exchequer, that an exclusive right of sporting over the allotments under a private Inclosure Act was reserved to the lord of the manor; although, before the Act, the lord did not have any right of free warren over the lands inclosed. The Act provided that the lord should have all rents, &c., piscaries, fishing, *hunting, hawking, and fowling, and all beasts and birds considered as game, &c.*, and all other royalties, liberties, privileges, franchises, pre-eminences, jurisdictions and appurtenances, *in as ample a manner* as they were then or had been theretofore used, exercised and enjoyed by him, or *as he might or could have held, used, &c. the same, in case the Act had not been passed.* The Court below (*i*) relied much on the inconveniences to the owners of the lands arising from the reservation to the lord of such a right; and they considered that the lord had no royalty, franchise or privilege of shooting game over the land, his right being merely that of the owner of the soil. But the Court of Exchequer Chamber were of opinion that the words of the Act were a sufficient expression of an intention to preserve to the lord the right of taking the game, to which he was previously entitled; although it was a right arising from his ownership of the soil, and not in the nature of a seignorial right. They relied upon a case in the House of Lords, of *Ewart* v. *Graham* (*k*). In that case there was no right of free warren in the manor; and an Inclosure Act provided that nothing therein contained should prejudice the right of Sir James Graham, his heirs and assigns, lords

Lord Leconfield v. Dixon.

Ewart v. Graham.

(*h*) L. R., 3 Exch. 30.   (*k*) 7 H. of L. Cas. 331.
i) L. R., 2 Exch. 202.

of the manor, of any seignory, &c. belonging to such
manor; but that the said Sir James Graham, his heirs
and assigns, should and might, at all times thereafter,
enjoy all rents, services, &c. and also *all rights of hunting,
shooting, fishing and fowling*, on, through and over the
said stinted pasture, which was allotted under the Act,
and every part and allotment thereof, and all other
seignories, royalties and privileges to the lord of the
manor for the time being incident or belonging (other
than those declared to be barred by the Act) in as full
a manner as if the Act had not been passed. It was
held by the House of Lords that this proviso did not
apply to mere manorial rights; but that the exclusive
right of hunting and shooting over the allotments was
thereby reserved to Sir James Graham. The last case

Sowerby v.
Smith.

upon this subject that I am aware of is that of *Sowerby*
v. *Smith* (*l*). This case is remarkable for the difference
of opinion which prevailed amongst the judges, both
in the Court below and in the Court of Appeal. The
majority of the Court of Appeal affirmed the decision of
the majority of the Court below, and decided that the
Inclosure Act, which was the subject of contest in that
case, did not reserve to the lady of the manor the right
of shooting, which she formerly possessed over the lands
allotted under the Act, by virtue of her ownership of the
soil. The reservation in this case was as follows:—That
nothing in the Act contained should prejudice the right,
title or interest of the lady of the manor, her heirs and
assigns, in or to the seignory or royalties incident or
belonging to the manor; but that she might hold and
enjoy all rents, quit rents and other rents, reliefs, duties,
customs and services, and all courts, perquisites and
profits of courts, rights of fishery, *and liberty of hawking,
hunting, coursing, fishing and fowling*, within the said
manor, and all tolls, fairs, &c., royalties, jurisdictions,

(*l*) L. R., 8 C. P. 514, affirmed by Exchequer Chamber, L. R.,
9 C. P. 524.

franchises, matters and things whatsoever *to the said manor, or to the lord or lady thereof, incident or belonging,* or which had been theretofore held and enjoyed by the lady of the manor or any of her ancestors, *other than and except such common right as could or might be claimed by the said lady of the manor as owner of the soil and inheritance of the said commons or waste grounds.* The Court distinguished the case from that of *Ewart* v. *Graham,* on the ground that, in that case, there was an express reservation of all rights of hunting, shooting, fishing, and fowling in the stinted pastures about to be inclosed; whilst, in the present case, there was no reservation of the previously existing right of sporting over the waste lands about to be inclosed, but only of a general right inherent in the lord as incident to the manor; which right failing, the reservation fails to have any effect. So difficult does it seem to be to frame a proper provision upon this subject. The framers of these Acts do not seem to have borne in mind the fact, that rights of sporting arise either from grants of free warren or from the ownership of the soil; and that, in the absence of a right of free warren, if you take away the ownership of the soil, you of course take away the right of sporting incidental to such ownership. The right of sporting which a lord of a manor has over a waste, in the absence of any grant of free warren, is merely a right incidental to the ownership of the soil; and if that right is intended to continue, after the ownership of the soil has been parted with, a new right is in fact intended to be given to him, and one of a kind most inconvenient to the owner of the land allotted. It must be reserved to the lord, not as a manorial right, which it is not (*m*), but as a new right, expressly created by the Inclosure Act, which intends to give the lord this privilege.

(*m*) *Pannell* v. *Mill*, 3 C. B. 625.

Rights of
sporting now
rateable to
the poor.

A right of sporting, like a right of common of pasture (*n*), was formerly not rateable to the poor; but by the Rating Act, 1874 (*o*), the Poor Rate Acts are extended, amongst other things, to rights of fowling, of shooting, and of taking or killing game or rabbits, when severed from the occupation of the lands.

(*n*) *Ante*, p. 202.   (*o*) Stat. 37 & 38 Vict. c. 54.

LECTURE XVII.

THE rights of common which I have hitherto spoken of, are, most of them, rights which arose in a primitive state of society, and which are unfitted for society as it now exists. The right of common of pasture was valuable in times when green crops were not thought of, and when the improvements which have now taken place in the breed of cattle and sheep, had not rendered these animals so tender and valuable as they now are. It came in process of time to be perceived, that it would be in every way more profitable, both to the owner of the soil of uncultivated ground, and to those who had rights of common upon it, that the land should be inclosed, and divided amongst them in proportion to their respective rights;—giving to the owner of the soil a part, in compensation for his rights of ownership of the soil; and dividing the rest amongst the commoners, in proportion to the value of their respective rights. And, whether the rights were rights of common of pasture, or rights of common of turbary, of estovers, or of digging sand and gravel, or the like, the same principle was equally applicable. In most cases, especially where the soil was good, it was to the advantage of all parties, that the land should be inclosed and divided amongst those who could substantiate any interest in it, in proportion to their respective rights. The statutes of Merton (a) and of Westminster the Second (b) were insufficient for this purpose. They related only to common of pasture; and all that they did was to enable the lord to approve or inclose a portion of the waste for his own benefit, provided he left for the commoner sufficient

Benefits of inclosure.

The statutes of Merton and Westminster the second insufficient.

(a) Stat. 20 Hen. III. c. 4;   (b) Stat. 13 Edw. I. c. 46;
ante, p. 103.   *ante*, p. 109.

pasture, with convenient rights of ingress and egress.
By these statutes no compensation was given to the
commoners for their rights; nor in fact were their rights
given up, for it was essential to an inclosure under these
statutes, that the owner of the soil should be able to
show that the approvement might take place without the
slightest injury to any of the commoners.

Agreements
between lord
and com-
moners.
　　　　The first attempts at an inclosure of waste lands
subject to common rights, appear to have been made by
mutual agreement between the lord, or owner of the
soil, of the one part, and the tenants having commonable rights of the other part; which agreements were
sometimes specifically enforced by the Court of Chancery
or Court of Exchequer which at that time had an equitable jurisdiction. And afterwards, when it came to be
doubted whether the decree of the Court of Chancery
was sufficient for the purpose, these agreements were
confirmed by private Acts of Parliament.

　　　　A specimen of a private agreement for the inclosure
of a portion of the lands, adjoining the manor house
Vill of Aston. of the lord of a manor, occurs in the case of the vill
or township of Aston and the hamlet of Cote, in the
county of Oxford, to which I called your attention in
a former Lecture (c). In that case Thomas Horde, Esq.,
was lord of the manor of Aston Boges, which comprised
a part, but by no means the whole, of the lands in the
vill of Aston and hamlet of Cote. And he had a large
manor house, in which he dwelt; and this house with
its immediate grounds was situate between a large waste
called Cote Moor on the one side, and open arable lands,
composing Cote common field, on the other side. And
the house, being exposed and lying open on every side
to great and wide fields, commons, and wastes, which
were frequently, and especially in the winter, wholly

(c) Lecture VII., *ante*, p. 86.

surrounded by water, became very unhealthy. An agreement was accordingly entered into between the lord of the one part and the landowners of the other part, dated the 20th of March, in the fourteenth year of the reign of Charles II., by which it was agreed that, not only the lord, but also any of the tenants and owners of land in Aston and Cote, might inclose all or any part of their respective arable lands there; and in particular, that Mr. Horde, the lord of the manor, might, as soon as he pleased, inclose fifty-four field acres of arable land, lying together in the field called Holwell Field, next to his capital messuage, in Cote aforesaid (d); which said fifty-four acres are thereby declared to be as much arable as usually belongs to two yard lands in Aston and Cote, thus showing that in this district a yard land consisted of the half of fifty-four, or twenty- seven acres of arable land, in addition to its due proportion of meadow and pasture. And two men were chosen on the part of the lord, and two on the part of the landowners, to settle all differences concerning the inclosures and exchanges and abatements of common. And the parties agreed to submit themselves to the order of the said four men, or any three of them, with powers to appoint others in case of the decease of any of them. The four persons so appointed duly made their award; and a great many exchanges of land in the common fields were made in pursuance of the above-mentioned agreement and award, all of which are detailed at length in a bill which was filed by the lord for the specific performance of the agreement. One of the parties to the agreement, however, was the dean and chapter of the cathedral church of Exeter; and they alleged that they were restrained by law from granting their lands for any longer time than twenty-one years, or three lives. And some of the copyholders alleged

(d) Mr. Horde's manor-house lay on the road to Old Shifford, a little out of the map, at p. 67, *ante*.

that they could not make any alienation of their copyhold lands, being only copyholders for lives.   And
some of the other persons who made the exchanges had
only particular estates in the lands exchanged by them,
there being several remainders settled and declared concerning divers of the same lands.   Moreover, some of
the persons who had made the exchanges objected that
the plaintiff could make no good title to them of several
parts of the lands they so had of the plaintiff in exchange as aforesaid, by reason of remainders, uses, and
estates limited or declared concerning the manor of
Aston, and other lands of the lord of the manor.   And
in order, as it appears, to overcome these objections, the
aid of the Court of Chancery was sought; and a bill
was filed accordingly for the specific performance of the
agreement, and for confirmation of everything that had
been done under it, and under the award made in pursuance thereof; and praying that the parties might
convey and assure the exchanged lands, each to other,
in such manner as the Court should appoint.   All the
defendants appeared and put in their answers; and in
Hilary Term, in the twenty-fourth year of Charles II.,
a decree was made by Sir Orlando Bridgman, knight
and baronet, lord keeper of the great seal of England,
that the said agreement should be duly performed, and
that the several exchanges and inclosures of lands theretofore made, and thereafter to be made, in pursuance of
the said agreement, and likewise all abatements of commons made or to be made in respect of any such inclosures, should remain and continue fixed and steadfast
at all times and for ever; the lands by any person to
be received in exchange to be for ever held or enjoyed
by such several respective person and persons, and for
such term, terms, and estates (I quote from the decree),
and upon such conditions, and under such rents and
services respectively, as the respective lands given or to
be given in exchange ought to have been holden and

Decree in Chancery confirming agreement.

enjoyed, by such person and persons respectively, by whom the same were or should be given in exchange, in case no such exchange had been made, without any suspension of any rent or rents whatsoever, by means of the said exchange; and that all such exchanges should be good and binding, as well against the dean and chapter of Exeter, as against all other persons making and agreeing to any such exchange, and against their and every of their respective successors, heirs, executors, administrators and assigns.

The power thus assumed by the Court of Chancery would, I apprehend, be at once disclaimed at the present day by any of the judges of the Chancery Division of the High Court of Justice. It is impossible for the Court to change the tenure of land, and to make what was formerly copyhold freehold, or what was formerly freehold or leasehold copyhold, as this decree purports to do. Accordingly we find that the agreements entered into by landowners and commoners were in most subsequent cases confirmed by Acts of Parliament—the process always being the same, of appointing persons, subsequently called commissioners, to allot and award the lands to be inclosed, amongst the landowners and the commoners in proportion to their respective interests therein. I can, however, find but two of such Acts of Parliament in the reign of King Charles II., and none in the reigns of James II. and William and Mary and Queen Anne. A few such Acts were passed in the reign of King George I.; and in subsequent reigns they became more common. The Acts, being private Acts, are not to be found in the usual collections of statutes. In the subsequent reigns these Inclosure Acts became more common; and it is said that about four thousand have been passed; of which about two thousand belong to the last century, and two thousand to the present century.

Acts of Parliament confirming agreements for inclosure.

General
Inclosure Act.

In the reign of George III. these Acts became so common that a General Inclosure Act was passed in the year 1801 (e). This Act is intituled "An Act for consolidating in one Act certain provisions usually inserted in Acts of Inclosure, and for facilitating the mode of proving several facts usually required on the passing of such Acts." It regulates the proceedings of the commissioners to be appointed, and contains many provisions with respect to inclosure of lands, which are from thenceforth to apply to future inclosures. And it

Saving of
lord's seigno-
ries, rights,
and royalties.

provides (f), "That nothing therein contained shall lessen, prejudice or defeat the right, title or interest of any lord or lady of any manor or lordship, or reputed manor or lordship, within the jurisdiction or limits whereof the lands and grounds thereby directed to be divided and allotted are situate, lying and being, of, in or to the seignories, rights and royalties incident or belonging to such manor or lordship, or reputed manor or lordship, or to the lord or lady thereof, or to any person or persons claiming under him or her ; but the same, other than and except the interest and other property as is or are meant or intended to be barred by such Act, shall remain in as full, ample and beneficial manner to all intents and purposes as he or she might or ought to have held or enjoyed such rights before the passing of such Act, or in case the same had never been made." The principal effect of this Act was to diminish the expenses attending Inclosure Acts; and the exceptions of royalties and seigniories belonging to the manor, or to the lord

Mines and
minerals not
saved to the
lord.

Townley v.
Gibson.

or lady thereof, was held not to include the mines and minerals under the lands inclosed. Thus in the case of *Townley* v. *Gibson* (g), a saving to the lord of all rents, fines, services, &c., and all other royalties and manorial jurisdiction whatsoever, was held not to reserve to the lord the mines and minerals under the allotments made

(e) Stat. 41 Geo. III. c. 109.　　　(g) 2 T. Rep. 701.
(f) Sect. 40.

to the tenants. Lord Kenyon, Chief Justice, observed, " The defendant's counsel has supposed that mines are a distinct right from the right to the soil; but I do not think so, where they are under the land of the lord of the manor. In cases of copyholds a lord may have a right under the soil of the copyholder; but where the soil is in the lord, all is resolvable into the ownership of the soil, and a grant of the soil will pass everything under it." In some cases, however, the mines and minerals are expressly reserved to the lord of the manor or some other person. Where this is the case a subsequent Act (*h*) provides that it must be specified whether or not a right to enter the lands when inclosed for the purpose of working the mines is to be reserved to such lord or other person, and whether or not any compensation is to be made for damage to the surface or other damage, and proper provisions are made as to the powers of working to be given, and as to the compensation to be made. By an Act of the reign of King William IV., to which I have before referred (*i*), provision was made for facilitating the exchange of lands lying in common fields. And by other Acts to which I have also before referred (*k*), provision was made for facilitating the inclosure of open and arable fields in England and Wales.

When minerals reserved, provision to be made for working and compensation.

Exchange of common field lands.

So things continued until the year 1845, when another general Inclosure Act was passed (*l*), to which I have before referred (*m*), and which has been amended several times (*n*), but which, as amended, is now in force; except in certain districts in the neighbourhood of the metropolis and large towns, to which I shall have

(*h*) Stat. 22 & 23 Vict. c. 43, ss. 1—6.

(*i*) Stat. 4 & 5 Will. IV. c. 30; *ante*, p. 77.

(*k*) Stat. 6 & 7 Will. IV. c. 115,

and 3 & 4 Vict. c. 31, *ante*, pp. 77, 78.

(*l*) Stat. 8 & 9 Vict. c. 118.

(*m*) *Ante*, p. 78.

(*n*) See *ante*, p. 78, note (*r*).

General Inclosure Act, stat. 8 & 9 Vict. c. 118.

occasion presently to refer. Prior to the passing of this Act, separate commissioners had been appointed for the purpose of each inclosure. But this Act provides (o) for the appointment of commissioners who are styled

Inclosure commissioners for England.

the inclosure commissioners for England, who are furnished with a common seal; and all awards and orders, purported to be sealed with the seal of the Board, are to be received in evidence, without any further proof thereof. These commissioners were appointed for a limited period only; but their appointment has been from time to time renewed, and the

Sect. 11.

Board are still in existence. By the 11th section, as we have already seen (p), all lands subject to any rights of common whatsoever are subject to be inclosed

Sect. 12.

under the Act. But, by the 12th section, no waste

Waste lands of manor.

land of any manor, on which the tenants of such manor have rights of common, nor any land whatsoever subject to rights of common which may be exercised at all times of every year, for cattle levant and couchant upon other land, or to any rights of common which may be exercised at all times of every year, and which shall not be limited by number or stints, shall be in-

Authority of Parliament for each inclosure.

closed under the Act, without the previous authority of Parliament in each particular case. The Act also provides (q), that no town green or village green shall

Village greens.

be subject to be inclosed under the Act; but provision may be made as thereby directed for preserving the surface and for fixing the boundaries of any such green. Subsequent Acts have provided for the protection of village greens from encroachments, inclosure, and other nuisances (r). The Act contains provisions in favour of the inhabitants of the neighbourhood, and also in favour of the labouring poor, which, up to that time, had not been enforced upon the landowners by public opinion.

(o) Stat. 8 & 9 Vict. c. 118, s. 2.

(p) *Ante*, p. 78.

(q) Sect. 15.

(r) Stat. 20 & 21 Vict. c. 31, s. 12; 39 & 40 Vict. c. 56, s. 29.

These provisions were, however, permissive only. The Act provides (s), that in the provisional order of the commissioners concerning the inclosure under the provisions of the Act, of such waste lands as were before forbidden to be inclosed without the previous authority of parliament, it shall be lawful for the commissioners to require and specify, as one of the terms of the inclosure, the appropriation of an allotment for the purposes of exercise and recreation for the inhabitants of the neighbourhood, not exceeding certain quantities, which limit is now, as we shall see, repealed; and if, in the provisional order for such inclosure, the commissioners shall not have required the appropriation of an allotment for the purposes of exercise and recreation, the commissioners shall, in their annual general report, state the grounds on which they shall have abstained from requiring such appropriation. The Act also provides (t), that in the provisional order concerning the inclosure of such waste lands as aforesaid, it shall be lawful for the commissioners to require and specify, as one of the terms and conditions of such inclosure, the appropriation of such an allotment for the labouring poor, as the commissioners shall think necessary, with reference to the circumstances of each particular case; such allotment, nevertheless, to be subject to a rent-charge, to be payable thereout to any person or persons who may be entitled to allotments under such inclosure as therein provided. But this provision as to rent-charge is now repealed. And if, in the provisional order for such inclosure, the commissioners shall not have required the appropriation of an allotment for the labouring poor, the commissioners shall, in their annual general report, state the grounds on which they shall have abstained from requiring such appropriation.

(s) Sect. 30.   (t) Sect. 31.

Remedy in defects in awards.

A very beneficial power is given by the Act (*u*) to the inclosure commissioners, of remedying defects and omissions in awards, made under local Inclosure Acts or under the Act of the 6 & 7 Will. IV. c. 115, for facilitating the inclosure of open and arable lands in England and Wales (*x*). The Act also contains a very beneficial

Exchanges.

provision (*y*), authorizing exchanges of land to be made by the commissioners by order under their seal, which exchanges are valid, notwithstanding any infirmity of estate or defect of title of the persons on whose application the same was made. This power has been extended to partition and otherwise by subsequent Acts (*z*); but this provision applies to all lands, whether subject or not to be inclosed under the Act, and is therefore beside my present purpose, which is to inform you of the different provisions which have been made with respect to inclosure of lands and the extinguishment of rights of common therein.

Common lands taken by railways, &c.

When any common or waste land is required by any railway or other public body under the provisions of the Lands Clauses Consolidation Act, 1845 (*a*), the compensation for the common rights is determined by agreement between the promoters of the undertaking and a committee of the parties entitled to the commonable rights (*b*), and if they fail to agree, the amount is determined as in other cases of disputed compensation (*c*). The amount received is then either apportioned by the committee (*d*), or paid into the Bank of

(*u*) Stat. 8 & 9 Vict. c. 118, s. 152.

(*x*) *Ante*, pp. 77, 78.

(*y*) Sect. 147.

(*z*) Stats. 9 & 10 Vict. c. 70, ss. 9—11; 11 & 12 Vict. c. 99, ss. 13, 14; 12 & 13 Vict. c. 83, ss. 7, 11; 15 & 16 Vict. c. 79, ss. 17, 31, 32; 17 & 18 Vict.

c. 97, ss. 2, 5; 20 & 21 Vict. c. 31, ss. 4—11; 22 & 23 Vict. c. 43, ss. 10, 11.

(*a*) Stat. 8 & 9 Vict. c. 18.

(*b*) Ib., ss. 99—107. See *Stoneham* v. *London and Brighton Railway Company*, L. R., 7 Q. B. 1.

(*c*) Sect. 105.

(*d*) Sect. 104.

England, and apportioned amongst the commoners in accordance with the statutory provisions which have been made for that purpose (e).

We now come to the Metropolitan Commons Act, 1866 (f), and the Metropolitan Commons Amendment Act, 1869 (g). The term "common" in these Acts means land subject, at the passing of the former Act, to any right of common, and any land subject to be included under the provisions of the statute 8 & 9 Vict. c. 118, of which I have been speaking. By the former of these Acts provision is made for the improvement, protection and management of commons near the metropolis; and the Act applies to any common, the whole or any part whereof is situate within the metropolitan police district, as defined at the passing of the Act, which common is referred to in the Act as a "metropolitan common." The Act enacts (h), that, after its passing, the inclosure commissioners shall not entertain an application for the inclosure of a metropolitan common, or any part thereof. And a scheme for the establishment of local management with a view to the expenditure of money on the drainage, levelling and improvement of a metropolitan common, and to the making of bye-laws and regulations for the prevention of nuisances and the preservation of order thereon, may be made under the Act on a memorial in that behalf presented to the commissioners by the lord of the manor, or by any commoners, or by the local authority, or in the case of a common extending into the districts of two or more of the bodies described in the first schedule of the Act as the local authority, then by any one or more of such bodies (i). The

Metropolitan commons.

Scheme for management of metropolitan common.

(e) Stats. 8 & 9 Vict. c. 18, s. 107; 17 & 18 Vict. c. 97, ss. 15—20.

(f) Stat. 29 & 30 Vict. c. 122.

(g) Stat. 32 & 33 Vict. c. 107.

(h) Stat. 29 & 30 Vict. c. 122, s. 5.

(i) Sect. 6.

scheme, when approved by the commissioners, is to be certified by them, and sealed by their common seal (*k*) ;

Scheme to be confirmed by Act of Parliament. but it has not of itself any operation unless confirmed by Act of Parliament; but when and as it is confirmed by Act of Parliament, it has full operation with such modification, if any, as to Parliament may seem fit (*l*). Several schemes for the regulation of commons in the neighbourhood of London under this Act have already been sanctioned by Parliament.

Regulation and improvement of commons. Commons Act, 1876. An Act has lately been passed for facilitating the regulation and improvement of commons, and for amending the Acts relating to the inclosure of commons (*m*). This Act is cited as the Commons Act, 1876. The first part of the Act relates to the law as to the regulation and inclosure of commons, and provides (*n*) that the inclosure commissioners may entertain an application made in the manner mentioned in the Act for a provisional order, first, for the regulation of a common ; secondly, for the inclosure of a common or parts of a common. And an application may be made as respects the same common for the regulation of part, and for the inclosure of the residue ; but the commissioners are not to proceed to carry any such application into effect, until it is made to appear to them that the persons making the application represent at least one-third in value of such interests in the common as are proposed to be affected by the provisional order.

Regulation of a common. A provisional order for the regulation of a common may provide generally or otherwise for the adjustment of rights in respect of such common, and for the improvement of such common, or for either of such purposes (*o*). The terms " adjustment of rights," and " improvement

(*k*) Stat. 29 & 30 Vict. c. 122, s. 18.

(*l*) Sect. 22.

(*m*) Stat. 39 & 40 Vict. c. 56,

amended by stat. 42 & 43 Vict. c. 37.

(*n*) Stat. 39 & 40 Vict. c. 56, s. 2.

(*o*) Sect. 3.

of a common," are explained in the Act by many sub-sections, showing the rights intended to be adjusted, and the mode in which improvements are to be carried out. And, in considering the expediency of the application, the commissioners are to take into consideration the question whether such application will be for the benefit of the neighbourhood; and shall, with a view to such benefit, insert in their order such of the following conditions as are applicable to the case, that is say:— First, that free access is to be secured to any particular points of view; 2ndly, that particular trees or objects of historical interest are to be preserved; 3rdly, that there is to be reserved, where a recreation ground is not set out, a privilege of playing games or of enjoying other species of recreation at such times and in such manner and on such parts of the common as may be thought suitable, care being taken to cause the least possible injury to the persons interested in the common; and 4thly, that carriage roads, bridle paths and footpaths over such common are to be set out in such directions as may appear most commodious; and 5thly, that any other specified thing is to be done which may be thought equitable and expedient, regard being had to the benefit of the neighbourhood (*p*). If the common is situate either wholly or partly in any town or towns, or within six miles of any town or towns, notice of any application under the Act is to be served, as soon as may be, on the urban sanitary authority or authorities, having jurisdiction over such town or towns, who may appear and make such representations as they may think fit with respect to the expediency or inexpediency of such application, regard being had to the health, comfort and convenience of the inhabitants of the town over which such authority has jurisdiction, and may propose such provisions as may appear to such urban sanitary authority to be proper, regard being had as afore-

Conditions to be inserted.
Views.
Historical objects.
Recreation.

Roads and ways.

Commons within six miles of a town.

(*p*) Sect. 7.

W.P.

Definition of a town for the purposes of the Act.

said (q). But a town, for the purposes of this section, means only any municipal borough or improvement Act district, or local government district, having a population of not less than five thousand inhabitants. Every report made by the inclosure commissioners certifying the expediency of any provisional order under the Act shall be presented to Parliament; and if at any time thereafter it is enacted by Act of Parliament that any order for the regulation or inclosure of a common, the expediency of which has been certified by the commissioners, shall be confirmed, the regulation or inclosure of the common shall be proceeded with and completed; but a provisional order until such Act of Parliament as aforesaid has been passed in relation thereto, shall not be of any validity whatever (r). The second part of the Act amends in several matters the Inclosure Acts already passed. And the third part of the Act, amongst other things, repeals (s) so much of sect. 30 of the Inclosure Act, 1845, as prescribes a limit to the quantity of land to be allotted to recreation grounds. There are also other provisions with respect to recreation grounds and field gardens, and allotments for the poor inhabitants of the parish, all tending to the greater benefit of the poor. The above is but a slight sketch of the Act, which contains many provisions of more or less importance, for which a reference must be made to the Act itself. The 31st section, as to giving notice of any intended inclosure or approvement otherwise than under the provisions of the Act, has already been referred to (t).

Provisional order to be confirmed by Parliament.

(q) Stat. 39 & 40 Vict. c. 56, s. 8.   (s) Sect. 34.
(r) Sect. 12, sub-s. 10.   (t) *Ante*, p. 118.

LECTURE XVIII.

WE now come to the consideration of rights of *)fishing*. Fishing.
And, first, of common of piscary. Common of piscary is Common of
a liberty of fishing in another man's water, in common piscary.
with the owner of the soil and perhaps also with others,
who may be entitled to the same right. It does not
very often occur. I apprehend, that common of piscary
may, like other common rights, be either appurtenant
to a house; in which case it would seem that the fish
taken ought to be consumed in the house, to which the
right is appurtenant; or it may be claimed as a right
in gross, and not attached to any tenement. And it
may arise either by grant or prescription. The incidents of common of piscary appear to be in every
respect analogous to those of common of estovers,
turbary and the like. The right of fishing which has
created most discussion is that which is called a *several* A several
)fishery, or sometimes a *free)fishery*, which is an exclusive fishery.
right of fishing, either with or without the ownership
of the soil. It is remarked by Mr. Justice Willes, in
delivering the opinion of the judges in the case of
Malcomson v. *O'Dea* (a), "that the only substantial distinction is between an exclusive right of fishery, usually
called 'several,' sometimes 'free' (used as in free
warren (b)), and a right in common with others, usually
called 'common of fishery,' sometimes 'free' (used as
in free port). The fishery in this case is sufficiently
described as a 'several fishery,' which means an exclusive right to fish in a given place, either with or
without the property in the soil." On this subject
a great deal of misapprehension seems to have pre-

(a) 10 H. of L. 593, 619.   (b) *Ante*, p. 238.

vailed; and the law is in this singular state, that whilst, according to authorities which must be submitted to, a several fishery implies the ownership of the soil, yet according to legal principles, and also according to more ancient authorities, a several fishery does not *primâ facie* imply the ownership of the soil, any more than a right of several pasture implies in it the ownership of the soil on which the grass grows. This subject was very much discussed in the case of *Marshall* v. *The Ulleswater Steam Navigation Company* (*Limited*) (*c*). The marginal note of that case on this point is as follows:—"The allegation of a several fishery *primâ facie* imports ownership of the soil; Cockburn, Chief Justice, dissenting, but holding the Court bound by the authorities to that effect."

Marshall v. The Ulleswater Steam Naviga- tion Company.

The judgment of Chief Justice Cockburn in this case explains the matter so clearly that I make no apology for reading it to you. It is as follows (*d*): "I am desirous to have it understood that in concurring with my learned brothers in discharging this rule I am acting, not upon my own conviction, but in deference to authorities by which, sitting here, I deem myself bound, but which, if I were sitting in a Court of Appeal, I should consider myself called upon to canvass. I agree with the rest of the Court in thinking that if the right to a several fishery, as such, is consistent with the ownership of the soil—*à fortiori* if *primâ facie* it is to be taken as implying such ownership—there is evidence in this case, in the reservation of the quit rent and the fact of the grant of the fishery to the plaintiff's predecessor having been accompanied by livery of seisin, to lead to the conclusion that the ownership of the soil was here united with the several fishery. My difficulty arises from my inability to assent to the doctrine that upon the grant of a several fishery the ownership of the soil and the right of

(*c*) 3 Best & Smith, 732.   (*d*) Ibid. 746.

fishery are to be taken to be united. It is certain that
both Bracton and Sir E. Coke considered a several fishery
as a thing essentially distinct from the ownership of the
soil. Lord Coke (e) expressly lays it down that by the
grant of a several fishery, even when accompanied by
livery of seisin *secundùm formam chartæ*, the soil does
not pass, but if the water becomes dry the grantor
shall have the soil. The language of Lord Coke is
precise and positive, and is well deserving of attention.
He says :—'If a man be seised of a river, and by deed
do grant *separalem piscariam* in the same, and maketh
livery of seisin *secundùm formam chartæ*, the soile doth
not pass nor the water, for the grantor may take water
there; and if the river become drie he may take the
benefit of the soile; for there passed to the grantee but
a particular right, and the livery being made *secundùm
formam chartæ* cannot enlarge the grant. For the same
reason if a man grant *aquam suam*, the soile shall not
passe, but the pischary within the water passeth therewith.' Now independently of the high authority of
Lord Coke on such a matter, I must say that this
doctrine appears to me the only one which is recon-
cilable with principle or reason. It is admitted on all
hands that a several fishery may exist independently
of the ownership of the soil in the bed of the water.
Why, then, should such a fishery be considered as
carrying with it, in the absence of negative proof, the
property in the soil? On the contrary, it seems to me
that there is every reason for holding the opposite way.
The use of water for the purpose of fishing is, when the
fishery is united with the ownership of the soil, a right
incidental and accessory to the latter. On a grant of
the land, the water and the incidental and accessory
right of fishing would necessarily pass with it. If,
then, the intention be to convey the soil, why not
convey the land at once, leaving the accessory to

(e) Co. Litt. 4 b.

follow? Why grant the accessory that the principal
may pass incidentally? Surely such a proceeding
would be at once illogical and unlawyer-like. The
greater is justly said to comprehend the less, but this
is to make the converse of the proposition hold good. A
grant of land carries with it, as we all know, the
mineral which may be below the surface. But who
ever heard of a grant of the mineral carrying with it
the general ownership of the soil? Why should a
different principle be applied to the grant of a fishery,
which may be said to be a grant of that which is above
the surface of the soil, as a grant of the mineral is a
grant of that which is below it? Nor should it be
forgotten that the opposite doctrine involves the startling
and manifest absurdity that, should the water be
diverted by natural causes, or become dry, the fishery,
which was the primary and principal object of the
grant, would be gone, and the property in the soil,
which only passed incidentally and as accessory to the
grant of the fishery, would remain. I must further
observe that, if I felt myself at liberty to follow my
own view of the law in this respect, I should not feel
any serious difficulty in dealing with the two principal
facts relied on as supporting the position that the
property in the soil passed with the grant of the fishery.
It may be that, in strictness, a quit rent is not properly
reservable on the grant of an incorporeal hereditament.
But if the law were clear that the grant of a several
fishery carried with it no right to the soil, the fact that
a quit rent had been reserved by the lord of the manor
by whom the grant was originally made would only
show that the parties had been mistaken in supposing
that a quit rent could be reserved on such a grant. So,
again, the fact that livery of seisin had been resorted to,
to give effect to the grant, would only show that the
parties erroneously supposed that this form of conveyance
was necessary, or at all events was available to effect

their purpose. These things would not, to my mind, convert a grant of the use of the surface of the soil for a specific purpose into a grant, inferentially, of the soil itself. Indeed, in the case put by Lord Coke, he assumes that the grant of the fishery has been accompanied by livery of seisin, yet lays down that this will not have the effect of making the freehold in the soil pass. Nevertheless, however strong may be my own opinion on this question, I think the authorities on it are too cogent to be overruled except in a Court of Appeal. In *Holford* v. *Bailey* (*f*), Lord Denman, in delivering the considered judgment of this Court, says, p. 1016, ' No doubt the allegation of a several fishery *primâ facie* imports ownership of the soil, though they are not necessarily united.' And the same doctrine is enunciated by Parke, B., in delivering the judgment of the Court of Exchequer Chamber in the same case (*g*). And though, in both instances, the doctrine may be said to have been extrajudicial, as being unnecessary to the decision, which turned on the question whether trespass would lie for disturbance of a several fishery, the affirmative of which was held on grounds altogether independent of the ownership in the soil, yet it cannot be denied that these dicta, occurring in the considered judgments of the Courts, are entitled to very great weight. And in the learned note to fol. 122a of Hargrave and Butler's edition of Coke upon Littleton, the annotator after passing in review the conflicting authorities on this subject concludes—I cannot but think contrary to the effect of his own reasoning—that the true doctrine on this subject is that a several piscary is presumed to comprehend the soil till the contrary appears. I feel that in disposing of this rule we ought to yield to the authority of these opinions, but entertaining myself individually a very different view, I am desirous to have it known that while I submit to

(*f*) 8 Q. B. 1000.   (*g*) 13 Q. B. 426, 444.

them I am far from acquiescing in them." I cannot help thinking that this reasoning will ultimately prevail, and that a right of several fishery will be considered, like a right of several pasture (h), to be merely an incorporeal hereditament, in the absence of any proof of ownership of the soil in the person entitled of the fishery.

Trespass.
Holford v.
Bailey.

It was held in the case of *Holford* v. *Bailey* (i) that an action of trespass will lie for fishing in a several fishery. This is in analogy to the cases of a several pasture (k), an exclusive right of mining (l), and a right of free warren (m) in respect of all of which an action of trespass may be maintained.

Several fishery may be appurtenant.

A several fishery may undoubtedly exist apart from any ownership of the soil of the river in which it exists. It may, like other rights of profit à prendre, be appurtenant to a manor (n). And the right may be confined to certain fish, as oysters, in a navigable tidal river; whilst the public have a right to catch all other fish (o). In the case of *The Duke of Somerset* v. *Fogwell* (p), the Duke of Somerset was the owner of a several fishery in the river Dart, which is a navigable tidal river, under ancient grant from the Crown prior to the reign of Henry II. And it was held that this was an incorporeal and not a territorial hereditament, the soil of the river remaining vested in the Crown, and the incorporeal right of exclusive fishing being alone vested in the Duke.

Duke of
Somerset v.
Fogwell.

Fishery in gross not within

The right to a several fishery, when claimed in gross,

(h) *Ante*, p. 21.
(i) 13 Q. B. 426.
(k) *Ante*, p. 21.
(l) *Ante*, p. 211.
(m) *Ante*, p. 239.

(n) *Rogers* v. *Allen*, 1 Campb. 309, 312.
(o) 1 Campb. 312.
(p) 5 B. & C. 875.

is not within the Prescription Act (*q*). This was decided in the case of *Shuttleworth* v. *Le Fleming* (*r*). In that case the defendant pleaded a right of free fishery in Coniston Water for sixty years and upwards, enjoyed by himself and his ancestors whose heir he was, as of right and without interruption, intending to avail himself of the provisions of the above statute. But the Court held that that statute only applied to cases in which there was a dominant tenement on the one hand and a servient tenement on the other hand, and had no reference to any claim, such as this, of a right in gross belonging to a man and his heirs, irrespective of any tenement to which the same may be appurtenant.

the Prescription Act.
Shuttleworth v. *Le Fleming.*

A right of fishing, when unconnected with the ownership of the soil, was formerly exempt from poor rates, being, like other common rights, only an incorporeal hereditament, and not therefore strictly speaking the subject of occupation: but, if any territorial right belonged to it, then it was rateable for the relief of the poor. A good deal of the law on this subject will be found in the case of *The King* v. *Ellis* (*s*). But by the Rating Act, 1874 (*t*), it is now provided that, after the commencement of that Act, the Poor Rate Acts shall extend, amongst other things, to rights of fishing when severed from the occupation of the land.

Fishery not formerly rateable to the poor.

The Rating Act, 1874. Rights of fishing now rateable.

With regard to the sea, the public have the right of fishing in the sea, and also in all navigable tidal rivers. The seashore, up to the point of high-water mark of medium tides, between the spring and the neap tides, is called the foreshore, and is ordinarily and *primâ facie* vested in the Crown (*u*); but it is so vested for the

The sea.

The foreshore.

(*q*) Stat. 2 & 3 Will. IV. c. 71; *ante*, p. 173.

(*r*) 19 C. B., N. S. 687.

(*s*) 1 M. & S. 652.

(*t*) Stat. 37 & 38 Vict. c. 54, s. 3.

(*u*) *Att.-Gen.* v. *Chambers*, 4 De Gex, M. & G. 206.

benefit of the Queen's subjects, who have by law, not only a right of fishing, but also a right of navigation, not only in the sea but also in all tidal navigable rivers (x). But the foreshore, though ordinarily vested in the Crown, may belong to a subject, either by itself or as part of an adjoining manor. And when vested in a subject it belongs to him as his private property (y). In many cases the right to the foreshore is derived under ancient grants from the Crown. It is a general principle, in the construction of ancient grants, that their meaning may be explained by modern user; and in cases where it is shown that acts of ownership have been exercised by a grantee under a grant which may or may not include the seashore, such acts of ownership, if exercised on the seashore between high and low water-mark, may be properly admitted as evidence to show that the grants in question included the seashore down to low water-mark (z). So in the case of *Calmady* v. *Rowe* (a), it was held that acts of ownership exercised by the lord of a manor upon the seashore adjoining between high and low water-mark, such as the exclusive taking of sand, stones and sea weeds, might be called in aid to show that the shore was parcel of a manor, where an ancient grant, under which the manor appeared to be held, and which professed to grant the manor with wreck of the sea, several fishery and other rights of an extensive description, did not purport expressly to convey the foreshore..

Foreshore may belong to a subject.

Ancient grants explained by modern user.

When high water-mark gradually alters.

When the boundary of high water-mark at medium tides is gradually altered, either by the gradual encroachment of the sea on the one hand, or by its gradual

(x) *Ward* v. *Creswell*, Willes, 265; *Bagott* v. *Orr*, 2 Bos. & Pul. 472; *Williams* v. *Wilcox*, 8 A. & E. 314, 333.

(y) *Mace* v. *Philcox*, 15 C. B., N. S. 600.

(z) *The Duke of Beaufort* v. *Mayor, &c. of Swansea*, 3 Ex. 413.

(a) 6 C. B. 861. See also *Att.- Gen.* v. *Mayor, &c. of Portsmouth*, Ex., 25 W. R. 559.

retirement on the other, by reason of the gradual formation of alluvium, the right of the Crown or of the Crown's grantee to the seashore gradually alters according as the boundary alters (b); and the land which gradually advances on the sea becomes the property of the adjoining owner. And so the land which has been gradually enroached on by the sea is gradually taken from the adjoining owner. The law on this subject is thus put by Baron Alderson *In the Matter of the Hull and Selby Railway* (c), "I think the question is precisely the same whether the claim is made as against the Crown or the Crown's grantee. Suppose the Crown, being the owner of the foreshore—that is, the space between high and low water-mark—grants the adjoining soil to an individual, and the water gradually recedes from the foreshore, no intermediate period of the change being perceptible; in that case the right of the grantee of the Crown would go forward with the change. On the other hand, if the sea gradually covered the land so granted, the Crown would be the gainer of the land. The principle laid down by Lord Hale, that the party who suffers the loss shall be entitled also to the benefit, governs and decides the question. That which cannot be perceived in its progress is taken to be as if it never had existed at all." But in the case of a sudden advance or recession the law is different. A sudden retirement of the sea does not deprive the grantee from the Crown of the foreshore of his title to the soil, which existed prior to such sudden retirement; and so, on the other hand, the sudden inundation of the sea does not deprive the owners of the land so inundated of their right to the soil.

Re Hull and Selby Railway.

Sudden advance or recession.

Primâ facie, as we have said (d), the soil of every

(b) *Gifford* v. *Lord Yarborough*, H. of L., 5 Bing. 163.

(c) 5 M. & W. 327, 332.

(d) *Ante*, p. 265.

tidal navigable river is vested in the Crown; and *primâ facie* the right of fishery therein belongs to the public.

Grant by Crown of several fishery.

But in ancient times the right to exclude the public from fishing in a tidal navigable river, and to create a several fishery therein, existed in the Crown; and the Crown might lawfully, before the passing of Magna Charta, have exercised this right; and the several fishery so created could afterwards be lawfully made the subject of a grant by the Crown to a private individual. This was one of the points decided by the House of Lords in the case of *Malcomson* v. *O'Dea* (e),

Malcomson v. O'Dea.

to which I have just referred (*f*). The part of the Magna Charta which relates to this subject, is cap. 16

Magna Charta, c. 16.

of the Magna Charta of 9 Hen. III., which provides that no river banks shall be defended from henceforth but such as were in defence in the time of King Henry our grandfather, by the same places and the same bounds as they were wont to be in his time. "That is," says Lord Coke (*g*), "that no owner of the banks of rivers shall so appropriate or keep the rivers several to him, to defend or bar others either to have passage or fish there, otherwise than they were used in the reign of King Henry II."

No public right in private waters.

Hudson v. Macrae.

The public have no right of fishing in any private waters; nor can they acquire such a right by any use, however long. This was decided in the case of *Hudson* v. *Macrae* (*h*). In that case the public had fished for sixty years and upwards, at their pleasure and without interruption, in the river Wandle, by angling from a footpath beside the river; and the defence of the appellant to an information against him before two justices for unlawfully fishing, was that, under the above circumstances, he had a right, as one of the public, to fish in that part of the river from the foot-

(e) 10 H. of L. 593. (g) 2 Inst. 30.
(f) *Ante*, p. 259. (h) 4 Best & Smith, 585.

path. And it was conceded on all hands that such a right could not exist. This case was followed by that of *Hargreaves* v. *Diddams* (i). In that case a river was *Hargreaves* v. *Diddams*. made navigable by a company, and the public were allowed to navigate it on payment of tolls under certain Acts of Parliament. The soil and rights of the owners on each side of the river remained untouched. The public had fished for many years in the river without interruption by the owner of the soil; but he caused a notice to be set up forbidding all fishing. The appellant afterwards fished in the river, and an information was taken out against him. At the hearing the appellant set up the right in the public. But it was held that the right set up could not exist in law—following the decision in *Hudson* v. *Macrae* to which I have just referred. In like manner a custom cannot be sustained for the inhabitants of a parish to angle and catch fish in Custom for inhabitants to fish, bad. certain waters; for a profit *à prendre*, as this is, cannot be established by custom (k). You will remember that in *Gateward's case* (l), it was decided that a custom for the inhabitants of a parish to pasture their cattle on a certain waste was held to be void.

With regard to rivers, other than those that are Rivers not tidal and navigable. tidal and navigable, the law is that the soil of one-half the river to the middle of the river belongs to the owner of the banks of the river on each side; the owner of the land on one side being entitled to the one-half next his land, and the owner of the land on the other side being entitled to the other half next his land. And each owner is entitled in common with the other to fish in the stream. And if the river should gradually and imperceptibly change its course, the same law holds as with regard to the seashore; and there accrues a gradual gain to the riparian owner from whose side

(i) L. R., 10 Q. B. 582.   B. 713, n.
(k) *Bland* v. *Lipscombe*, 4 E. &   (l) 6 Rep. 59; *ante*, p. 13.

the river gradually recedes, and a gradual loss to the other riparian owner upon whom the river gradually incroaches. But in case of any sudden advance or recession of the water of the river, the law is the same as with regard to any sudden advance or recession of the sea. Such sudden advance or recession does not alter the rights of the respective riparian owners. And even where a river gradually shifts its course, if it in course of time leaves the soil of A., and flows through the soil of B., the right of fishing which belonged to A. whilst the river ran through his land, is lost by him so soon as the river forsakes his land. Thus in the case of the *Mayor of Carlisle* v. *Graham* (*m*), the plaintiffs claimed a several fishery in a portion of the river Eden called the Goat, about half a mile in length. The river Eden is a tidal river; and the plaintiffs were entitled to two fisheries derived under ancient grants from the Crown, confirming other more ancient grants anterior to Magna Charta. The river Eden in process of time entirely left its former channel, and formed for itself a new one. And it was held that the corporation of the city of Carlisle thereby lost its right of fishing in the river.

Mayor of Carlisle v. Graham.

Johnson v. Bloomfield.

In the recent case of *Johnson* v. *Bloomfield* (*n*), it was held by the Court of Exchequer Chamber in Ireland that the presumption that the bed and soil of a stream belongs to the riparian proprietors, does not apply to a large inland non-tidal and navigable lake. It was also held in the same case that the public has not a common law right to fish in a non-tidal lake, although it may be navigable.

Inland lake.

(*m*) L. R., 4 Ex. 361 ; 18 W. R. 318. See, however, *Foster* v. *Wright*, 4 C. P. D. 438.

(*n*) 8 Irish Reports, Common Law, 68.

LECTURE XIX.

I now come to the consideration of other franchises Franchises. which may be claimed either by grant from the Crown, or by prescription from long enjoyment. Many of these franchises not unfrequently belong to lords of manors, and are in fact appurtenant to their several manors. It is laid down by Lord Coke (*a*), that to treasure trove, waifs, estrays, wreck of sea, to hold pleas, Court of leets, hundreds, &c., in-fang thief, out-fang thief, to have a park, warren, royal fishes, as whales, sturgeons, fairs, markets, frank foldage, the keeping of a gaol, toll, a corporation by prescription, and the like, a man may make a title by usage and prescription only, without any matter of record.

I now proceed to take some of these franchises more particularly. A very common franchise annexed to a manor is a right of the lord to hold a *Court leet*. The Court leet. Court leet is thus described by Blackstone in his Commentaries (*b*), "The Court leet or view of frank-pledge, is a Court of record, held once in the year and not oftener, within a particular hundred, lordship or manor, before the steward of the leet, being the King's Court granted by charter to the lords of those hundreds or manors. Its original intent was to view the frank-pledges, that is, the freemen within the liberty; who, we may remember, according to the institution of the great Alfred, were all mutually pledges for the good behaviour of each other. Besides this, the preservation of the peace and the chastisement of divers minute offences against the public good, are the objects both of

(*a*) Co. Litt. 114 b.   (*b*) 4 Bl. Com. 273.

the Court leet and the sheriff's tourn; which have exactly the same jurisdiction, one being only a larger species of the other, extending over more territory but not over more causes. All freeholders within the precinct are obliged to attend them and all persons *commorant* therein, which commorancy consists in usually lying there; a regulation which owes its original to the laws of King Canute." [I may add that the persons commorant within the place are also fre-

Resiants.

quently called "resiants."] "But persons under twelve and above sixty years old, peers, clergymen, women, and the king's tenants in ancient demesne, are excused from attendance there; all others being bound to appear upon the jury, if required, and make their due presentments. It was also anciently the custom to summon all the king's subjects as they respectively grew to years of discretion and strength to come to the Court leet and there take the oath of allegiance to the king. The other general business of the leet and tourn was to present by jury all crimes whatsoever that happened within their jurisdiction; and not only to present, but also to punish all trivial misdemeanors, as all trivial debts were recoverable in the Court baron, and county Court : justice in these minuter matters of both kinds being brought home to the doors of every man by our ancient constitution." But, as Blackstone observes, both the tourn and the leet have been for a long time in a declining way, this business for the most part having gradually devolved upon the quarter sessions. As a Court leet may be claimed by prescription, so the mode of summoning the jury may be by prescription varied from the ordinary mode. This was

The King v. *Joliffe.*

decided in the case of *The King* v. *Joliffe* (c), to which I called attention in a former Lecture (d). It was there held that where, for twenty years and upwards, it had been the custom for the steward of the manor to

(c) 2 B. & C. 54.   (d) *Ante*, p. 5.

nominate the persons to serve on the jury, instead of their being chosen by the bailiff of the manor in the usual way, this was evidence from which, if uncontradicted, the jury were justified in finding that such had been the practice from time immemorial; and it was held that this was a good custom belonging to the Court leet, which also was claimed to have been held by prescription from time immemorial. In that case the person holding the Court leet was not the lord of a manor but the mayor of the borough of Petersfield, which is an ancient borough. The Court leet when held by the lord of a manor must be carefully distinguished from the Court baron and also from the copyhold Court of the manor. All three Courts are not unfrequently held together. But the Court leet is a criminal Court and can only be claimed by a grant from the Crown, or by prescription from immemorial user, whereas the Court baron is incident to every manor (e). It is the Court of the freeholders, and in it they are both suitors and judges, whilst the Court of the copyholders is only for them, and in it the lord or his steward presides as judge (f).

The right of holding a Court leet may be forfeited by long neglect to hold a Court. But in the case of *The King* v. *The Steward and Suitors of the Manor of Havering-atte-Bower in the County of Essex* (g), decided in the year 1822, it was held that a Court established by charter in that manor (which was a manor of ancient demesne (h)) was not lost by non-user for fifty years, except for the purpose of levying fines and suffering recoveries, which at that time were levied and suffered in the manor Court in all manors of ancient demesne.

Forfeiture of Court by neglect.

The King v. *The Steward, &c. of Havering-atte-Bower.*

(e) Lectures on the Seisin of the Freehold, p. 15.

(f) *Ibid.* p. 36.

(g) 5 B. & Ald. 691.

(h) See Lectures on the Seisin of the Freehold, p. 31.

W.P.   T

Infangthief and outfang-thief.

With regard to the franchises of *infangthief* and *out-fangthief* mentioned by Lord Coke in the passage that I have read (*i*), they have both long become obsolete. *Infangthief* was a liberty or privilege, granted to the lords of certain manors, to judge any thief taken within their fee. And in some old charters you may find that

Gallows.

the privilege of having a gallows to hang felons upon is expressly granted to the lord of the manor. The right of *outfangthief* is a liberty for the lord of a manor to call any man, dwelling in his manor, and taken for felony in another place out of his fee, to judgment in his own Court. The last statute which I am aware of by which these privileges were recognized is the statute

Stat. 1 & 2 Phil. & Mary, c. 15, s. 3.

1 & 2 Philip & Mary, c. 15, which was "An Act to confirm the liberties of the Lord Marchers in Wales." And that Act provides (*k*), that persons having lord-ships marchers or lordships royal shall have, within the precincts of their lordships, amongst other things, *infangthief* and *outfangthief*, as they had had in times past, and as such privileges were granted unto them by

A hundred.

point of charter. The franchise of a *hundred*, which Lord Coke mentions, consists of a right to hold a hundred Court, which belongs of common right to the Crown; but which a subject may have by grant from the Crown, or, as Lord Coke tells us, by prescription

Keeping a gaol.

from long enjoyment. I apprehend that the franchise of keeping a gaol, like the privilege of having a gallows, is now long obsolete.

Frank foldage.

Another prescriptive right mentioned by Lord Coke (*l*), is a right of *frank foldage* (*faldagium*), on which it may be as well to say a few words, especially as the right has been sometimes confounded with the right of *fold course*, which is a totally distinct right, as we shall presently see. *Frank foldage* is one of those

(*i*) *Ante*, p. 271.　　　　　(*l*) Co. Litt. 114 b; *ante*, p.
(*k*) Sect. 3.　　　　　　　　271.

oppressive rights, which the law permitted in early days, but which I think would now be scarcely tolerated. It is the right of a lord of a manor or other person to have all the sheep within his manor, or within a certain vill or town or other district, folded at night on his land, for the purpose of manuring it (*m*). So that the unfortunate tenants of the manor, or other land owners in the vill, are forbidden to exercise their ordinary common law right of ownership, by folding their own sheep on their own land, but must take them every night to be folded on the land of the lord of the manor, or other person having the prescriptive right of frank foldage, in order that thereby his lands may be the better manured at the expense of theirs. The duty of the tenants to fold their sheep on the lord's land was called suit of fold, *secta faldæ* (*n*). An early instance Suit of fold. of this right occurs in the third year of King Edward III. (*o*). John de Sedgeford and his brother brought a writ of trespass against William, Prior of the Trinity of Norwich, and others, because they by force of arms broke down his fold, and set their dogs to bite his sheep which were there, so that a great part of the sheep died. And the defence set up was this;— that the Prior of the Trinity of Norwich was lord of the vill of Sedgeford, where the usage of the town was, and had been from time whereof the memory of man ran not to the contrary, that no man in the same vill might erect a sheep fold without the leave and licence of the lord of the vill, namely, the prior and his predecessors; with the exception only of one person, who and whose ancestors had from time immemorial been used to erect a fold of their own will. And because the aforesaid plaintiffs, tenants of the aforesaid prior, erected a fold,

(*m*) Keilway, 198 a; see also Year Book, Hil. 1 Edw. III. pl. 4; Pasch. 1 Hen. VII. pl. 17.

(*n*) Spelman's Glossary, voce *Faldagium*.

(*o*) Year Book, Hil. 3 Edw. III. fol. 3 a, pl. 7.

T 2

contrary to the leave and licence of the said prior, they
came and abated the fold, as well they might without
breaking the peace. This case is mentioned in 2nd
Brownlow (*p*), in a case of *Waggoner* v. *Fish*, and also
in Lord Coke's Reports (*q*), as an instance of frank
foldage. And in the same report at the same page
Lord Coke mentions another instance of the same sort ;
namely, a case in which one Jeffery at Hay brought
an action of trespass against two persons for breaking
his fold at Hastings in the county of Sussex ; and the
defence was that Johan de Frichborn, the lady of the
manor of Hastings, and her ancestors, and all the lords
of the manor whose estate she had, from time immemorial had the franchise to have a free fold (*liberam
faldam*) through the whole town of Hastings, and to
have a lock of the wool of the sheep ; so that none in
the town of Hastings ought to have a free fold without
agreement made with her ; and if any did erect a fold
without agreement made with her or her ancestors,
that the lords for the time being had used to abate it.
Jeffery at Hay, the plaintiff, set up a new fold without
agreement, wherefore the defendants, as servants to the
said Johan de Frichborn, came and disjoined the hurdles
and abated them. And it was objected that it was
against common right ; for a man, of common right,
might have a fold in his own land, and also that it was
unreasonable to oust him of that which the common
law gives him ; but the objections were overruled, for
it was said that every prescription was against common
right, and that, although the folding of sheep is for
the maintenance of tillage, which is so much esteemed
and favoured in law, yet by custom and usage a man
may be barred thereof upon his own land, and another
than he by whom the land is held may have it. I
should hardly suppose, however, that such a custom

(*p*) Page 287.   (*q*) Vol. 8, p. 125 b, in *The
                                        City of London's case.*

now exists; but the right is curious as showing the state of the country in ancient times. You observe that in the reign of Edward III. the lord who claimed the right was not said to be the lord of the manor, but the lord of the vill. This is another instance of a prescriptive right affecting a *vill* in early days, rather than a manor; although it is said that the land owners were tenants of the lord of the vill.

Lord of the vill.

This right of *frank foldage* must not be confounded with the right of *fold course*, which is a right grown out of the ancient right of frank foldage, and cannot, I apprehend, exist except in cases where the lord of the manor, or other lord paramount, claimed the right of frank foldage. The right of fold course is a compound right. It is the right of a man to have a fold of his own on certain land, or on his own submanor, instead of sending his sheep to the fold of the superior lord, and a right for the sheep so folded to run for pasture over the commonable grounds of the manor or superior lordship. It is accordingly called in old books *libertas faldagii et cursus ovium* (*r*). It sometimes includes the land itself on which the fold is privileged to be erected (*s*). But in modern times it is nothing more than a right of common for so many sheep appurtenant to certain lands where the sheep-fold formerly stood (*t*). The distinction between frank foldage and fold course is well explained in a case of *Sharp* v. *Bechenowe* (*u*), where it is said that the prescription to have *foldage* cannot extend to depasturing the sheep of the person who claimed under the prescription; because "the nature of *foldage* is only to have the sheep, but not my own,

Fold course.

Sharp v. Bechenowe.

<hr>

(*r*) West's Symboleography, Fines, p. 11, sect. 32; Punsany and Leader's case, 1 Leon. 11.

(*s*) Co. Litt. 6 a.

(*t*) *Fielding* v. *Wren*, Cary, 65; *Musgrave* v. *Gave*, Willes, 319;

2 Wms. Saund. 327, n. 11; *Robinson* v. *Maharajah Duleep Singh*, C. A., 27 W. R. 21; L. R., 11 Ch. D. 798.

(*u*) Lutwyche, pp. 398, 399 of Nelson's translation.

folded in my lands in the night time. It is true that he hath prescribed likewise for a *fold course*, which is a sheep walk or a feeding for sheep; but this," we are told, "is inconsistent with *foldage*, for that is a liberty to have another man's sheep folded on my land; and a fold course is to have pasture for a certain number of my own sheep upon another man's land." There is a case of *Spooner* v. *Day* (x), in which a fold course for 300 sheep was claimed by prescription, as a right appurtenant to a manor. Part of the manor, together with the fold course, had been demised to the plaintiff for five years; and it was held that the right was in the nature of common certain, and might be well divided or annexed to a parcel of the manor. A right of a similar kind was claimed in the more modern case of *Ivatt* v. *Man* (y). In this case it appeared that from time immemorial, two flocks of sheep had depastured upon the open fields and commons of Rampton Lyles, in the county of Cambridge, namely, the town flock, consisting of sheep put in by the occupiers of ploughed land in the vill; and the manor flock, consisting of sheep belonging to, and levant and couchant upon, the manor farm. In that case, the occupier of the manor farm claimed a separate right of feeding and folding an unlimited number of sheep to his own use; but his claim was disallowed, the evidence showing that the right of the manor flock was only with respect to sheep levant and couchant upon the manor farm.

Spooner v. *Day*.

Ivatt v. *Man*.

Town flock.

Another prescriptive right or franchise is that of a lord of a manor to compel all the tenants and inhabitants within the manor to bake bread at his bakehouse, or to grind their corn at his mill. Thus in the case to which I have already referred, the *City of London's*

To bake bread at the lord's bakehouse.

(x) Cro. Car. 432; *S. C.* nom. *Day* v. *Spoone*, Sir W. Jones, 375.

(y) 3 Man. & Gr. 691, anno 1842.

case (z), an instance is given of this prescription. Sir George Farmour brought an action on the case against one Brook, and showed that he was seised of the manor of Torcester, in the county of Northampton, in fee ; and that all the tenements of the said town are held of the said manor ; and showed that, from time immemorial, he and all those whose estate he had, had had a bakehouse, parcel of the said manor, maintained at their charge, and that this bakehouse was sufficient to bake bread for all the inhabitants and for all passengers through the same town ; and that the bread so baked used to be sold at reasonable prices ; and that no other person within the said town had used to bake any bread to sell to any person.   And it was adjudged a reasonable custom by Sir Christopher Wray and the whole Court.   So in the case of *Hex* v. *Gardiner* (a) it was held that the lord of a manor might bind *resiants*, that is, persons dwelling within his manor (b), and inhabitants within the same, to come and grind their corn at his mill.   It was held in that case that the claim would be clearly good by way of tenure ; that is, where the tenants of a manor held by such a service ; but it was also held to be a good prescription, as against *resiants* and inhabitants, as well as against tenants.

To grind corn at the lord's mill.

You may have observed in this case how very nearly prescription and custom run together.   The distinction between the two, you may remember, as mentioned by Lord Coke (c), is that a prescription is personal, applying to a man and his ancestors, or those whose estate he hath, or in bodies politic or corporate and their predecessors ; but a custom is local, is alleged in no person, but laid within some manor or other place. It seems, in truth, that the same claim may be spoken of either as a prescription or as a custom, according to

Prescription and custom.

(z) 8 Rep. 125 b. (b) *Ante*, p. 272.
(a) 2 Bulst. 195. (c) Co. Litt. 113 b; *ante*, p. 1.

the manner in which it is viewed. Thus where the right is claimed that all the inhabitants of a place should bake bread at the lord's bakehouse, or grind their corn at the lord's mill, this claim, viewed in regard to the lord of the manor, is a claim by prescription ; because he prescribes that he is lord of the manor, and that he and all those whose estate he hath, have, from time immemorial, had this right. But viewed in regard to the *resiants* within the manor, who are under an obligation to conform to the right so claimed, it is a *custom* laid within the manor, and therefore local. So that, with regard to a right of this kind, it may be called either a prescription or a custom, according as it is viewed in the light of the person claiming it, or in the light of those who are bound by the claim.

Treasure trove.

Treasure trove is another franchise often claimed by lords of manors by grant from the Crown or by prescription. Treasure trove is thus explained by Blackstone in his Commentaries (*d*). "Treasure trove (derived from the French word *trover*, to find), called in Latin *thesaurus inventus*, is where any money or coin, gold, silver, plate or bullion is found hidden *in* the earth or other private place, the owner thereof being unknown ; in which case the treasure belongs to the king ; but if he that hid it be known or afterwards found out, the owner and not the king is entitled to it. Also if it be found in the sea, or *upon* the earth, it doth not belong to the king, but the finder, if no owner appears. So that it is the *hiding* and not the *abandoning* of it that gives the king a property ; Bracton defining it in the words of the civilians to be ' *vetus depositio pecuniæ*.' This difference clearly arises from the different intentions which the law implies in the owner. A man that hides his treasure in a secret

(*d*) Vol. 1, p. 295.

place evidently does not mean to relinquish his property ; but reserves a right of claiming it again when he sees occasion ; but if he dies, and the secret also dies with him, the law gives it to the king in part of his royal revenue. But a man that scatters his treasure 'into the sea or upon the public surface of the earth is construed to have absolutely abandoned his property, and returned it into the common stock without any intention of reclaiming it ; and therefore it belongs, as in the state of nature, to the first occupant or finder, unless the owner appear and assert his right, which then proves that the loss was by accident and not with an intent to renounce his property." Nothing but gold and. silver comes within the description of treasure trove.

Waifs are another prescriptive right, often belonging Waifs. to lords of manors by grant from the Crown, or by prescription. "Waifs," says Blackstone in his Commentaries (e), " *bona waviata*, are goods stolen and *waived* or thrown away by the thief in his flight, for fear of being apprehended. These are given to the king by the law as a punishment upon the owner, for not himself pursuing the felon and taking away his goods from him. And therefore if the party robbed do his diligence immediately to follow and apprehend the thief (which is called making *fresh suit*) or do convict him afterwards, or procure evidence to convict him, he shall have his goods again. Waived goods do also not belong to the king till seized by somebody for his use ; for if the party robbed can seize them first, though at the distance of twenty years, the king shall never have them. If the goods are hid by the thief, or left any where by him so that he had them not about him when

(e) Vol. 1, p. 297.

he fled, and therefore did not throw them away in his flight, these also are not *bona waviata*, but the owner may have them again when he pleases. The goods of a foreign merchant, though stolen and thrown away in flight, shall never be waifs; the reason whereof may be, not only for the encouragement of trade, but also because there is no wilful default in the foreign merchant's not pursuing the thief; he being generally a stranger to our laws, our usages, and our language."

tolen goods.

I may add, with regard to stolen goods, that if the thief should sell the goods, even to a *bonâ fide* purchaser (so that the sale is not made in open market, or *market overt* as it is called), yet the true owner of the goods may recover his property from the purchaser. And it is not necessary for this purpose that he should first have prosecuted the felon. Thus in the case of *Lee* v. *Bayes* (*f*), a person *bonâ fide* bought a horse, which had been stolen, at a repository for horses which was out of the city of London, and not in law a market overt. The owner of the horse, finding it there, brought an action against the owner of the repository and the purchaser, for the wrongful conversion of the horse to their own use ; and he was held entitled to recover. With regard to the duty of a person whose goods have been stolen to prosecute the thief, it has been held in a recent case in the Queen's Bench, that, although undoubtedly that is his duty, and although the right of redress by action is suspended until the party inflicting the injury is prosecuted, yet this rule is not always capable of being enforced. The case I refer to is that

Fells v. *1braham*.

of *Wells* v. *Abraham* (*g*). In that case an action of trover and trespass for a valuable brooch was brought against the defendant; and the jury found a verdict for

(*f*) 18 C. B. 599.   (*g*) L. R., 7 Q. B. 554.

the plaintiff. Whereupon a rule for a new trial was obtained on the ground that it appeared from the evidence that the brooch was taken by the defendant under such circumstances as to prove a charge of felony ; and that the judge ought, therefore, to have nonsuited the plaintiff. The defendant, you will ob- serve, in this case endeavoured to get off from the action on the ground that the evidence showed that he must have stolen the brooch ; and so the plaintiff could not recover in a civil action, until he had prosecuted the defendant for felony. But, as the Chief Justice said (h), " Having obtained a rule founded upon the hypothesis that the facts proved at the trial amounted to a felony, he, the counsel for the defendant, yet per- sists in denying that his client has committed a felony ; so that he seeks to have the benefit of something, the existence of which he denies. When the case has thus been explained, it is manifest that the defendant has no *locus standi* to make this application. He can only apply to us on the ground that he has committed a felony ; but at the same time he denies that he is a criminal. Can it be said that my learned brother at the trial did anything beyond that which he was called upon to do, namely, try the issues brought before him ? I think therefore there is no ground for making the rule absolute." It appears therefore that unless a stealer will confess that he is indeed a thief, he cannot resist a civil action brought against him, for the re- covery of the goods, by the person from whom they have been stolen.

A sale in *market overt* gives the purchaser a valid Market overt. title to the goods he has purchased, subject however to the rule already mentioned with regard to waifs (i) that, if the true owner of the goods prosecutes the felon

---

(h) Page 559. (i) *Ante*, p. 281.

to conviction, the property in the goods vests in him,
whether they have been sold in market overt or not.
The law on this subject is now contained in the statute
24 & 25 Vict. c. 96, which enacts (k) that, if a person
guilty of stealing any chattel, money, valuable security,
or other property whatsoever, shall be indicted for such
offence by or on the behalf of the owner of the property
or his executor or administrator, and convicted thereof,
in such case the property shall be restored to the owner
or his representative, with this exception, that if it shall
appear that any valuable security shall have been *bonâ
fide* paid or discharged by some person or body corporate liable to the payment thereof, or, being a nego-
tiable instrument, shall have been *bonâ fide* taken or
received by transfer or delivery by some person or body
corporate, for a just and valuable consideration, without
any notice, or without any reasonable cause to suspect
that the same had by any felony or misdemeanor been
stolen, obtained or disposed of, in such case the Court
shall not order the restitution of such security. But
this section is not to apply to the case of any prosecu-
tion of any trustee, banker, merchant, attorney, factor,
broker or other agent intrusted with the possession of
goods, or documents of title to goods, for any misdemeanor against the Act. A further provision in
favour of a *bonâ fide* purchaser, which perhaps may not
often be of much value, has been made by the statute
30 & 31 Vict. c. 35 (l), which provides that where any
prisoner shall be convicted, either summarily or otherwise, of larceny or other offence, which includes the
stealing of any property, and it shall appear to the
Court by the evidence that the prisoner has sold the
stolen property to any person, and that such person has
had no knowledge that the same was stolen, and that
any monies have been taken from the prisoner on his

Marginal notes:

Stat. 24 & 25 Vict. c. 96, s. 100.

Stat. 30 & 31 Vict. c. 35, s. 9.

(k) Sect. 100.   (l) Sect. 9.

apprehension, it shall be lawful for the Court, on the application of such purchaser, and on the restitution of the stolen property to the prosecutor, to order that out of such monies a sum not exceeding the amount of the proceeds of the said sale be delivered to the said purchaser. The remedy given by this section depends, you will observe, upon the precarious fact of the prisoner having money upon him and taken from him at the time of his apprehension.

LECTURE XX.

ANOTHER of those rights, to which, as Lord Coke tells us, a title may be made by prescription, is the right to *Estrays*. Estrays are thus described by Blackstone in his Commentaries (a) : "Estrays are such valuable animals as are found wandering in any manor or lordship, and no man knoweth the owner of them; in which case the law gives them to the king as the general owner and lord paramount of the soil, in recompense for the damage which they may have done therein : and they now most commonly belong to the lord of the manor, by special grant from the Crown. But, in order to vest an absolute property in the king or his grantees, they must be proclaimed in the church and two market towns next adjoining to the place where they are found: and then, if no man claims them, after proclamation and a year and a day passed, they belong to the king or his substitute without redemption, even though the owner were a minor, or under any .other legal incapacity." If the owner claims the estray within the year and a day, he must pay the charges of finding and keeping and proclaiming it. Animals upon which the law sets no value, as a dog or cat, and

animals *feræ naturæ*, cannot be estrays. Swans, however, being royal fowl, may be estrays, but not any other fowl. An estray is an animal of value, tame and reclaimable, such as a horse, an ox, a sheep, or a pig.

The advantage which the lord of a manor may gain by having a right of estrays is no doubt very precarious; for cattle, when they go astray, frequently

(a) Vol. 1, p. 297.

commit trespass on the lands of other persons than their owners, doing damage, of course, to the grass or crops that may be growing there. When this occurs Distress of cattle damage feasant. in consequence of any defect in the fences of the lands, the owner of the cattle is bound to remove them within a reasonable time (*b*) ; and if he do not, or if the cattle have broken down the fencing, the cattle may be seized or distrained *damage feasant*, as it is called. This may be done by the owner of the land summarily and without legal process; but the cattle must be actually on the premises when distrained and doing damage thereto; and if there are more beasts than one, each beast can only be seized and detained for the damage actually done by itself only, and not for any part of the general damage done by the others (*c*). The distress may be taken at any time, either at the night or in the day, when the cattle are found upon the premises. And the remedy is not confined to the mere owner of the soil upon which they may be found; for a person who has Commoner may distrain stranger's cattle damage feasant. a right of common on a waste may distrain the cattle of a stranger *damage feasant*, found on that waste, on account of the injury done to his right of common (*d*). If the owner of the cattle makes a sufficient tender for the damage done before the cattle are actually taken, the taking is unlawful. And if, after the cattle are taken, and before they are impounded, sufficient tender is made for the damage done, they can no longer be lawfully detained. The right to impound *damage feasant* Dogs and inanimate objects may be distrained damage feasant. extends not only to cattle, but also to dogs and other animals, and even to inanimate objects, such as nets and oars on a several fishery (*e*), and an engine unduly placed on and incumbering a railway (*f*).

(*b*) *Goodwin* v. *Cheveley*, 4 H. & N. 631. See also *Singleton* v. *Williamson*, 7 H. & N. 410.

(*c*) Vin. Abr. tit. Distress (A).

(*d*) *Morris's case*, Godbolt, 185; Vin. Abr. tit. Distress (C), 1.

(*e*) Vin. Abr. tit. Distress (A); *ante*, p. 259.

(*f*) *Ambergate, &c. Railway Co.* v. *Midland Railway Co.*, 2 Ellis & Bl. 793.

Person
impounding
cattle to
supply them
with food and
water.

The person who impounds cattle is now bound
to supply them with food and water, a measure of
humanity which did not exist at the common law, by
which the owner of the cattle was bound to feed them
while they were in an open pound ; and if the owner
did not know where they were, they ran a risk of
dying of starvation.   The Act of 12 & 13 Vict. c. 92,
for the more effectual prevention of cruelty to animals
(which repeals a prior Act for the same purpose) (*g*),
provides (*h*) that every person who shall impound or
confine, or cause to be impounded or confined, in any
pound or receptacle of the like nature any animal,
shall provide and supply, during such confinement, a
sufficient quantity of fit and wholesome food and water
to such animal, under a penalty of twenty shillings.
And (*i*) if any animal shall be impounded without fit
and sufficient food and water for more than twelve
successive hours, any person may enter the pound, and
supply such animal with fit and sufficient food and
water, so long as it remains confined ; and the reasonable cost of such food and water shall be paid by the
owner of such animal, before such animal is removed,
to the person who shall supply the same.   And by a
later statute (*k*) every person impounding an animal,
and supplying it with food and water, may recover
from the owner of the animal not exceeding double the
value of the food and water so supplied, or if he thinks
fit, he may, instead of proceeding for the recovery of
the value thereof, after the expiration of seven clear
days from the time of impounding the same, sell any
such animal openly at any public market (after having
given three days' public printed notice thereof) for the
most money that can be got for the same, and may
apply the produce in discharge of the value of such

Power to sell
animal for
value of food
supplied.

(*g*) Stat. 5 & 6 Will. IV. c. 59.   (*i*) Sect. 6.
(*h*) Stat. 12 & 13 Vict. c. 92,   (*k*) Stat. 17 & 18 Vict. c. 60,
s. 5.   s. 1.

food and water so supplied as aforesaid, and the expenses of and attending such sale, rendering the overplus, if any, to the owner of such animal.

Wrecks of the sea are thus described by Blackstone in his Commentaries (*l*): "Another maritime revenue is that of shipwrecks; which are also declared to be the king's property by the prerogative statute 17 Edw. II. c. 2; and were so, long before, at the common law. It is worthy observation how greatly the law of wrecks has been altered, and the rigour of it gradually softened in favour of the distressed proprietors. Wreck, by the ancient common law, was where any ship was lost at sea, and the goods or cargo were thrown upon the land; in which case these goods, so wrecked, were adjudged to belong to the king; for it was held, that, by the loss of the ship, all property was gone out of the original owner. But this was undoubtedly adding sorrow to sorrow, and was consonant neither to reason nor humanity. Wherefore it was first ordained by King Henry I. that if any person escaped alive out of the ship it should be no wreck; and afterwards King Henry II., by his charter, declared that, if on the coasts of either England, Poictou, Oleron or Gascony, any ship should be distressed, and either man or beast should escape or be found therein alive, the goods should remain to the owners, if they claimed them within three months; but otherwise should be esteemed a wreck, and should belong to the king, or other lord of the franchise. This was again confirmed with improvements by King Richard I.; who, in the second year of his reign, not only established these concessions by ordaining that the owner, if he was shipwrecked and escaped, ' *omnes res suas liberas et quietas haberet*,' but also that, if he perished, his children, or, in default of them, his brethren and sisters, should retain the

Wrecks of the sea.

(*l*) Vol. 1, p. 291.

property ; and in default of brother or sister, then the goods should remain to the king. And the law, as laid down by Bracton in the reign of Henry III., seems still to have improved in its equity. For then, if not only a dog (for instance) escaped, by which the owner might be discovered, but if any certain mark were set on the goods, by which they might be known again, it was held to be no wreck. And this," says Blackstone, " is certainly most agreeable to reason ; the rational claim of the king being only founded upon this, that the true owner cannot be ascertained. Afterwards, in the Statute of Westminster the First, the time of limitation of claims given by the charter of Henry II. is extended to a year and a day, according to the usage of Normandy ; and it enacts : that if a man, a dog, or a cat escape alive, the vessel shall not be adjudged a wreck. These animals, as in Bracton, are only put for examples ; for it is now held, that not only if any live thing escape, but if proof can be made of the property of any of the goods or lading which come to shore, they shall not be forfeited as wreck."

"It is to be observed," continues Blackstone (*m*), " that in order to constitute a legal wreck, the goods must come to land. If they continue at sea, the law distinguishes them by the barbarous and uncouth appellations of *jetsam, flotsam*, and *ligan*. *Jetsam* is where goods are cast into the sea, and there sink and remain under water : *flotsam* is where they continue swimming on the surface of the waves : *ligan* is where they are sunk in the sea, but tied to a cork or buoy, in order to be found again. These are also the king's, if no owner appears to claim them ; but, if any owner appears, he is entitled to recover the possession. For even if they be cast overboard without any mark or buoy, in order to lighten the ship, the owner is not by this act of

Jetsam, flotsam, and ligan.

(*m*) Vol. 1, p. 292.

necessity construed to have renounced his property: much less can things ligan be supposed to be abandoned, since the owner has done all in his power to assert and retain his property. These three are therefore accounted so far a distinct thing from the former, that by the king's grant to a man of wrecks, things jetsam, flotsam, and ligan will not pass."

The right to wreck of the sea was in ancient times frequently granted by the Crown to lords of manors and other persons; and it may be claimed by a subject either by express grant or by prescription. But, as Lord Hale remarks (n), "He that hath wreck of the sea or royal fish by prescription *infra manerium*, it is a great presumption that the shore is part of the manor, as otherwise he could not have them" (o).

The procedure in case of wreck is now governed by the Merchant Shipping Act, 1854 (p), amended by the Merchant Shipping Act Amendment Acts, 1855 (q) and 1862 (r). The Board of Trade has now throughout the United Kingdom the general superintendence of all matters relating to wreck; and it may, with the consent of the Treasury, appoint any officer of customs, or of the coastguard, or any officer of inland revenue, or, when it appears to such board to be more convenient, any other person to be a *receiver of wreck* in any district (s). The receiver is authorized to summon such number of men as he thinks necessary, to require aid from any ship or boat near at hand, or to demand the use of any waggon, cart, or horses that may be near

Right to wreck of the sea by grants or prescription.

Receivers of wreck.

(n) Hale, de Jure Maris, part 1, c. 6; Hargrave's Law Tracts, p. 27.

(o) See *ante*, p. 266.

(p) Stat. 17 & 18 Vict. c. 104, part 8.

(q) Stat. 18 & 19 Vict. c. 91, ss. 19, 20.

(r) Stat. 25 & 26 Vict. c. 63, ss. 49—53.

(s) Stat. 17 & 18 Vict. c. 104, s. 439.

at hand, with a view to the preservation of any ship or boat stranded or in distress at any place on shore, or her cargo and apparel (*t*). In cases where any lord of a manor or other person is entitled for his own use to any unclaimed wreck, such person must deliver to the receiver a statement containing the particulars of his title, and the address to which notices are to be sent; and upon such statement being so delivered, and proof made to the satisfaction of the receiver of the validity of such title, it shall be his duty, whenever he takes possession of any wreck, to send within forty-eight hours thereafter a description of the same, and of any marks by which it is distinguished, directed to such address as aforesaid (*u*). In the event of no owner establishing a claim to the wreck within a year from its coming into the possession of the receiver, the wreck must be given up, on payment of all expenses, fees, and salvage, to the person who has so given notice of and proved his title thereto (*x*). And if no owner establishes his claim to wreck so found before the expiration of a year as aforesaid, and no lord of a manor or person other than her Majesty, either in right of her Crown or of the Duchy of Lancaster or Cornwall, is proved to be entitled to the same, then it is to be sold by the receiver, and the proceeds thereof, after payment of all expenses, fees, and salvage, are to be paid into the Exchequer and dealt with as provided by the Acts (*y*).

Royal ɣfishes, which Lord Coke mentions, are whales and sturgeons, which, when taken, belong of right to the Crown; but the right to them may be vested in the lord of a manor or other subject by grant from the Crown, or by prescription. There were other franchises

Marginal notes:

Where lord of a manor entitled to wreck.

Sale for benefit of the Crown.

Royal fishes.

(*t*) Stat. 17 & 18 Vict. c. 104, s. 442.
(*u*) Sect. 454.
(*x*) Sect. 471.

(*y*) Stats. 17 & 18 Vict. c. 104, s. 475; 25 & 26 Vict. c. 63, s. 53.

which have now been abolished, but which in former days were often vested in subjects by grants from the Crown, though they could not be claimed by prescription (z). One of these was the right to the *goods of felons*. But Goods of felons. the Act to abolish forfeitures for treason and felony, Forfeitures and to otherwise amend the law relating thereto (a), abolished. provides (b), that from and after the passing of that Act—which took place on the 4th of July, 1870—no conviction of treason, felony, or *felo de se* shall cause any forfeiture; although nothing in the Act is to affect the law of forfeiture consequent upon outlawry, and which accordingly still exists (c). Another right frequently granted to subjects was the right to *deodands*, Deodands. which are thus described in Cruise's Digest (d): "Where a person comes to a violent death by mischance, the animal or thing which was the cause of his death becomes forfeited, and is called a *deodand*; as if given to God to appease his wrath: and the forfeiture accrues to the king or the lord of the manor, having this franchise by grant from the Crown or by prescription." The right to deodands, however, like the right to the goods of felons, could not have been claimed by prescription, according to the passage from Coke upon Littleton, which I cited in my first Lecture (e). And now, by the Act to abolish deodands (f), it is provided Now that, after the 1st of September, 1846, there shall be abolished no forfeiture of any chattel for or in respect of the same having moved to or caused the death of man.

Another franchise mentioned by Lord Coke is that of Fairs and holding *fairs and markets*, in which is usually, but not markets. Tolls. necessarily, comprised the right of taking toll for goods

---

(z) *Ante*, p. 3.

(a) Stat. 33 & 34 Vict. c. 23.

(b) Sect. 1.

(c) By stat. 42 & 43 Vict. c. 59, s. 3, outlawry in civil proceedings

is now abolished.

(d) Vol. 3, tit. Franchise, p. 261.

(e) Co. Litt. 114 a; *ante*, p. 3.

(f) Stat. 9 & 10 Vict. c. 62.

sold in the fair or market, and also for pickage and stallage, or the right of picking up the ground and setting up booths and stalls in the market or fair (*g*). When a person has a right to hold a market within a certain district, the presumption is that the original grant from the Crown is for the holding of the market at any convenient place within that district; and ac-

cordingly the owner of the market may change the site of it to any other place within the district within which it is to be held. But this removal cannot be made, if it interferes with the prescriptive rights of other persons, the origin of which might have been a condition contained in the original grant, that such persons should enjoy some particular privilege, connected with the market, which they cannot enjoy if the market place

is removed. Thus in the case of *Ellis* v. *The Mayor, Aldermen and Burgesses of the Borough of Bridgnorth* (*h*), it appeared that, from time immemorial, a weekly market had been held in the High Street of Bridgnorth. The market belonged to the corporation of Bridgnorth, who were also lords of the manor in which the borough is situate. The plaintiff was the owner of a house in the High Street, and he and the previous owners and occupiers of that house, as well as several other occupiers of houses in High Street, had from time immemorial erected, on market days, stalls opposite their respective houses, and had exposed thereon goods for sale in the market, or let the stalls for hire to others who had done so; and no payment had ever been made or claimed by the corporation for stallage, or for tolls of things sold at such stalls, though they took tolls of similar produce exposed elsewhere in the market. The corporation removed the market to another place within the borough, at a small distance from the High Street: and so necessarily injuriously affected the interests of

(*g*) See *Yard* v. *Ford*, 2 Wms.   R., 12 Ch. Div. 468.
Saund. 172; *Elwes* v. *Payne*, L.   (*h*) 15 C. B., N. S. 52.

those who had rights in the old market. And it was held that the plaintiff was entitled to maintain an action against the corporation for the unlawful disturbance by them of his enjoyment of this right.

The right of *stallage* is a right for a payment to be made, to the owner of the market, in respect of the exclusive occupation of a portion of the soil, for the purpose of selling goods in the market. And in the case of *The Mayor, Aldermen and Burgesses of Great Yarmouth* v. *Groom* (i), it was held that, in order to enable the owner of a market to claim payment for stallage, it was not necessary that the stall should be fixed into the soil; but that if the person selling goods used a chair and a large wooden basket (in this case four feet long, two feet and a half wide, and two feet high) with a lid which formed a table, on which provisions were exposed for sale, he was liable for stallage, quite as much as if he had had a stall in the market fixed in the ground. The right of stallage, being a right to the exclusive occupation of a portion of the soil, is liable to be rated for the poor. But tolls taken by the owner of a market in respect of cattle brought into the market for sale, which tolls become due as soon as the cattle are brought into the market place, and before the cattle are put into a pen or tied up, are mere market tolls, and are not in the nature of stallage, or tolls taken in respect of the use of the soil; and, in assessing the lessee of the market and tolls to the poor rate, in respect of his occupation of the market place, such tolls cannot be taken into account as enhancing the value of the occupation. This was decided in the case of *The Queen* v. *Casswell* (k).

A practice has grown up in modern times of selling

Stallage.

Mayor, &c. of Great Yarmouth v. Groom.

Stallage rateable.

Tolls not rateable.

The Queen v. Casswell.

(i) 1 H. & C. 102.
(k) L. R., 7 Q. B. 328. See   *Percy* v. *Ashford Union*, C. A., 34 L. T., N. S. 597.

Sale by
sample not
sale in
market overt.

corn and seeds by sample, instead of in bulk. And it is held that such a sale is not a sale in *market overt* or open market, and does not give the purchaser by sample an indefeasible title to goods bought, which, as we have seen (*l*), a sale in open market generally does. Thus

Crane v.
London Dock
Company.

in the case of *Crane* v. *The London Dock Company* (*m*), it was held that a sale made by sample in a shop in the city of London, in which, by the custom of the city, every shop is a market overt for the goods sold therein, was not a sale in market overt. Mr. Justice Blackburn remarked (*n*), "It is pretty clear that the privilege given by law to a sale in market overt of binding property against the true owner, was originally given in consequence of its policy of encouraging markets and commerce. I agree with the plaintiff's counsel so far. But I think that for that purpose the vendor [purchaser] must buy the goods under circumstances such as would induce him to think the sale a good sale in market overt; namely, he must buy a thing which is openly exposed in market overt, under such circumstances that he might say to himself, no person but the owner would dare to expose them for sale here, and therefore I have a right to assume that the shopkeeper has a right to sell them. I think this principle runs through all the cases, that the goods must be corporally present and exposed in the market." A sale of goods

Disturbance
of market.

by sample, within a market, is a disturbance of the market, and renders the vendor liable in damages to the owner of the market for the tolls of which he is thus deprived. But such a sale of goods, near to, but without the market, is not necessarily actionable. Thus

Mayor, &c. of
Brecon v.
Edwards.

in the case of *The Mayor, Aldermen and Burgesses of the Borough of Brecon* v. *Edwards* (*o*), the plaintiffs claimed a market within the town of Brecon, and brought an action against the defendant for selling corn by sample

---

(*l*) *Ante*, p. 283.   (*n*) Page 320.

(*m*) 5 Best & Smith, 313.   (*o*) 1 Hurl. & Colt. 51.

within the borough. It appeared that the defendant's son went, as his agent, on a market day to the shop of a person within the borough, near the market place, and there sold him by sample some oats, which were delivered on the following market day. And it was held that the defendant was entitled to the judgment of the Court, there being, in the opinion of the Court, no infringement of the plaintiff's market by this transaction. The substance of the decision seems properly summed up in the marginal note, which is, " That a sale by sample on a market day, near to but without the limits of the market, is not a disturbance of the market, unless it is done designedly and with the intention to evade payment of toll."

Markets and fairs are frequently established by Act of Parliament. And in the year 1847 an Act was passed for consolidating in one Act certain provisions usually contained in Acts for constructing or regulating markets and fairs, called the Markets and Fairs Clauses Act, 1847 (p). It has been held, in a case in Ireland, that the protection attendant upon a sale in market overt is not confined to ancient markets, created by charter or by prescription, but extends to modern markets established under powers conferred by Act of Parliament (q). And with regard to sales, it has been held, in another case in Ireland (r), that a person, not being a licensed hawker, was liable to be committed and fined for selling corn by sample in a place other than his own dwelling-place or shop, within the municipal boundary of the city of Londonderry, the bulk of the corn being at the time of sale within the municipal boundary. The sale by sample, the corn being within the boundary, was held to be a breach of the 13th

Markets and fairs established by Act of Parliament.

Sale by sample.

(p) Stat. 10 & 11 Vict. c. 14.
(q) *Gauly* v. *Ledwidge*, 10 Ir. p. Com. Law, Q. B. 33.
(r) *Mayor of Londonderry* v. *M'Elhiney*, 9 Ir. Rep., Com. Law, C. P. 71.

section of the Markets and Fairs Clauses Act, 1847, which provides that, after the market-place is open for public use, every person, other than a licensed hawker, who shall sell or expose for sale in any place within the prescribed limits, except in his own dwelling-place or shop, any articles in respect of which tolls are, by the special Act, authorized to be taken in the market, shall for every such offence be liable to a penalty not exceeding 40s.

Change of fair days.

The Act to amend the law relating to fairs in England and Wales (s), which may be shortly cited as "The Fairs Act, 1873," empowers the secretary of state (t), upon representation duly made to him by the justices acting in and for the petty sessional division in which any fair is held, or by the owner of any fair in England or Wales, that it would be for the convenience and advantage of the public that any such fair should be held in each year on some day or days other than that or those on which such fair is used to be held, or on the day or days on which such fair is used to be held and any preceding or subsequent day or days, or on or during a less number of days than those on which such fair is used to be held, it shall be lawful for a secretary of state to order the same to be held accordingly. This Act repeals a former Act on the same subject (u). And by a previous Act, called "The Fairs Act, 1871" (x), it is provided (y) that, in case it shall appear to the secretary of state for the home department, upon representation duly made to him by the magistrates of any petty sessional district, within which any fair is held, or by the owner of any fair in England or Wales, that it would be for the convenience and advantage of the public that any such fair shall be

(s) Stat. 36 & 37 Vict. c. 37.   (x) Stat. 34 & 35 Vict. c. 12.
(t) Sect. 6.   (y) Sect. 3.
(u) Stat. 31 & 32 Vict. c. 51.

abolished, it shall be lawful for the secretary of state Power to abolish fairs. for the home department, with the previous consent in writing of the owner for the time being of such fair, or of the tolls or dues payable in respect thereof, to order that such fair shall be abolished accordingly. But notice of such representation, and of the time for taking it into consideration, shall be published as provided by the Act. And, by a further section (z), so soon as any such order shall have been made by the secretary of state for the home department, notice Notice. thereof is to be published in the London Gazette, and in some one newspaper of the county, city or borough in which such fair is usually held, or, if there be no newspaper published therein, then in the newspaper of some county adjoining or near thereto; and thereupon such fair shall be abolished.

The right of toll may also be in respect of a way. Tolls. Tolls of this kind are divided into toll traverse and toll thorough. *Toll traverse* is properly where a man pays Toll traverse. a certain toll for passing over the soil of another man, in a way which is not a high street. *Toll thorough* is Toll thorough. properly where a toll is taken of men for passing through a vill in the high street, or for passing over a public ferry or a public bridge. A good deal of the law with respect to tolls will be found in the case of *Lawrence* v. *Hitch*, in the Exchequer Chamber (a). In *Lawrence* v. *Hitch*. that case a toll of 1s. for every cartload of vegetables exposed for sale in a street within the town and manor of Cheltenham, and for which no toll had been paid in the market, was claimed by the lord of the manor, under a grant in the reign of King Henry III., confirmed by King Charles I. in a grant of the manor in fee to persons under whom the plaintiff claimed, with all the tolls due by reason of markets, &c. within the lordship. One objection made to the toll was on the

(z) Sect. 4. (a) L. R., 3 Q. B. 521.

ground that it was rank, that is to say, that, according to the value of money in early days, it was impossible that so large a sum as 1s. should have been ever sanctioned as a moderate and proper toll to be paid for

Rankness. a mere cartload of vegetables. And this doctrine of rankness is well known to the law; and, before tithes were commuted, a *modus* or composition which had been long paid in lieu of tithes, was often defeated on the ground of *rankness;* that is, that it could not have existed from time immemorial, because, in ancient times, the sum paid would, according to the then value of money, have been too large a sum for the tithe for which it was substituted. And in a case about the

Bryant v. Foot. same time in the Exchequer Chamber, namely, *Bryant* v. *Foot* (b), in which the judges differed very much in opinion, the question was whether a fee of 13s. on every marriage, namely, 10s. to the rector, and 3s. to the clerk, was not rank, as too large a sum to have been paid in the times of Richard I., when, as you may remember, legal memory began (c). However, in the case of *Lawrence* v. *Hitch* (d), the Court seemed disposed to think that 1s. for every cartload of vegetables was not void for rankness; but that, if it were so, the Court might dispense with the claim by prescription, and presume a lawful origin of the toll by means of a contemporaneous dedication of the streets to the public, and a reservation of this toll on the part of the Crown—such dedication and reservation having been made within the time of legal memory. It was also held that the claim might be sustained as a claim to a reasonable toll only, the amount of which might vary from time to time with the value of money.

(b) L. R., 3 Q. B. 497.   (d) *Ante*, p. 299.
(c) *Ante*, p. 4.

LECTURE XXI.

I now come to consider the law of *Easements*. An easement is defined in Mr. Gale's Treatise on Easements (*a*), as a privilege without profit, which the owner of one neighbouring tenement hath of another, existing in respect of their several tenements, by which the servient owner is obliged to suffer or not to do something on his own land for the advantage of the dominant owner. Easements are therefore incorporeal rights, imposed upon corporeal property ; but, unlike most of the rights which we have been hitherto considering, they do not confer any right to a participation in the profits arising from the servient tenement. In order to constitute an easement, there must be a dominant tenement on the one hand, and a servient tenement on the other hand. In the case of *Rangeley* v. *Midland Railway Company* (*b*), the present Lord Chancellor remarked that "there can be no easement properly so called unless there be both a servient and a dominant tenement. There can be no such thing according to our law, or according to the civil law, as what I may term an easement in gross. An easement must be connected with a dominant tenement." A right of common of pasture, a right of several pasture, a right of mining in common, or an exclusive right of mining, or an exclusive right of sporting, may be given to a person in gross, irrespective of the enjoyment of any tenement. But easements or privileges with respect to land, which confer no right to participate in the profits of the land, cannot be granted to a man and his heirs, irrespective of the enjoyment of any tene-

Easements, definition of.

No easement in gross.

(*a*) Part 1, chap. 1.　　　(*b*) L. R., 3 Ch. 306, 310, 311.

ment. If they are unconnected with the enjoyment of any tenement, they are mere personal privileges, and they cannot be assigned by the grantee to any other person. Thus, if I give a man leave to walk across my land, this is a mere privilege, personal to himself, and no one but he can enjoy it. But if I grant to him and his heirs and assigns, owners and occupiers of a neighbouring house, a right of way across my land, to and from his house, this is an easement and may be enjoyed at all times by my grantee and by everyone to whom the house may belong or be let.

An easement, if appendant or appurtenant to land, must relate to the land to which it is appendant or appurtenant. This rule is in analogy to the rules with regard to *profits à prendre*. A right of *profit à prendre*, in respect of a tenement, must be for something or other to be consumed upon. that tenement (*c*). So an easement, appendant or appurtenant to a tenement, must relate to that tenement. Thus, if a way is appurtenant to a house, and belongs to the house, it must be a right of way to and from that house, and not a right to enjoy a road for other purposes than those connected with the house. This was decided in the

important case of *Ackroyd* v. *Smith* (*d*). In that case the plaintiff brought an action of trespass against the defendant for using a road ; and the defendant pleaded a conveyance by lease and release made between one Ellis Cunliffe Lister and other persons, by which certain premises were conveyed to one John Smith, his heirs and assigns, and by the deed of release the said Ellis Cunliffe Lister granted to John Smith, his heirs and assigns, that he and they respectively, being owners and occupiers for the time being of the close, pieces or parcels of land thereby released, or any of them, and all persons having occasion to resort

(*c*) *Ante*, pp. 192, 205.   (*d*) 10 C. B. 164.

thereto, should have the privilege of passing and re-passing *for all purposes* in, over and through the road in the plea first mentioned, or in, over and through some other road in the same direction, to be formed by and at the expense of the plaintiff, his heirs or assigns, such other road passing in a manner prescribed by the deed. Here you observe an attempt to give to the owners and occupiers for the time being of the land conveyed, not only a right to pass and repass over a certain road for the purpose of going to and from the house, which would have been good enough; but also a right of passing over that road *for all purposes whatever*, which of course might include a right of passing over the road for the purpose of going to and fro between two totally distinct tenements; and this, being too wide a purpose, was considered to be illegal. The Court in their judgment held (*e*) that, if the right conferred by the deed set out was only to use the road in question for purposes connected with the occupation and enjoyment of the land conveyed, it did not justify the acts confessed by the plea. And if the grant were more ample, and extended to using the road for purposes unconnected with the enjoyment of the land, which they thought was the true construction of it, it became necessary to decide whether the assignee of the land and appurtenances would be entitled to it. And they held that the privilege or right in question did not inhere in the land, did not concern the premises conveyed or the mode of occupying them, and was not appurtenant to them. And they considered that it would be a novel incident annexed to land, that the owner and occupier should, for purposes wholly unconnected with that land, and merely because he is owner and occupier, have a right of road over other land.

This case has sometimes been considered as having

(*e*) Page 187.

decided more than it appears to have actually done ; but the decision itself is in complete analogy with the decisions with respect to all other prescriptive rights, which, when claimed in respect of a tenement, must be for the use and enjoyment of the tenement in respect of which they are claimed (*f*). The following remarks on the case of *Ackroyd* v. *Smith* were made in the case of *Thorpe* v. *Brumfitt* (*g*). Lord Justice James observed, "The case of *Ackroyd* v. *Smith* has been misapprehended. It was there in substance said to the defendants, ' In any view of the case you are wrong. If this was a right of way appurtenant to a particular property, it could only be used for purposes connected with that property, and you have been using it for other purposes. If it was not, then it was a right in gross, and could not be assigned to you.' " Lord Justice Mellish observed (*h*), that in that case the close to which it was sought to make the way appendant was not at the end of the road. And he quotes the remark of Mr. Justice Cresswell, who said in his judgment, " It is not in the power of a vendor to create any rights not connected with the use or enjoyment of the land and annex them to it ; nor can the owner of land render it subject to a new species of burden, so as to bind it in the hands of an assignee. It would be a novel incident annexed to land that the owner and occupier should, for purposes wholly unconnected with that land, and merely because he was owner and occupier, have a right of road over other land."

Remarks on Ackroyd v. Smith in Thorpe v. Brumfitt.

Affirmative and negative easements.

Easements are divided into affirmative easements and negative easements. On this subject I cite a passage in Gale on Easements (*i*). " From the civil law may be taken a practically useful division of easements into two principal classes, which may be termed

(*f*) *Ante*, pp. 192, 205.   (*h*) Page 657.
(*g*) L. R., 8 Ch. 650, 655, 657.   (*i*) Chap. 2, p. 19, 4th ed.

affirmative and negative. Those coming under the head of *affirmative easements* authorize the commission of acts which, in their very inception, are positively injurious to another, as a right of way across a neighbour's land, or a right to discharge water, every exercise of which rights may be the subject of an action. *Negative easements* are injuries consequentially only restricting the owner of the soil in the exercise of the natural rights of property, as where he is prevented building on his own land to the obstruction of lights. With respect to this latter class, it is evident that no cause of action can arise from their exercise; they can be opposed only by an obstruction to their enjoyment." Easements are also divided into *continuous easements* and *easements which are not continuous*. Continuous easements are those of which the enjoyment is or may be continual, without the necessity of any actual interference by man, as a waterspout, or right to light and air. *Discontinuous easements* are those, the enjoyment of which can only be had by the interference of man, as rights of way, or a right to take water, of which I gave an instance in my Second Lecture (*k*); referring to the case of *Race* v. *Ward* (*l*), in which it was held that a right to take water from a spring was not a *profit à prendre*, but an easement. The enjoyment of such an easement can only be had by man's interference, so that it is one of a discontinuous kind.

Continuous and discontinuous easements.

Now easements being prescriptive rights may be gained either by prescription or by grant. And first with regard to the title by prescription. A right to an easement may be gained from enjoyment as of right, and without interruption, from time whereof the memory of man runneth not to the contrary; or it may be gained from enjoyment of a sufficient length to cause the Courts to presume that a grant of it must have been made at some time or another; or it may

Title by prescription.

(*k*) *Ante*, p. 18.   (*l*) 4 El. & Bl. 702.

W.P.   x

be gained by an enjoyment, either for twenty or forty
years, according to the provisions of the Prescription
Act (*m*), to which I shall have to call your attention.

Immemorial enjoyment.

And first, an easement may be gained by immemorial
enjoyment, from time whereof the memory of man
runneth not to the contrary. On this point I wish to call

Aynsley v. Glover.

your attention to the important case of *Aynsley* v. *Glover*,
decided in the first instance by the present Master of
the Rolls (*n*), and affirmed on appeal by the Lord
Justices (*o*). In that case it was held that the Prescription Act of 2 & 3 Will. IV. c. 71, did not take away
any of the modes of claiming easements, which existed
before its passing. The contest was with regard to
ancient lights in a building forming part of an inn; and
the question was, whether the plaintiff had made out
his right to the light, in respect of four windows mentioned in the pleadings. And during the course of the
argument it was observed by Lord Justice Mellish, "It
is every-day practice to plead, first, enjoyment for
twenty years before action; second, enjoyment for
forty years before action; third, enjoyment from time
immemorial; fourth, a lost grant; and it has always
been understood that a right may be supported on the
third ground, although it may be incapable of being
supported under the first or second. There are no
negative words in the statute to take away rights
existing independently of it." The enjoyment which
the Lord Justice mentions for twenty and forty are the
periods mentioned in the Prescription Act; and you see,
he says distinctly the right may be supported on the third
ground, that is, on the ground of enjoyment from time
immemorial, although it may be incapable of being
supported under the first and second, that is, under the
provisions of the Prescription Act. And in delivering
judgment his Lordship proceeds as follows (*p*). "The

(*m*) Stat. 2 & 3 Will. IV. c. 71.   (*o*) L. R., 10 Ch. 283.
(*n*) L. R , 18 Eq. 544.   (*p*) Page 285.

objection that is made to them is, that although they have been erected more than twenty years, yet there has been a unity of possession at any rate from the year 1849, if not before, up to within a very short time before the filing of the bill. In my opinion it is unnecessary to consider whether the plaintiff could have made out his right under the statute 2 & 3 Will. IV. c. 71; because I am of opinion that, under the circumstances of the case, the plaintiff has clearly made out a right from time immemorial. The statute 2 & 3 Will. IV. c. 71 has not, as I apprehend, taken away any of the modes of claiming easements which existed before this statute. Indeed, as the statute requires the twenty years or forty years (as the case may be), the enjoyment during which confers a right, to be the twenty years or forty years next immediately before some suit or action is brought with respect to the easement, there would be a variety of valuable easements which would be altogether destroyed, if a plaintiff was not entitled to resort to the proof which he could have resorted to before the Act passed. Now in this case there is an old man above eighty years old, who says, that he recollects these windows all his life; that before the cottages, in which the windows in question are, became part of the inn to which they now belong, they were occupied as separate cottages; that he was born in one of them; and that the windows were there as far back as he knew the cottages, subject to this, that two of the windows had been considerably enlarged in the year 1846. It also appears that the cottages were in existence in the year 1808; for in a deed dated in that year they are conveyed as being then in existence. I quite agree with the Master of the Rolls that it must, of course, be inferred that the windows were in existence then. Beyond that, we know nothing about them, and therefore the proof is that the cottages, with the lights in them, have existed as far back as living memory goes, and we have no evidence as to when they were built; and although there is clear evidence of unity of possession in the year 1849, and there is a question whether that unity of possession may not have commenced between the years 1830 and 1840, still it is clear that there were a great number of years before during which there was no unity of possession, and there is no evidence that there ever was any unity of title at all. Under those circumstances there is, I apprehend, clear evidence of a right to the light from time immemorial, which is not in any way taken away by the statute. I am, therefore, of opinion that the plaintiff has proved his right to these four lights." It must, however, always be remembered that a prescriptive right, claimed by virtue of immemorial user, may always be destroyed by proof on the other side that there was any time, subsequent to the commencement of legal memory, namely, the first year of King Richard I., at which the right did not exist. For if the right began within legal memory, it cannot have been used from time immemorial (q).

Lost grant.   The next mode of proving a title is, by such a measure of enjoyment as would warrant the Court to direct the jury to presume that there must have been a grant of the easement, which was lost. One of the cases with respect to a lost grant most frequently referred to, is that of *Cowlam* v. *Slack* (r), which I mentioned in a former Lecture (s). In these cases, as is mentioned by Mr. Taylor in his Law of Evidence (t), it seems now to be finally settled that juries in such cases should not be required to find, as a fact, that a deed of grant has been actually executed, but that, without believing any grant to have been made, they may often, under the instruction of the Court, presume its existence, for the simple purpose of quieting possession. But the presumption of the grant can only arise when the person against

(q) *Ante*, p. 5.   (s) *Ante*, p. 170.
(r) 15 East, 108.   (t) Vol. 1, p. 146, 6th ed.

whom the right is claimed might have interrupted or prevented the user relied on.

Another, and the most usual mode of acquiring an easement, is by enjoyment for the period mentioned in the Prescription Act (*u*), to which I referred in former Lectures, when speaking of rights of common and other *profits à prendre* (*x*). The two periods mentioned in the Act in the first section, with respect to these rights, are, as you may remember, respectively thirty and sixty years (*y*) ; but with regard to rights of way, and other easements, the periods are different. For it is enacted in the second section that no claim, which may be lawfully made at the common law, by custom, prescription, or grant, to any way or other easement, or to any watercourse or the use of any water, to be enjoyed or derived upon, over or from any land or water of our said lord the king, his heirs or successors, or being parcel of the duchy of Lancaster or of the duchy of Cornwall, or being the property of any ecclesiastical or lay person, or body corporate, when such way or other matter as herein last before mentioned, shall have been actually enjoyed by any person claiming right thereto, without interruption, for the full period of *twenty years*, shall be defeated or destroyed by showing only that such way or other matter was first enjoyed at any time prior to such period of twenty years ; but nevertheless such claim may be defeated in any other way by which the same is now liable to be defeated ; and where such way or other matter as herein last before mentioned shall have been so enjoyed as aforesaid, for the full period of *forty years*, the right thereto shall be deemed absolute and indefeasible, unless it shall appear that the same was enjoyed by some consent or agreement expressly given or made for that

The Prescription Act.

Sect. 2.

Twenty years' enjoyment.

Forty years' enjoyment.

(*u*) Stat. 2 & 3 Will. IV. c. 71.   (*y*) *Ante*, p. 173.
(*x*) *Ante*, p. 173.

purpose by deed or writing. Here you observe that
the claim must be one which may be lawfully made;
and if any such claim has been actually enjoyed by a
person claiming right thereto, without interruption, for
twenty years, it cannot now be defeated merely by showing that it was first enjoyed at some time within legal
memory. And a similar enjoyment for forty years
makes the right absolute and indefeasible, unless some
express consent or agreement is shown to have been
given or made by deed or writing.

There is a separate provision in the third section
with respect to the access and use of light, to which I
hope to call your attention in a future Lecture, when
speaking of that subject.

Defeat of
claim raised
by twenty
years' enjoy-
ment.

You will observe that a mere twenty years' enjoyment may be defeated in any other way by which the
same was, at the passing of the Act, liable to be
defeated. Instances of the way in which such a claim
might have been defeated at the time of the passing of
the Act, are given by Mr. Baron Parke in his judgment
in the case of *Bright* v. *Walker* (*z*); he remarks (*a*):
"Again, such claim may be defeated in any other way
by which the same is now liable to be defeated; that
is, by the same means by which a similar claim, arising
by custom, prescription or grant would now be defeasible: and therefore it may be answered by proof of
a grant, or of a licence, written or parol, for a limited
period; comprising the whole or part of the twenty
years, or of the absence or ignorance of the parties interested in opposing the claim, and their agents, during
the whole time that it was exercised." And, accordingly, in that case of *Bright* v. *Walker*, it was held that,
where a way had been used adversely and under a claim
of right for more than twenty years, over land which,

Baron Parke
in *Bright* v.
Walker.

(*z*) 1 Cro. Mee. & Rosc. 211.   (*a*) Page 219.

during the whole of that period, was in the possession of a lessee for lives under the Bishop of Worcester, that this user gave no right as against the Bishop, nor did it give any title as against the lessees. For, before the passing of the Act, user as of right for twenty years, when the land during the whole period was in the possession of a lessee for life, was not sufficient to cause a presumption of immemorial user as against the owner of the fee simple. Indeed, the case of a tenancy for life is distinctly provided for in the 7th section of the Act to which I have already called your attention (b).

The provisions of the 4th, 5th, 6th, and 7th sections, which apply to claims of rights of common and *profits à prendre*, apply also to claims to ways or other easements, and to watercourses and the use of water. These provisions I have already mentioned (c). With regard to the 6th section, it is observed by Lord Chancellor Westbury in the case of *Hanmer* v. *Chance* (d), that the meaning seems to be, that no presumption or inference in support of the claim shall be derived from the bare fact of user or enjoyment for less than the prescribed number of years; but where there are other circumstances in addition, the statute does not take away, from the fact of enjoyment for a shorter period, its natural weight as evidence, so as to preclude a jury from taking it, along with other circumstances, into consideration as evidence of a grant.

Meaning of sect. 6. Lord Westbury in *Hanmer* v. *Chance*.

The 8th section has no application to claims of rights of common or other *profits à prendre*. It provides, that "when any land or water, upon, over or from which any such way or other convenient watercourse (which words are supposed to be a misprint for other easement or watercourse,) or use of water shall have been or shall be

Sect. 8.

(b) *Ante*, p. 175.
(c) *Ante*, pp. 174, 175.

(d) 4 De Jones & Smith, 626, 631.

enjoyed or derived, hath been or shall be held under or
by virtue of any term of life or any term of years, exceeding three years from the granting thereof, the time
of the enjoyment, of any such way or other matter as
therein last before mentioned, during the continuance
of such term, shall be excluded in the computation of
the said period of forty years, in case the claim shall,
within three years next after the end or sooner determination of such term, be resisted by any person entitled
to any reversion expectant on the determination thereof."
So that in these cases an enjoyment, even of forty
years, does not give an absolute and indefeasible title;
for if the servient tenement is held for the life of any
person, or for any term of years exceeding three from
the time of granting thereof, the life of the tenant for
life, or the term of years during which the property
is held, is excluded in the computation of the period of
forty years. But this exception only applies in case the
claim is resisted within three years next after the end or
sooner determination of the life estate, or the term of
years subsisting in the servient tenement.

In the case of *Bright* v. *Walker*, to which I have
just referred (*e*), there are some remarks with regard to
the construction of the 8th section of the statute, which
have been dissented from and corrected in the more

Palk v.
Skinner.

recent case of *Palk* v. *Skinner* (*f*). In *Bright* v. *Walker*,
Baron Parke considered that the 8th section applied not
only to the term of forty years appointed by the Act,

Section 8 does
not apply to
the period of
twenty years.

but also to the term of twenty years. This, however,
was denied in the case of *Palk* v. *Skinner*, in which the
facts were as follows :—The way had been used for
twenty years. The land over which the right of way
was claimed had been demised in 1831 for a term of
fourteen years ; and again in 1838 by a fresh lease for
a term of eight years, ending in 1846. No resistance

(*e*) *Ante*, p. 310.   (*f*) 18 Q. B. 563.

had been made to the user at any time during or after
the determination of the leases until the 1st of June,
1851, when the defendant obstructed the way. And
it was held that by this user a right of way had been
acquired, as against the owner of the fee. Lord Camp-
bell remarks (*g*), "I am of opinion that the plaintiff
is entitled to our judgment. I think that there was
evidence from which the jury might find that he was
entitled to claim a right of way under sect. 2 of the
Act 2 & 3 Will. IV. c. 71. I do not say that the
evidence was conclusive; but it was sufficient to justify
their finding; and that finding ought not to be disturbed unless the plaintiff's claim is defeated by sect. 8.
I am of opinion that it is not. The period during
which the land, over which the right of way is claimed,
has been leased for a term exceeding three years is not,
under that section, to be excluded from the computation
of a twenty years' enjoyment; though it is no doubt to
be excluded from the computation of an enjoyment
for forty years. Sect. 7 excludes certain times, including that of a tenancy for life, but not that of a tenancy
for years, from the computation of the periods thereinbefore mentioned; and a twenty years' enjoyment is
one of those periods. But sect. 8 provides for the
exclusion of certain other times, among which is a
tenancy of more than three years, not from the periods
thereinbefore mentioned, but from one particular period
only, expressly mentioned, namely, that of an enjoyment for forty years. It is clear, therefore, that it
was not intended to exclude them from the computation of an enjoyment for twenty years. Great reliance
was placed upon *Bright* v. *Walker;* but on examination
into that case, it appears that there was no necessity
for the Court to give any opinion as to the effect of
sect. 8, for the right of way there claimed was clearly
destroyed under sect. 7 by reason of a tenancy for

(*g*) Page 573.

life." And Mr. Justice Erle remarked (*h*), " If this case had arisen before the statute, there would have been good evidence to go to the jury of a user as of right for twenty years, notwithstanding the existence of the tenancy for years. And the question is still to be left to the jury in the same way; for the statute makes no difference in the various modes of defeating the user, except as it provides that it shall not be defeated by proof of origin at some time prior to the twenty years. The question then arises whether, under sect. 8, the tenancy for years is to be excluded from the computation of twenty years' enjoyment. That section applies expressly to the computation of an enjoyment for forty years; and it would be contrary to all rules of construction to hold that it applies also to the computation of an enjoyment for twenty years. The only possible ground for such a conclusion is found in *Bright* v. *Walker*. But there the question was as to the exclusion of a tenancy for life, and the Court was clearly right in holding that such tenancy must be excluded from the computation of a twenty years' enjoyment. It is so excluded under sect. 7, and I do not see that its exclusion is made more clear by sect. 8. But I do not think the learned judge ever meant to say that a tenancy for years must be excluded from the computation of an enjoyment for twenty years."

(*h*) Page 575.

LECTURE XXII.

ANOTHER mode of acquiring easements is by *grant* Grant.
either express or implied. With regard to an express
grant, if clearly made by the owner of the servient
tenement to the owner of the dominant tenement his
heirs and assigns, owners and occupiers for the time
being of the dominant tenement, there is little to be
said. But a great many cases, and some of them conflicting, have arisen as to the grant of easements by
mere *general words*, as they are called, and also as to an General
implied grant of easements being made under certain words.
circumstances without any general words. With regard
to the use of *general words*, as they are called, it seems
clear that any easement or right whatsoever, whether Easements
appendant or appurtenant to land, will, if it be strictly pass by con-
appendant or appurtenant, pass by a conveyance of the veyance of
dominant tenement, without any express mention, and tenement.
without the use of the words " with the appurtenances ;"
although these words no doubt are much better to be
used, in order to show clearly the intent that every
right appurtenant to the land should pass with it. The
conveyance of the principal carries that which is accessory.
In the times when writing was not necessary to the
conveyance of land, a feoffment of the land carried
with it all incorporeal rights, which were appendant or
appurtenant to the land ; although if any such rights
had been conveyed in gross, or apart from anything
corporeal, a deed of grant would have been abso-
lutely necessary. So in the case of *Skull* v. *Glenister* (*a*), *Skull* v.
a demise had been made of land, to which a way led, *Glenister.*
for a term less than three years at a rack rent. Such a

(*a*) 16 C. B., N. S. 81.

demise, you may remember, is excepted out of the Statute of Frauds (*b*), which requires most other demises to be in writing. And accordingly the demise in the present case had been made by parol. And it was

Parol demise.

held that the parol demise carried with it the right to use the way belonging to the land during the term granted by the parol demise.

Easement extinguished by unity of possession.

But in some cases an easement, or other appurtenant right, which formerly belonged to land, may have been extinguished by unity of possession. Thus, there may have been a right of way to field A. over field B. whilst the ownership of the fields was different. Afterwards the two fields may have belonged to the same owner; by which the right of way to field A. over field B.

Regrant by general words.

would be extinguished. If then the owner of the two closes should convey field A., together with all easements to the same belonging, or therewith usually held or enjoyed, the way, having formerly existed as an easement, and having been, up to the date of the conveyance, actually enjoyed in practice, (not of course as an easement, which a man cannot have in his own soil, but as what may be called *a quasi easement*,) would pass as an easement enjoyed with the land. A grant of field A. with the easements usually held therewith, would pass the right of way, as, in point of law, a new easement, created by the deed, and granted, by means of the above general words, to the grantee of A. his heirs and assigns, and to be for ever thereafter enjoyed by him and them over the field B. as such easement was anciently enjoyed before the ownership of the two closes had destroyed it.

But, more than this, it is now held that it is not absolutely necessary that the easement in question should ever have existed as a legal easement, enjoyed

(*b*) Stat. 29 Car. II. c. 3.

in respect of one property over another property. For if the two properties have all along been enjoyed by the same owner, and he and his servants have been accustomed to use a watercourse, or a way, from one part of his property to the other, for the quasi benefit of that other property, either in the case of a watercourse, for aiding its fertility, or in the case of a way, for more convenient access to it; and afterwards he conveys to a stranger that part of the property which may be called the quasi dominant tenement, namely, that part of the property which has enjoyed this, which might have been a right had the ownership been different; then he creates, if he use such general words as I have mentioned, a new easement of a similar kind, and conveys the same to the grantee. Thus in the case of *Watts* v. *Kelson* (c), it appeared that in the year 1860 the owner of properties A. and B. made a drain from a tank on property B. to a lower tank on the same property, and laid pipes from the lower tank to cattle sheds on property A., for the purpose of supplying them with water; and they were so supplied till 1863, when the owner sold property A. to the plaintiff, with all waters, watercourses, &c. to the same hereditaments and premises belonging or appertaining, or with the same or any part thereof held, used, enjoyed, or reputed as part thereof, or as appurtenant thereto. The plaintiff had the use of the water after his conveyance until the defendant, a subsequent purchaser of property B., stopped it. It was held that the general words were sufficient to pass the right to the flow of water. It was also held (but this is a point I am coming to presently) that the plaintiff would have been entitled to the use of the water, without any express words of grant. Here you see the easement or right to water was not created whilst the properties were in distinct ownership, but arose from the act of the owner of both

(c) L. R., 6 Ch. 166.

Kay v. *Oxley*. properties, while they were both in his own possession. Another case on the same subject is that of *Kay* v. *Oxley* (d). In that case the defendant Oxley was the owner in fee of a dwelling house, with a cottage and stable belonging to it, called " Roseville ; " and he was also owner in fee of an adjoining farmstead and farm, having a private road, which led from a high road to the farm buildings, and passed close by one side of the stable of Roseville. By indenture of the 1st of May, 1860, the defendant demised Roseville to one Hudson for ten years. Hudson entered on the premises, and built over the stable a hay loft, with two openings towards the private farm road, having first obtained permission from the defendant to do so, and also permission from the defendant and the then tenant of the farm, to use the farm road for the purpose of bringing hay, straw, &c. to the loft, that being the only access to the openings in the loft. Hudson, and the sub-tenants occupying Roseville, continued during the term to use the road up to May, 1870. At that time the plaintiff agreed to purchase Roseville of the defendant ; and, by a deed of the 2nd of August, 1870, the defendant conveyed Roseville to the plaintiff in fee, with the following general words, amongst others, " together with all ways, and rights of way, easements, and appurtenances to the said dwelling-house, cottage, and hereditaments, or any of them appertaining, or with the same or any of them now or heretofore demised, occupied or enjoyed, or reputed as part or parcel of them, or any of them, or appurtenant thereto." It was strongly contended that there never had been any right of way existing over this private road in respect of Roseville. But the Court held that the right to use the farm road for the purposes of the loft passed to the plaintiff under the above words. The Court in that case takes notice of and comments upon other decisions

(d) L. R., 10 Q. B. 360.

on similar points, with which I think it scarcely necessary to trouble you ; as these two cases appear to me to have established the principle that a quasi easement actually enjoyed at the time of the conveyance may be newly created as an actual easement by the grant of easements usually enjoyed with the premises, or reputed as part of them, or appurtenant thereto.

In some cases, however, an easement will pass by implication, by conveyance of property, without any grant for that purpose. This arises in the case of an easement, which is an easement of necessity and a continuous easement, as distinguished from a right of way or other easement, which is not continuous, but which requires to be exercised from time to time. It was said by Chief Justice Erle in the case of *Polden* v. *Bastard* (e), in a passage which has been often quoted and relied upon, "There is a distinction between easements, such as a right of way or easement used from time to time, and easements of necessity or continuous easements. The cases recognize this distinction, and it is clear law that, upon a severance of tenements, easements used as of necessity, or in their nature continuous, will pass by implication of law without any words of grant; but with regard to easements which are used from time to time only, they do not pass, unless the owner, by appropriate language, shows an intention that they should pass." Such an implication may arise upon the grant of part of a tenement, when there will pass to the grantee all those continuous and apparent easements over the other part of the tenement, which are necessary to the enjoyment of the part granted and have been hitherto used therewith (f). It may also arise in the case of a devise to different persons of tenements previously in the ownership of the same

Implied grant.

Easement necessary and continuous.

Chief Justice Erle in Polden v. Bastard.

(e) L. R., 1 Q. B. 156, 161.   (f) *Wheeldon* v. *Burrows*, L. R., 12 Ch. D. 31.

person (*g*). Moreover, upon a sale *at one and the same time* to different persons of tenements belonging to the same vendor, it has been held that necessary and continuous easements, to be enjoyed in right of one of the tenements so sold, over another of them, may pass by implication (*h*). But although, as we have seen, a *grant* of easements for the benefit of a grantee may be implied, yet, as a general rule, upon a severance of tenements there is no corresponding implication in favour of the grantor of a *reservation* of continuous and apparent easements to be exercised in right of a tenement retained by him over a tenement granted. This

Wheeldon v. *Burrows*.

was laid down in the recent case of *Wheeldon* v. *Burrows* (*i*), where the Court dissented from the principle expressed in a previous case of *Pyer* v. *Carter* (*k*). In the case of *Wheeldon* v. *Burrows*, a workshop and an adjoining piece of land belonging to the same owner were put up for sale by auction. The workshop was not then sold, but the piece of land was sold, and was soon afterwards conveyed to the purchaser. A month after this the vendor agreed to sell the workshop to another person, and in due time conveyed it to him. The workshop had windows overlooking and receiving their light from the piece of land first sold. And it was held by Vice-Chancellor Bacon, and afterwards by the Court of Appeal, that, as the vendor had not when he conveyed the piece of land reserved the right of access of light to the windows, no such right passed to the purchaser of the workshop, and that the purchaser of the piece of land could build so as to obstruct the windows of the workshop; and that, whatever might

(*g*) *Barnes* v. *Loach*, L. R., 4 Q. B. D. 494; see also *Pearson* v. *Spencer*, 3 B. & S. 761.

(*h*) *Compton* v. *Richards*, 1 Price, 27; *Swansborough* v. *Coventry*, 9 Bing. 305; see also *Barnes* v.

Loach, L. R., 4 Q. B. D. 494.

(*i*) L. R., 12 Ch. D. 31; see also *Ellis* v. *Manchester Carriage Co.*, L. R., 2 C. P. D. 13.

(*k*) 1 H. & N. 916.

have been the case had both lots been sold at the same sale by auction, there was, under the circumstances, no implied reservation of any right over the piece of land first sold. Of the law with regard to the access of light, I hope to speak in a subsequent Lecture (*l*).

Lord Justice Thesiger, in a judgment which contains a critical examination of all the authorities, states the law of the implication of easements as follows (*m*): "We have had a considerable number of cases cited to us, and out of them I think that two propositions may be stated as what I may call the general rules governing cases of this kind. The first of these rules is, that on the grant by the owner of a tenement of part of that tenement as it is then used and enjoyed, there will pass to the grantee all those continuous and apparent easements (by which of course I mean *quasi* easements), or, in other words, all those easements which are necessary to the reasonable enjoyment of the property granted, and which have been and are at the time of the grant used by the owners of the entirety for the benefit of the part granted. The second proposition is that, if the grantor intends to reserve any right over the tenement granted, it is his duty to reserve it expressly in the grant. Those are the general rules governing cases of this kind, but the second of those rules is subject to certain exceptions. One of these exceptions is the well-known exception which attaches to cases of what are called ways of necessity; and I do not dispute for a moment that there may be, and probably are, certain other exceptions to which I shall refer before I close my observations upon this case. Both of the general rules which I have mentioned are founded on a maxim which is as well established by authority as it is consonant

(*l*) *Post*, Lecture XXIV.   (*m*) L. R., 12 Ch. D. 49.

to reason and common sense, viz., that a grantor shall not derogate from his grant."

Exceptions to rule.
The nature of the exceptions to the rule mentioned by the Lord Justice was discussed by him in a subsequent part of his judgment (*n*), and also by Vice-Chancellor Bacon in delivering the judgment of the Court below (*o*). The following appear to be the grounds of exception :—the necessity of the case, as in the instance of a way of necessity (*p*) ; the intention of the parties, upon which depends the rule of the implication of easements, upon a sale at one and the same time to different persons of tenements previously belonging to the same vendor (*q*) ; or mutual benefit in cases where reciprocal easements may be implied, which may be illustrated by the implication of reciprocal rights of support in the case of houses built together (*r*). It thus appears, that if, upon the alienation of a piece of land, the owner should desire to reserve to himself any easements over it, all the easements to be reserved should be fully and clearly defined in the deed of conveyance.

An easement such as a way may, under certain circumstances, be erected by a mere conveyance of land. Thus if I grant a person a piece of land in the middle of my field, he has, by implication of law, a **Way of necessity.** *way of necessity* over my land for the purpose of getting at it, otherwise the grant would be of no avail (*s*). And, under the grant of any easement, that which is necessary for the enjoyment of the easement passes by **Necessary repairs.** implication. Thus, under the grant of a drain, there

(*n*) 12 Ch. D. 57—60.

(*o*) 12 Ch. D. 44.

(*p*) *Pinnington* v. *Galland*, 9 Ex. 1; *Davies* v. *Sear*, L. R., 7 Eq. 427.

(*q*) *Ante*, p. 320.

(*r*) *Richards* v. *Rose*, 9 Ex. 218. See also Lord Justice Thesiger's explanation of *Pyer* v. *Carter*, 1 H. & N. 916, at 12 Ch. D. 59.

(*s*) 2 Bl. Com. 36.

passes, by implication of law, a right to enter and repair the drain, in case at any time it should get out of order (*t*).

If an easement be not necessary and continuous it will not be created by the conveyance of the land, in respect of which it has been used, but to which it is not strictly appendant or appurtenant, without the use of some general words comprising "easements therewith usually held or enjoyed." Thus in the case of *Worthington* v. *Gimson* (*u*), certain lands, part lying at Naneby, a hamlet of Market Bosworth in the county of Leicester, and part lying in the parish of Newbold Vernon, belonged in the year 1822 to the late Sir E. C. Hartopp and Mr. John Pares, each being seised of an undivided moiety. A right of way existed from a farm which was part of this property and situate at Naneby, across certain lands in Newbold Vernon, part of the same farm, to another farm on the same property in Newbold Vernon; and this right of way had for many years been used by the occupiers of either farm. So that the way, you perceive, was not appendant or appurtenant strictly to either farm; because the whole belonged in moieties to Sir E. C. Hartopp and Mr. Pares. In the year 1820, a deed of partition was executed between them; and Sir E. C. Hartopp conveyed his undivided moiety of that part of the property which was in the parish of Newbold Vernon to Mr. Pares; including, among other farms, so much of the farm lying at Naneby and Newbold Vernon as was in Naneby, "with their and every of their rights, members, easements and appurtenances." Mr. Pares also, by the deed, conveyed his undivided moiety of that part of the property lying in Newbold Vernon to Sir E. C. Hartopp. The deed

Easement not necessary and continuous will not pass without express grant.

Worthington v. *Gimson.*

(*t*) *Pomfret* v. *Ricroft*, 1 Wms. Saund. 321, 323; *Richard Liford's case*, 11 Rep. 52 a.

(*u*) 2 Ellis & Ellis, 618; see also *Bolton* v. *Bolton*, L. R., 11 Ch. D. 968.

Y 2

contained no express reservation of the right of way to either party. The plaintiff, who was then the occupier, and the previous occupiers, of the farm at Naneby, used the right of way from 1820 to 1859; when it was obstructed by the defendant, the then occupier of the farm in Newbold Vernon. In an action by the plaintiff for such obstruction, it was held that he could not recover, because the right of way did not pass under the deed of partition, not being an apparent and continuous easement necessarily passing upon the severance of the property, as incident to the separate enjoyment of the portion severed. Now if, instead of a right of way, this had been a right of drainage, it is clear, on the authorities I have mentioned, that it would have passed, being a necessary and continuous easement. It seems also clear that if the deed of partition, in addition to the words "with their and every of their rights, members, easements and appurtenances," had contained a grant of ways or easements "therewith usually held or enjoyed," that the way would have passed as a new creation of a right of way, analogous to the *quasi* right, which had, previously to the deed of partition, been enjoyed by the occupiers of the two farms.

Ways.

I now proceed to consider a few points respecting the law of ways. I do not propose to consider public rights of way, as they are not, properly speaking, easements. A way may be either a footway, or a bridleway, or a driftway for cattle, or a right of way with carts and carriages for agricultural purposes, or for mining purposes, or for all purposes whatever; indeed it is difficult to say how many kinds of ways there may be. On this subject I may cite a passage from Coke upon Littleton (*x*), in which he divides ways into three kinds. He says,

The different kinds of ways.

"there be three kind of ways whereof you shall read in our ancient books. First, a footway, which is called *iter*,

(*x*) Co. Litt. 56 a.

quod est jus eundi vel ambulandi hominis; and this was the first way. The second is a footway and horse-way, which is called *actus, ab agendo;* and this vulgarly is called *packe* and *prime way*, because it is both a footway, which was the first or *prime way*, and a *packe* or *drift way also.* The third is *via* or *aditus*, which contains the other two, and also a cartway, &c., for this is *jus eundi, vehendi et vehiculum et jumentum ducendi;* and this is two-fold, viz. *regia via*, the king's highway for all men, *et communis strata*, belonging to a city or town, or between neighbours and neighbours. This is called in our books *chimin*, being a French word for a way, whereof cometh *chiminage, chiminagium* or *chimmagium*, which signifieth a toll due by custom for having a way through a forest; and in ancient records it is sometime also called *pedagium*."

A right to one kind of way, gained by prescription from long enjoyment, or by an enjoyment under the Prescription Act (*y*), or acquired by grant, does not authorize the use of the way for any more extensive purpose than that for which it has been acquired or granted. Thus in the case of *Wimbledon and Putney Commons Conservators* v. *Dixon* (*z*), it was held that the immemorial user of a right of way for all purposes for which a road was wanted in the then condition of the property, does not establish a right of way for all purposes, in an altered condition of the property; where that would impose a greater burden on the servient tenement. It was also held that, where a road had been immemorially used to a farm, not only for agricultural purposes, but, in certain instances, for carrying building materials to enlarge the farm-house, and rebuilding a cottage on the farm, and for carting away sand and gravel dug out of the farm, that this did not establish a right of way for carting the materials required for

A way can only be used for the purpose for which it was acquired.

Wimbledon and Putney Commons Conservators v. Dixon.

building a number of new houses on the land. The
principle of cases of this kind of course is, that immemorial user implies a grant for the purpose for which
the road has been immemorially used; and such a grant
by no means necessarily includes a right to use the road
for other purposes, which would impose upon the
servient tenement a greater burden than was already

*Bradburn v.
Morris.*

laid upon it. So in the case of *Bradburn v. Morris*, in
the Court of Appeal (*a*), it was held that the user for
twenty years of a way to a field, used only for agricultural purposes, does not give a right of way for
mineral purposes.

Division of
dominant
tenement.

If, however, the dominant tenement should be divided
into more tenements than one, a right of way granted
to the owners and occupiers for the time being of the
dominant tenement, gives a right of way to the owner
and occupier for the time being of every part of the
severed lands. This was decided in the recent case of

*Newcomen v.
Coulson.*

When right
of way ac-
quired for all
purposes.

Newcomen v. *Coulson*, in the Court of Appeal (*b*).
Another question decided in this case was as to the
extent of a right of way, granted by an award made in
1760, under an Inclosure Act. It awarded that the
owner and owners for the time being of the lands
thereby allotted should for ever thereafter have a way,
right, and liberty of passage, for themselves and their
respective tenants and farmers, of the said lands, as well
on foot as on horseback, as with carts and carriages, and
to lead and drive their horses, oxen, and other cattle
between certain points therein named, doing as little
damage to the soil, corn, grass, or herbage as might be.
In case the owners for the time being of the respective
allotments should street out the same way leading
through their allotments, the same should be made and
ever after remain eleven yards broad at the least,

(*a*) L. R., 3 Ch. D. 812.   *Western Railway Co.*, Ex. Div.,
(*b*) 25 W. R. 469; 5 Ch. D.   28 W. R. 229.
133. See also *Finch* v. *Great*

between the quick sets; but such way was not to be a right of way for any other person whomsoever. The land forming one of the allotments which, at the time of the award, was used only for agricultural purposes, had been severed, and part of it had been recently purchased by the defendant, and by him laid out in building plots; and he intended to construct a macadamized road, for the use of the new houses, over that part of the land in respect of which the right of way had been granted. The plaintiff, who was lord of the manor and the owner of the adjoining land, brought an action against the defendant for an injunction. But it was held, affirming the decision of Vice-Chancellor Malins, that the right was a general right of way, for all reasonable purposes, to all the houses which might be built on the lands in question, and that the plaintiff was not entitled to the relief claimed by him.

It is clear, however, that if a right of way be acquired by prescription or grant to one close or parcel of land, the owner of the right of way will not be justified in using the way for the purpose of going to any other land, beyond or beside that to which the way was granted. The grant expressed or implied was only a right of way to one particular close; and it would subject the servient tenement to a burden, not contemplated by the original grant, if it were made use of for the purpose of going to other closes beyond or beside that to which the way originally led. Thus, in the case of *Skull* v. *Glenister* (c), by an indenture dated the 4th September, 1861, made between the plaintiffs of the one part, and Robert Wheeler and Thomas Wheeler of the other part, the plaintiffs conveyed to them a piece of land, which afterwards came into the possession of the defendant, together with the right of way or passage, ingress, egress, and regress with horses, carts,

Way to one close cannot be used to another close.

Skull v. Glenister.

(c) 16 C. B., N. S. 81; *ante*, p. 315.

or carriages, or otherwise, upon or over a certain bridge, and in, through and over the several closes in the declaration mentioned, as belonging and appertaining to the piece of land then in the possession of the defendant Glenister. And the plaintiff contended that the defendants had used the right of way for the purpose of going beyond Wheeler's close, and delivering materials on to their own land. It appeared in evidence that the defendants, who had hired Wheeler's close, used it for a place of deposit for building materials to be used upon their own land adjoining. It was contended on the part of the plaintiffs that if Wheeler's close was used merely as a means of getting to Glenister's close, that was not a user of the way within the terms of the grant. The question which the learned judge left to the jury was whether the defendants used the way as a way to Wheeler's land, or was it a mere colorable use of it for the purpose of getting at their own land; or did the defendant use the way merely for the purpose of carrying the building materials through Wheeler's close to their own land. The jury decided that the use was a mere colorable use of the way, and found for the plaintiff with 3*l.* damages. The Court were of opinion that that was the correct way to leave the question.

Repairs of road.

Grantee may repair.

With regard to the repairs of a road or way, the person that has the right of way has the right of repairing the way; and the owner of the servient tenement is not bound to repair the way, in the absence of any duty on his part cast upon him by the act or agreement, either of himself or of his predecessors in title. As the grantee of a right of way may repair it if he pleases, so,

No right to deviate.

in case it should become impassable for want of repair, he has no right to deviate from the way. In this respect there is a difference between public and private ways; for, with regard to a public way, it is generally considered that, if it should become impassable for want of repair, the public may deviate from it and go over the adjoining ground. On this subject, I may perhaps mention the recent case of *Arnold* v. *Holbrook* (*d*), in which it was held that a footpath across an arable field might be dedicated to the public with a reservation of the right to plough across it; and if it were so dedicated, the public would not, on its becoming impassable after being ploughed up, have any right to pass over the adjoining parts of the field, unless they had gained such right by prescription from immemorial user.

Arnold v. *Holbrook.* Dedication of way with right to plough across it.

A right of way is a right to go from one point to another point; and as was said by Lord Justice Mellish in the case of *Wimbledon and Putney Commons Conservators* v. *Dixon* (*e*), to which I have just referred (*f*), "If a person has land bordering on a common and it is proved that he went on the common at any place where his land might happen to adjoin it, sometimes in one place and sometimes in another, and then went over the common, sometimes to one place and sometimes to another, it would be difficult from that to infer any right of way. But if you can find the terminus *a quo* and the terminus *ad quem*, the mere fact that the owner does not go precisely in the same track for the purpose of going from one place to the other would not enable the owner of the servient tenement to dispute the right of road. Suppose the owner of this common had granted by deed to Mr. Dixon the right to go from the gate leading out of Cæsar's Camp to the highway by the National School with carriages and horses at his free will and pleasure. I cannot suppose that the grant would fail in point of law, because it did not point out the precise definite track between the one terminus and the other, in which he was to go in using the

When way not defined. Lord Justice Mellish in *Wimbledon and Putney Commons Conservators* v. *Dixon.*

(*d*) L. R., 8 Q. B. 96.   (*f*) *Ante*, p. 325.
(*e*) L. R., 1 Ch. D. 362, 369.

right of way. If the owner of the servient tenement does not point out the line of way, then the grantee must take the nearest way he can. If the owner of the servient tenement wishes to confine him to a particular track, he must set out a reasonable way; and then the person is not entitled to go out of the way, merely because the way is rough and there are ruts in it, and so forth."

LECTURE XXIII.

I now proceed to consider a few points with respect to the law of *Watercourses*. And the subject naturally divides itself into two heads, namely, 1st, the right of the riparian proprietor to the *use* of the water of a stream which runs through or along his land; and 2ndly, the right of the riparian proprietor to have the water which flows down come to him in its pure and natural state, *unpolluted* with extraneous matter.

Water-courses.

Use.

Pollution.

On the first point the law is concisely laid down by Sir John Leach in the case of *Wright* v. *Howard* (a). He says, "The right to use of water rests on clear and settled principles. Primâ facie the proprietor of each bank of a stream is the proprietor of half the land covered by the stream, but there is no property in the water. Every proprietor has an equal right to use the water which flows in the stream; and, consequently no proprietor can have the right to use the water to the prejudice of any other proprietor. Without the consent of the other proprietors who may be affected by his operations, no proprietor can either diminish the quantity of water, which would otherwise descend to the proprietors below, nor throw the water back upon the proprietors above. Every proprietor, who claims a right either to throw the water back above, or to diminish the quantity of water which is to descend below, must, in order to maintain his claim, either prove an actual grant or licence from the proprietors affected by his operations, or must prove an uninterrupted enjoyment of twenty years; which term of twenty

Wright v. *Howard*.

(a) 1 Sim. & Stu. 190, 203.

years is now adopted upon a principle of general convenience as affording conclusive presumption of a grant."
This was laid down in the year 1823, before the
passing of the Prescription Act (b), which was not
passed until the year 1832. Prior to the Act the
presumption of a grant certainly arose from twenty
years' uninterrupted user as of right; but, as we have
seen (c), the presumption was not always quite conclusive; and in that respect perhaps the law, as laid down
by the Vice-Chancellor, might require a little modification. But, with regard to the right of each riparian
proprietor to the benefit of the water of every natural
stream, unaffected by the acts of any proprietor either
above or below him, the law as laid down in *Wright* v.
Howard still remains; although in many points the
exact rights of the respective proprietors have in recent
times been more particularly ascertained by subsequent
decisions.

With regard to the use of the water which may be
made by a riparian proprietor, the law is more particu-

Baron Parke
in *Embrey* v.
Owen.

larly expounded by Baron Parke in the case of *Embrey*
v. *Owen* (d). The question in that case turned upon
the quantity of water, which a riparian proprietor

Irrigation.

might take from the stream, for the purpose of irrigat-
ing meadows belonging to him, situate on the bank of
the stream. And in that case it was held that a diversion for the purpose of irrigation, which was not continuous, and which caused no diminution of the water
cognizable by the senses, was a diversion which might
be lawfully used. And, in delivering the judgment of
the Court, Baron Parke makes the following remarks,
speaking of irrigation: "Nor do we mean to lay down
that it would in every case be deemed a lawful enjoyment of the water, if it was again returned into the

(b) Stat. 2 & 3 Will. IV. c. 71.   (d) 6 Exch. 353, 371.
(c) *Ante*, p. 5.

river with no other diminution than that which was caused by the absorption and evaporation attendant on the irrigation of the lands of the adjoining proprietor. This must depend upon the circumstances of each case. On the one hand it could not be permitted that the owner of a tract of many thousand acres of porous soil abutting on one part of the stream, could be permitted to irrigate them continually by canals and drains and so cause a serious diminution of the quantity of water, though there was no loss to the natural stream than that arising from the necessary absorption and evaporation of the water employed for that purpose; on the other hand one's common sense would be shocked by supposing that a riparian owner could not dip a watering-pot into the stream, in order to water his garden, or allow his family or his cattle to drink it. It is entirely a question of degree; and it is very difficult, indeed impossible, to define precisely the limits which separate the reasonable and permitted use of the stream, from its wrongful application; but there is often no difficulty in deciding whether a particular case falls within the permitted limits or not; and in this we think that, as the irrigation took place, not continuously, but only at intermittent periods, when the river was full, and no damage was done thereby to the working of the mill, and the diminution of the water was not perceptible to the eye, it was such a reasonable use of the water as not to be prohibited by law. If so, it was no infringement of the plaintiff's right at all; it was only the exercise of an equal right, which the defendant had to the usufruct of the stream." In accordance with this principle the case of the *Medway Company* v. *Earl of Romney and others* (e) was decided. In that case the defendants erected works on the banks of the river for the purpose of raising, and thereby raised, water from the river, for the supply of the county lunatic asylum

Medway Company v. Earl of Romney.

(e) 9 C. B., N. S. 575.

and county gaol. And it was held by the Court that these purposes were more extensive than those for which a riparian proprietor, as such, could insist upon appropriating the stream as it passed by his land. So in the case of *The Wilts and Berks Canal Navigation Company* v. *Swindon Waterworks Company* (*f*), the canal company had, under their Act, power to supply their canal with water from the neighbouring streams, and they bought a mill and turned the mill stream into the canal. Many years afterwards the waterworks company diverted part of the mill stream, and thereby supplied with water the town of Swindon, which had then a population of 7,000 or 8,000 inhabitants, brought there of late years by the establishment of the Great Western Railway Company's works; but which before had been very badly supplied with water. And it was held that the canal company, both under their Act and as owners of the mill, were riparian proprietors, and had power to prevent the unlawful use of the water by other riparian proprietors; and that the supply of the neighbouring town of Swindon with water was such an unlawful use. Lord Justice Mellish observed in the course of his judgment (*g*), "It is quite plain, indeed I do not know that it is disputed, that the diversion of the water of a stream for the purpose of sending it in large quantities to a reservoir to supply a town, is not within the right of a riparian proprietor."

The Lord Chancellor, Earl Cairns, in his judgment in the same case in the House of Lords (*h*), summarized the law on this subject as follows:—"Undoubtedly the lower riparian owner is entitled to the accustomed flow of the water for the ordinary purposes for which he can use the water, that is quite consistent with the right of the upper owner also to use the water for all ordinary

(*f*) L. R., 9 Ch. 451; 7 H. L. 697.

(*g*) L. R., 9 Ch. 461.

(*h*) L. R., 7 H. L. 704, 705.

purposes, namely, as has been said, *ad lavandum et ad potandum*, whatever portion of the water may be thereby exhausted and may cease to come down by reason of that use. But farther, there are uses no doubt to which the water may be put by the upper owner, namely, uses connected with the tenement of that upper owner. Under certain circumstances, and provided no material injury is done, the water may be used and may be diverted for a time by the upper owner for the purpose of irrigation. That may well be done; the exhaustion of the water which may thereby take place may be so inconsiderable as not to form a subject of complaint by the lower owner, and the water may be restored after the object of irrigation is answered, in a volume substantially equal to that in which it passed before. Again, it may well be that there may be a use of the water by the upper owner for, I will say, manufacturing purposes, so reasonable that no just complaint can be made upon the subject by the lower owner. Whether such a use in any particular case could be made for manufacturing purposes connected with the upper tenement would, I apprehend, depend upon whether the use was a reasonable use. Whether it was a reasonable use would depend, at all events, in some degree on the magnitude of the stream from which the deduction was made for this purpose over and above the ordinary use of the water. But, my lords, I think your lordships will find that, in the present case, you have no difficulty in saying whether the use which has been made of the water by the upper owner, comes under the range of those authorities which deal with cases such as I have supposed,—cases of irrigation and cases of manufacture. Those were cases where the use made of the stream by the upper owner has been for purposes connected with the tenement of the upper owner. But the use which here has been made by the appellants of the water, and the use which they claim the right to make of it, is not for the purpose of their tenements at all, but is a use which virtually amounts to a complete diversion of the stream—as great a diversion as if they had changed the entire watershed of the country, and in place of allowing the stream to flow towards the south, had altered it near its source so as to make it flow towards the north. My lords, that is not a user of the stream which could be called a reasonable user by the upper owner; it is a confiscation of the rights of the lower owner; it is an annihilation, so far as he is concerned, of that portion of the stream which is used for those purposes; and that is done, not for the sake of the tenement of the upper owner, but that the upper owner may make gains by alienating the water to other parties who have no connection whatever with any part of the stream."

Pollution.

Again, every riparian proprietor has the right to have the water of the stream which flows down through or beside his land, preserved by those above him in its pure and natural state, free from all pollution. But the right may exist to interfere with the course of nature by altering, not only the quantity, but also the quality of the water; and such a right is an easement which may be claimed by prescription, or by twenty years' enjoyment under the terms of the Prescription Act, 2 & 3 Will. IV. c. 71. Thus in the case of *Baxendale* v. *McMurray* (i), the defendant was the owner of an ancient paper mill, where paper had been made from rags; but he introduced a new vegetable fibre, and carried on the works upon the same scale, for making paper from this new material. For more than twenty years before this change, the refuse arising from the paper manufacture had been discharged into a stream which ran past the plaintiff's house. And it was held that the defendant had acquired a right, by long user, to discharge into the stream the washings produced by

Baxendale v.
McMurray.

(i) L. R., 2 Ch. 790.

the manufacture of paper, in the reasonable and proper course of such manufacture, using any proper materials for the purpose, so that he did not increase the pollution of the stream ; and that the onus lay on the plaintiff to prove any increase of pollution. The plaintiff contended that although the defendant had a right to pollute the stream by making paper from rags, as had been done for many years, yet he had no right in a similar way to pollute the stream by making paper of a new vegetable fibre; but on that point the judgment of the Court was against him. This case, therefore, shows that a right to pollute a stream may be gained by upwards of twenty years' user, providing the pollution carried on during the whole of that time be not increased in its quantity.

In most cases, however, the pollution is gradual, especially in cases where the pollution takes place by drainage from towns, which sometimes gradually increase in population to such an extent as to cause a pollution, imperceptible at first, to become in course of time a very great nuisance. And in that case it seems, according to the principle which pervades all cases of prescriptive right, that in order to gain a right by a user for twenty years, the user must, during the whole of the twenty years, be such a user as is claimed. And the consequence is that if, at the beginning of the twenty years, the pollution of the water was materially less than at the end of the period, no right to pollute the water can be gained by the twenty years' user, beyond the amount of pollution which existed at the commencement of the term. Thus in the case of *Crossley* v. *Lightowler* (*k*), it was laid down by Lord Chelmsford, Lord Chancellor (*l*), that the user which originates the right must also be its measure. He observes: "The first question to be determined in this

Gradual pollution.

Lord Chelmsford in Crossley v. Lightowler.

(*k*) L. R., 2 Ch. 478.　　　(*l*) Page 480.

W.P.　　　　　　　Z

case is, whether the Messrs. Irving, the occupiers of the former dye works, had acquired a prescriptive right to foul the stream. The evidence appears to me to be sufficient to establish that, for twenty years prior to 1839, when the dye works were discontinued, the foul water from those works had been discharged into the stream. The extent to which the fouling of the water took place in Messrs. Irving's time cannot of course be absolutely determined; but, looking to the evidence on the subject, it appears to me, that although similar in kind, it was considerably less in degree than since the defendants' works have been in operation. The defendants contend that, whatever may be the increased extent of the Messrs. Lightowler's buildings or of their business, their rights must be measured by the means which they had of discharging their foul water into the Hebble, and that if the watercourses which Messrs. Irving used have not been enlarged, and the means of discharge into the stream have remained the same, the plaintiffs have no ground of complaint. In answer to this argument, however, it may be observed that the right upon which the defendants insist is, not to pour water but to pour foul water into the Hebble. It may be difficult to fix a limit to such a right, where the quantity of fouling to which the prescription extends has not been far exceeded; but, where the excess is considerable, the proof will be comparatively easy. The user which originated the right must also be its measure, and it cannot be enlarged to the prejudice of any other person."

tural
eams, what
The principles above laid down apply only to natural streams. In some cases it is not easy to determine whether a stream may or may not be called a natural stream, so as to carry with it the rights and duties of riparian proprietors. A question of this kind occurred

in the case of *Holker* v. *Poritt* (*m*). In that case a natural stream divided itself at a certain point into two branches; one branch ran down to the river Irwell, and the second branch passed into a farm-yard, where it supplied a watering trough; and the overflow from the trough was formerly diffused over the ground, and found its way ultimately into the river Irwell. This branch appeared to have been made by artificial means, but was of immemorial age. In the year 1847 the owner of the land on which the watering trough stood, and thence down to the Irwell, collected the overflow into a reservoir, and conducted it by a culvert to a mill situated on the banks of the Irwell. In 1865 he became the owner of all the rest of the land through which the second branch flowed. And in 1867 he sold the mill, with all water rights, to the plaintiff. A riparian owner on the stream above the point of divergence, obstructed the flow of the water; and the plaintiff, in respect of his right to the flow of water to the mill, brought an action against the owner on the upper part of the stream for so obstructing the flow of the water. And it was held that the plaintiff was, under the circumstances, such a riparian owner as might bring an action for the obstruction of the stream against the riparian owner above the point at which the stream divided. The contention was, that the stream was merely an artificial stream, and consequently the plaintiff was not a riparian owner. But it was held that the stream was analogous to a natural stream, and that its character as a natural stream was not destroyed by the pains which had been taken to collect the water, and to pass it down to the mill by means of a culvert.

With regard to artificial watercourses, a claim similar in its nature to that of a right to pollute flowing water by manufactures or otherwise, is that which is

(*m*) L. R., 8 Ex. 107.

z 2

Right to discharge refuse water.

sometimes claimed of discharging refuse water from mines and other works, over lands belonging to other people. Such a discharge is an actionable injury (*n*); although an increased percolation of water into a neighbouring mine, caused by the proper working of a mine adjoining, does not give any right of action; such working being only the natural use which every man has a right to make of his own land (*o*). But an uninterrupted burdening of one's neighbour's land with a servitude which in its inception is actionable, or which may be prevented by him, in time gives a right to the continuance of the servitude. A right thus acquired, to let off water impregnated with mineral substances into a neighbouring watercourse, was claimed in the case of

Wright v. Williams.

Wright v. *Williams* (*p*). It was held in that case that a claim of this nature was a claim to a watercourse, within the meaning of the second section of the Prescription Act (*q*), and that accordingly a user of this kind for forty years next before the commencement of the suit gave the defendant a legal right so to dispose of his refuse water.

Right to surplus water.

Refuse water may sometimes be of great advantage to the owner of the servient tenement; and the question then arises whether, by long user, he may not only be bound to receive the water, but whether he has not by long user acquired a right to the water, so as to compel the owner of the tenement from which the water proceeds to keep up the supply of the water for the benefit of the owner of the servient tenement. An

Arkwright v. Gell.

important case on this subject is that of *Arkwright* v. *Gell* (*r*); and under the circumstances of that case it was considered that the watercourse was an artificial watercourse, made for a particular and temporary pur-

---

(*n*) *Hardman* v. *North Eastern Rail. Co.*, L. R., 3 C. P. D. 168.

(*o*) *Wilson* v. *Waddell*, L. R., 2 App. Cas. 95. See also *West Cumberland Iron and Steel Co.* v.

Kenyon, L. R., 11 Ch. D. 782.

(*p*) 1 Mee. & Wels. 77.

(*q*) Stat. 2 & 3 Will. IV. c. 71; *ante*, p. 309.

(*r*) 5 Mee. & Wels. 203.

pose, and that its water was originally taken by the owner of the servient tenement, with notice that it might be discontinued. The circumstancês of the case, therefore, did not afford any presumption of a grant of the stream, by the owners of the mines from which it issued. And it was accordingly held that the owner of the land through which the stream passed did not acquire a right to have it continued by force of the 2nd section of the statute 2 & 3 Will. IV. c. 71.

On the other hand, in the case of *Magor* v. *Chad-* wick (s), the Court of Queen's Bench held that, in the absence of a special custom, artificial watercourses are not to be distinguished in law from natural ones, a proposition with respect to which the Judicial Committee of the Privy Council have observed that as a general proposition it would be too broad (t). In the case of *Magor* v. *Chadwick*, mine owners had made an adit through their lands to drain the mines, which they afterwards ceased to work; and the owner of a brewery, through whose premises the water flowed for twenty years after the working had ceased, had, during that time, used it for brewing. And it was held that he thereby gained a right to the undisturbed enjoyment of the water, and that the mines could not afterwards be so worked as to pollute the stream. In the subsequent case of *Wood* v. *Waud* (u), it was held that no action will lie for the diversion of an artificial watercourse when, from the nature of the case, it is obvious that the enjoyment of it depends upon temporary circumstances, and is not of a permanent character; and where the interruption is by a person who stands in the nature of a grantor. And it was also held that, where water has flowed in an artificial and covered watercourse

Magor v. *Chadwick.*

Wood v. *Waud.*

(s) 11 A. & E. 571.

(t) *Rameshur Pershad Narain Singh* v. *Koonj Behari Pattuck,*

L. R., 4 App. Cas. 121, 127.

(u) 3 Exch. 748. See also *Gaved* v. *Martyn,* 19 C. B., N. S. 732.

for more than sixty years, from a colliery into an immemorial and natural stream, upon whose banks the plaintiff's mills are situated, the plaintiff, in such case, has no right of action for diversion of the water of such artificial watercourse against a party, through whose land it passes, even if he does not claim under or is unauthorized by the colliery owners. The case, however, would perhaps be different if the water were polluted. These cases seem to shadow out the law with respect to artificial watercourses. In many respects it resembles the law of natural watercourses; but the rights with regard to them vary in this respect, that, whereas a natural watercourse is the gift of nature, and exists by the bounty of providence, an artificial stream may have been created for a mere temporary purpose; and, if so created, no right to its continuance can be acquired by its enjoyment; although a sufficient length of the enjoyment of such water in a pure state may give a right to prevent the water from being polluted.

The principles which regulate the rights of owners of land in respect to water flowing in known and defined channels, whether upon or below the surface of the ground, do not apply to underground water, which

Percolation of water underground.

merely percolates through the strata in no known channels. The leading authority on this subject is that of *Chasemore* v. *Richards* in the House of Lords (x).

Chasemore v. *Richards*.

The plaintiff in that case was a mill-owner near the town of Croydon in Surrey. The mill was situate on the river Wandle; and the river was fed and supplied, above the plaintiff's mill, from the water produced by the rainfall on a district of many thousand acres in extent, comprising the town of Croydon and its vicinity. The defendant represented the Local Board of Health for the town of Croydon. The board, in order to supply

(*x*) 7 H. of L. Cas. 349.

the town of Croydon with water, and for other sanitary purposes, sank a large well to the depth of seventy-four feet in a piece of land belonging to them in the town of Croydon. The distance of this well from the commencement of the river Wandle was about a quarter of a mile. From this well they pumped up very large quantities of water, namely, between 500,000 and 600,000 gallons a day. And the result was that the water which flowed to the plaintiff's mill was sensibly diminished in quantity, and in its value as a power towards working the mill. The question was whether under these circumstances the plaintiff, the mill-owner, had any right of action against the Local Board for the injury by this means to the river Wandle. The House of Lords summoned the judges, there having been some differences of opinion in the Court below. And the judges present delivered a unanimous opinion, which was followed by the House of Lords, that, under the circumstances, the plaintiff had no right of action against the defendant for the damage done by means of their well to the quantity of water which flowed down the river.

The opinion delivered by Mr. Justice Wightman on the part of the judges, deserves perusal. Lord Kingsdown in his judgment (y) observes that the house was greatly indebted to those learned persons for· the admirable reasoning, by which they appear to have removed all doubt upon one of the most important questions that ever came under the consideration of a Court of Justice. After stating the facts of the case, Mr. Justice Wightman proceeds (z) as follows:—" The law respecting the right to water flowing in definite visible channels, may be considered as pretty well settled by several modern decisions, and is very clearly enunciated in the judgment

(y) Page 390.   (z) Page 366.

of the Court of Exchequer in the case of *Embrey* v.
Owen (*a*). But the law, as laid down in those cases, is in-
applicable to the case of subterranean water not flowing
in any definite channel, nor indeed at all in the ordinary
sense; but percolating or oozing through the soil more or
less according to the quantity of rain that may chance to
fall. The inapplicability of the general law respecting
rights to water, to such a case, has been recognized and
observed upon by many judges, whose opinions are of
the greatest weight and authority." The learned judge
then proceeds to mention several cases in which this
distinction was taken, and proceeds (*b*), " The question
then is, whether the plaintiff has such a right as he
claims *jure naturæ* to prevent the defendant sinking
a well in his own ground at a distance from the mill,
and so absorbing the water percolating in and into his
own ground beneath the surface, if such absorption has
the effect of diminishing the quantity of water which
would otherwise find its way into the river Wandle;
and by such diminution affects the working of the
plaintiff's mill. It is impossible to reconcile such a
right with the natural and ordinary rights of land
owners, or to fix any reasonable limits to the exercise of
such a right. Such a right as that contended for by
the plaintiff would interfere with, if not prevent, the
draining of land by the owner. Supposing, as it was
put at the bar in argument, a man sank a well upon
his own land, and the amount of percolating water
which found a way into it had no sensible effect upon
the quantity of water in the river which ran to the
plaintiff's mill, no action would be maintainable; but if
many landowners sank wells upon their own lands, and
thereby absorbed so much of the percolating water, by
the united effect of all the wells, as would sensibly and
injuriously diminish the quantity of water in the river,
though no one well alone would have that effect—could

(*a*) 6 Exch. 353; *ante*, p. 332.   (*b*) 7 H. of L. Cas. p. 370.

an action be maintained against any one of them, and if any, which? for it is clear that no action could be maintained against them jointly. In the course of the argument one of your Lordships [Lord Brougham] adverted to the French artesian well at the Abattoir de Grenelle, which was said to draw part of its supplies from a distance of forty miles, but underground, and, as far as is known, from percolating water. In the present case the water which finds its way into the defendant's well is drained from and percolates through an extensive district; but it is impossible to say how much from any part. If the rain which has fallen may not be intercepted whilst it is merely percolating through the soil, no man could safely collect the rain water as it fell into a pond; nor would he have a right to intercept its fall before it reached the ground, by extensive roofing from which it might be conveyed to tanks, to the sensible diminution of water which had, before the erection of such impediments, reached the ground, and flowed to the plaintiff's mill. In the present case, the defendant's well is only a quarter of a mile from the river Wandle; but the question would have been the same if the distance had been ten or twenty or more miles distant: provided the effect had been to prevent underground percolating water from finding its way into the river, and increasing its quantity, to the detriment of the plaintiff's mill. Such a right as that claimed by the plaintiff is so indefinite and unlimited that, unsupported as it is by any weight of authority, we do not think that it can be well founded, or that the present action is maintainable; and we, therefore, answer your Lordships' question in the negative." The question was whether, under the circumstances stated in the case, the Croydon Local Board of Health was legally liable to the action of the appellant for the abstraction of the water in the manner described. Another case of the same kind, decided on the authority of *Chasemore* v. *Richards*, is that of *The Queen v. The Metropolitan Board of Works* (c), to which I think I need not do more than refer.

The limits of the doctrine of these cases may be found in the subsequent case of *The Grand Junction Canal Company* v. *Shugar* (d). In that case the defendant represented the Local Board of Health of the town of Tring; and the suit was brought against them by the Grand Junction Canal Company, for the purpose of restraining them from diverting certain water belonging to the canal company. This water belonged to the company by virtue of interceptions made by them, under the powers of their Acts, of a certain stream, flowing from the Silk Millpond near Tring; which interceptions caused the water to flow into a branch of their canal at a high level. The Local Board of Health made a drain near and below the Silk Millpond. It was not disputed that the drain and other works of the Local Board had lowered the water in the Silk Millpond, and that the water now came out at a lower level, and had to be pumped up by the plaintiffs; but there was considerable conflict of evidence as to the manner of the interference. However, in the view which the Lord Chancellor took of the evidence, it was established that some of the water flowing in the stream was withdrawn from the stream by the action of the drain. And his Lordship was of opinion that although a landowner will not in general be restrained from drawing off the subterranean waters in the adjoining land, yet he will be restrained if, in so doing, he draws off the water flowing in a defined surface channel through the adjoining land. His Lordship observes (e), that the distinction is plain. "If you are simply using what you have a right to use, and leaving your neighbour to use the rest of the water as

(c) 3 Best & Smith, 710.   (e) Page 487.

(d) L. R., 6 Ch. 483.

it flows on, you are entitled to do so; but you must not appropriate that which you have no right to appropriate to yourself. In this case there is *ex concessis*, a defined channel in which this water was flowing; and I think the evidence is clear that some of it is withdrawn by the drain which the Local Board have made. As far as regards the support of the water, all one can say is this: I do not think *Chasemore* v. *Richards* or any other case has decided more than this; that you have a right to all the water which you can draw from the different sources which may percolate under ground; but that has no bearing at all on what you may do with regard to water which is in a defined channel, and which you are not to touch. If you cannot get at the underground water without touching the water in a defined surface channel, I think you cannot get at it at all. You are not by your operations or by any act of yours to diminish the water which runs in this defined channel, because that is not only for yourself but for your neighbours also, who have a clear right to use it, and have it come to them unimpaired in quality and undiminished in quantity. That appears to me to be clearly the course which the Local Board have taken, and, therefore, they have clearly and plainly given ground for the injunction."

You observe that in *Chasemore* v. *Richards* the action was brought in respect of water which, but for the well, would have gone into the stream. The suit in *The Grand Junction Canal Company* v. *Shugar* was in respect of water which, by means of the drains made by the defendant, was actually abstracted from the stream, after it had become a stream. In this I conceive lies the difference between the two cases.

LECTURE XXIV.

Light.

I now come to consider claims to the use of light, air, and a few other matters. The Prescription Act (*a*) shortens the time of prescription in favour of the enjoyment of light in a much more peremptory way than it does with respect to ways, watercourses, and other easements. So that, in the case of light, the Prescription Act is generally relied upon as giving a title. But, as in the case of other prescriptive rights, so in the case of a claim to light, the claim may be founded upon Immemorial enjoyment. immemorial enjoyment; and this, in fact, was the case *Aynsley* v. *Glover.* in the suit of *Aynsley* v. *Glover* (*b*), to which I called your attention in a former Lecture (*c*).

Access of light enjoyed for twenty years.

The third section of the Prescription Act (*a*) enacts "that when the access and use of light to and for any dwelling-house, workshop, or other building, shall have been actually enjoyed therewith for the full period of twenty years without interruption, the right thereto is to be deemed absolute and indefeasible, any local usage or custom to the contrary notwithstanding, unless it shall appear that the same was enjoyed by some consent or agreement expressly made or given for that purpose by deed or writing." This period, like the other Sect. 4. periods, must, by the fourth section, be deemed and taken to be the period next before some suit or action, wherein the claim or matter, to which such period may relate, shall have been or shall be brought into question. And in this, as in the other cases, by the same section, no act

(*a*) Stat. 2 & 3 Will. IV. c. 71.   283.
(*b*) L. R., 18 Eq. 544; 10 Ch.   (*c*) *Ante*, p. 306.

or other matter shall be deemed to be an interruption within the meaning of the Act, unless the same shall have been or shall be submitted to or acquiesced in for one year after the party interrupted shall have had or shall have notice thereof and of the person making or authorizing the same to be made. You will observe that, in this case, actual enjoyment of the access and use of light for twenty years without interruption makes the right absolute and indefeasible, unless enjoyed by consent or agreement expressly made or given by deed or writing. The seventh section of the Act, therefore, which excludes from the computation of certain periods the times during which any person otherwise capable of resisting the claim shall have been an infant, idiot, non compos mentis, feme covert, or tenant for life, or during which any action or suit shall have been diligently prosecuted until abated by death of any party or parties thereto, does not apply in the case of lights; because that section excepts cases in which the right or claim is by the Act declared to be absolute and indefeasible. Nor does the eighth section apply to the case of light; for the eighth section relates only to the period of forty years mentioned in the Act; and the period of forty years has nothing whatever to do with any claim to the access and use of light. *Sect. 7 does not apply.* *Sect. 8 does not apply.*

It follows, therefore, that if I erect a house on my own land, with windows overlooking my neighbour's land; and the access and use of light to and for my house through those windows continues to be actually enjoyed therewith for the full period of twenty years without interruption, I get an absolute and indefeasible right to the use of the light from that time forward; unless it can be shown that I enjoyed the right by some consent or agreement of my neighbour expressly made or given for that purpose by deed or writing. That being so, the question not unfrequently occurs, on the *Landowner's remedy in respect of* part of landowners whose neighbours begin building houses with windows overlooking their lands, as to what course they should take in order to prevent the windows becoming, by a twenty years' user, permanent injuries to the landowner's property. Now one answer to this question is, that the landowner, under such circumstances, has no right to prevent his neighbour from building upon his own land, and from making windows in the houses so built, overlooking the landowner's property, whatever the nature of that property may be; whether it be a garden in which he wishes for privacy, or land on which he may intend himself to build some day. In truth, his only remedy is to interrupt the access and use of light to the buildings, which have been erected with windows overlooking his own land; and this he can only do by erecting, which he has a perfect right to do, any building, screen or other erection on his own land in such a way as to block out his neighbour's lights. And this he must do before these lights have been enjoyed for the full period of twenty years; but he may do it, and do it with impunity, at any time prior to the expiration of the period of twenty years from the making of the windows.

One of the leading cases with regard to the right to light is that of *Tapling* v. *Jones* (e). It was an action brought by the respondent Jones against the appellant Tapling for obstructing the respondent's lights, and the facts were substantially as follows: Jones, the plaintiff below, was a silk mercer, and at the time of the action carried on business at Nos. 107, 108, and 109, Wood Street, Cheapside. He had been in possession of Nos. 108 and 109 for several years. They were on the west side of Wood Street, and abutted in the rear or eastward on premises belonging to the defendant Tapling, numbered 1 to 8, and called Gresham Street property. In

(e) 11 H. of L. 290.

the year 1852 the plaintiff pulled down Nos. 108 and 109, Wood Street, and erected on their site new warehouses, in doing which he altered the position and enlarged the dimensions of the windows previously existing, increased the height of the buildings, and set back the rear line of them so as to approach nearer to the defendant's premises. With regard to No. 107, Wood Street, the lights in which were the cause of the dispute, the plaintiff became possessed of it in the year 1857; up to that time it had been a public-house known as the "Magpie and Pewter Platter," which possessed ancient windows, entitled to access of light and air from an open space belonging to the defendant, and called "The Flying Horse Court," situate between the plaintiff's premises and those of the defendant. On obtaining possession of No. 107, the plaintiff began to make alterations in it, in order to make the floors of all his premises correspond with each other. He lowered the first and second floors, and lowered the windows in them to agree with the floors. One of the windows was brought down about one foot lower than before; the other was about the same size as the old one, and both occupied parts of the old apertures. One small window in the first floor was blocked up. The plaintiff also built two additional stories, in the first of which he opened a new window, and in the other he placed a window extending across the whole width of the building. These new windows were so situated that it was impossible for the defendant, the owner of the Gresham Street property, to obstruct or block them, without also obstructing or blocking to an equal or greater extent that portion of the windows in the new building which occupied, but with an enlarged space, the site of the ancient windows in the "Magpie and Pewter Platter." The plaintiff's alterations were completed in August, 1857. At the end of the year 1856, the defendant Tapling had pulled down the buildings then standing

on the Gresham Street property, in order to erect
thereon a warehouse; and in 1857, after the plaintiff's
buildings had been completed, the defendant proceeded
to erect his warehouse, and built up the eastern wall
thereof to such a height as to obstruct the whole of the
windows and lights in the premises of No. 107. This
wall was completed by the end of October, 1857. On
the subject of these buildings a correspondence took
place between the attornies for the plaintiff and defendant during the months of September and October,
1857; each insisted that the other was exceeding his
rights, and notices of opposition were mutually given.
Before the 4th February, 1858, the plaintiff, by the
advice of counsel, caused the altered windows in the
building formerly the "Magpie and Pewter Platter,"
to be restored to their original state as to size and
position, and he caused the new windows in the new
portion of the building to be blocked up by filling up
the spaces with brickwork. On the 4th February,
1858, the plaintiff's attorney gave notice to the defeu-
dant, Tapling, to pull down the wall he had erected,
and to "restore Jones' premises to their former light
and air." The case found that the new windows of
No. 107 could not have been obstructed in a more
convenient manner than by building up a wall of
sufficient height on the defendant's premises. The
action, you will observe, was by the plaintiff Jones, for
obstructing the ancient lights belonging to No. 107,
the title to which was obtained while the windows
formed part of the ancient public-house known as the
"Magpie and Pewter Platter." There was a great
difference amongst the judges, both in the Court below
and in the Court of Exchequer Chamber; but the
majority were in favour of the plaintiff. And on
appeal the House of Lords were of the same opinion
as the majority of the judges, but not for the same
reasons, and held that the defendant Tapling was

liable to an action for obstructing the ancient lights of No. 107, notwithstanding the fact that the plaintiff by his alteration had considerably enlarged the windows. Lord Westbury, then Lord Chancellor, in his judgment observes (*f*): "Before dealing with the present appeal it may be useful to point out some expressions, which are found in the decided cases, and which seem to have a tendency to mislead; one of these expressions is the phrase 'right to obstruct.' If my adjoining neighbour builds upon his land, and opens numerous windows, which look over my garden or my pleasure grounds, I do not acquire from this act of my neighbour any new or other right than I before possessed. I have simply the same right of building or raising any erection I please on my own land, unless that right has been by some antecedent matter either lost or impaired, and I gain no new or enlarged right by the act of my neighbour. Again, there is another form of words which is often found in cases on this subject, namely, the phrase 'invasion of privacy by opening windows.' That is not treated by the law as a wrong, for which any remedy is given. If A. is the owner of beautiful gardens and pleasure grounds, and B. is the owner of an adjoining piece of land, B. may build on it a manu-factory with a hundred windows overlooking the pleasure grounds, and A. has neither more nor less than the right, which he previously had, of erecting on his land a building of such height and extent as will shut out the windows of the newly-erected manufac-tory." "If," Lord Westbury continues, "in lieu of the words 'the access and use of light to and for any dwelling-house,' in the 3rd section of the statute, there be read, as there well may, 'any window of any dwell-ing-house,' the enactment, omitting immaterial words, will run thus:—'When any window of a dwelling-house shall have been actually enjoyed therewith for

Judgment of Lord Westbury.

(*f*) Page 305.

W.P.   A A

the full period of twenty years without interruption, the right to such window shall be deemed absolute and indefeasible.' Suppose then that the owner of a dwelling-house with such a window, that is, with an absolute and indefeasible right to a certain access of light, opens two other windows, one on each side of the old window, does the indefeasible right become thereby defeasible? By opening the new windows he does no injury or wrong in the eye of the law to his neighbour, who is at liberty to build up against them, so far as he possesses the right of so building on his land; but it must be remembered that he possesses no right of building so as to obstruct the ancient window; for to that extent his right of building was gone, by the indefeasible right which the statute has conferred." Again (*g*), "In the present case an ancient window in the plaintiff's house has been preserved and remained unaltered, during all the alterations of the building; and the access of light to that window is now obstructed by the appellant's wall. A majority of the Court below has held that the obstruction was justified whilst the new windows, which the plaintiff some time since opened, remained, but was not justifiable when those new windows were closed, and the house, so far as regards the access of light, was restored to its original state. But on the plain and simple principles I have stated, my opinion is that the appellant's wall, so far as it obstructed the access of light to the respondent's ancient unaltered window, was an illegal obstruction from the beginning; and I have great difficulty in acceding to the reasoning that this permanent building of the plaintiff in error was a legal act when begun and completed, but has subsequently become illegal through a change of purpose on the part of the defendant in error. On such a principle, the person who opens new lights might allow them to remain until his neighbour, acting legally according to

(*g*) Page 307.

these judgments, has, at great expense, erected a dwelling-house, and then, by abandoning and closing the new lights, might require his neighbour's house to be pulled down. I think the judgment ought to be affirmed, but not on the ground or for the reasons given by the majority of the judges in the Courts below." The other learned judges, Lord Cranworth and Lord Chelmsford, concurred with Lord Westbury, both in the decision of the case, and also in the reasons on which he considered that the judgment of the majority of the judges should be affirmed. Lord Cranworth observed (h), " The opening of a window is not an unlawful act. Every man may open any number of windows looking over his neighbour's land ; and, on the other hand, the neighbour may, by building on his own land within twenty years after the opening of the window, obstruct the light which would otherwise reach it. Some confusion seems to have arisen from speaking of the right of the neighbour in such a case as a right to obstruct the new lights. His right is a right to use his own land by building on it as he thinks most to his interest; and if by so doing he obstructs the access of light to the new windows, he is doing that which affords no ground of complaint. He has a right to build, and if thereby he obstructs the new lights he is not committing a wrong. But what ground is there for contending that, because his building so as to obstruct a new light would afford no ground of complaint, therefore, if he cannot so build without committing a trespass, he may commit a trespass? I can discover no principle to warrant any such inference."

Judgment of Lord Cranworth.

You will observe that in this case the plaintiff Jones need not have stopped up his new windows, as he did under the advice of counsel. The House of Lords held that he had, like every one else, a perfect right to put

(h) Page 311.

in new windows into his house; and the fact that he put in new windows was held by the House of Lords to be no derogation of his right to light through the ancient windows which remained. This case has been followed in the Court of Chancery in the case of *Staight* v. *Burn* (*i*). In that case the defendant built a wall to the north of the windows of the plaintiff's house, by which his ancient lights were interfered with. The plaintiff was at the same time enlarging his own premises, whereby he diminished the light coming to his own windows, by shutting off some of the light from the south and south-west. It was held, reversing the decision of Vice-Chancellor Stuart, that the plaintiff was entitled to an injunction to restrain the defendant from building the wall. In the course of his judgment Lord Justice Giffard, before whom the case came, observed (*k*), "If there is a house with three ancient windows, and it is desirable to add, at no great distance from those three ancient windows, two other windows, is it to be said that, because those two other windows are to be placed in that position, the plaintiff is not to come into Court to preserve what has been decided, in *Tapling* v. *Jones*, to be his clear legal right? Such a conclusion would not be either according to principle or to the course of this Court. I take the course of this Court to be that, when there is a material injury to that which is a clear legal right, and it appears that damages, from the nature of the case, would not be a complete compensation, this Court will interfere by injunction."

When lights are interfered with, the nature of the remedy depends upon the amount and nature of the injury sustained. In order to enable the plaintiff to maintain an action for obstructing light, it is sufficient to show that the easement cannot be enjoyed in so full and ample a manner as before, or that the premises are,

Staight v. *Burn*.

Judgment of Lord Justice Giffard.

Remedies.

Damages.

(*i*) L. R., 5 Ch. 163. (*k*) Page 167.

to a sensible degree, less fit for the purpose of business or occupation. For an obstruction of this kind the owner of the lights may obtain damages (*l*). If, however, damages are not a sufficient remedy, and if it appear that there will be a diminution of a substantial amount of light, so as to substantially make the house less comfortable, then an injunction will be granted to **Injunction.** restrain the defendant from building so as to diminish the light. And, even if the building has been already begun, yet, if the plaintiff loses no time, he may obtain a mandatory injunction requiring the defendant to pull **Mandatory** down any building already erected, by which substantial **injunction.** diminution has been made of the amount of light to which the plaintiff is entitled. Cases of this kind are often practically of great difficulty. Generally speaking, if a street be narrow, and if a wall be erected to such a height, as that a line drawn from the top of it to the base of an ancient window, forms an angle of forty-five **Forty-five** degrees with a horizontal line drawn also from the base **degrees.** of the window; then the wall will not be allowed to be carried higher; as any height beyond this would generally produce a substantial diminution of the light. On this point the following remarks were made by Lord Selborne, in the case of *The City of London Brewery* **Lord Selborne** *Company* v. *Tennant* (*m*) : " With regard to the forty-five **in** *City of* degrees, there is no positive rule of law upon that *Brewery Co.* subject; the circumstance that forty-five degrees are left **v.** *Tennant.* unobstructed being merely an element in the question of fact, whether the access of light is unduly interfered with; but undoubtedly there is ground for saying that, if the legislature, when making general regulations as to buildings, considered that, when new buildings are erected, the light sufficient for the comfortable occupation of them will, as a general rule, be obtained if the buildings to be erected opposite to them have not a greater angular elevation than forty-five degrees, the

(*l*) See *Allen* v. *Scckham*, L. R.,   (*m*) L. R., 9 Ch. 212, 220.
11 Ch. D. 790, 798.

fact that forty-five degrees of sky are left unobstructed may, under ordinary circumstances, be considered *primâ facie* evidence that there is not likely to be material injury; and, of course, that evidence applies more strongly where only a lateral light is partially affected and all the lights are not obstructed. I make that observation not imagining that either at law or in this Court any judge has ever meant to lay down, as a general proposition, that there can be no material injury to light if forty-five degrees of sky are left open; but I am of opinion that if forty-five degrees are left, this is some *primâ facie* evidence of the light not being obstructed to such an extent as to call for the interference of the Court — evidence which requires to be rebutted by direct evidence of injury and not by the mere exhibition of models." This case was followed by the present Master of the

Hackett v. *Baiss.*

Rolls in the case of *Hackett* v. *Baiss* (n), in which he cites the passage of Lord Selborne's judgment which I have just quoted. In the case of *Hackett* v. *Baiss*, a building was erected in a somewhat narrow street in the city of London, and had already reached a height which would subtend an angle of forty-five degrees at the foot of the ancient lights of the plaintiff's houses on the opposite side of the street. And it was held that the plaintiff was entitled to an injunction restraining the raising of the new building to a greater height. So much then as to the right to light.

Air.

Right to air not an easement.

Light and air generally go together; and that which obstructs one usually obstructs the other. It is not, however, always so. A right to air, as distinguished from a right to light, is not an easement, and cannot be claimed by long enjoyment, either from time immemorial or within the periods limited by the Prescription Act (o), with respect to the enjoyment of easements.

(n) L. R., 20 Eq. 494.   (o) Stat. 2 & 3 Will. IV. c. 71.

This was decided in the case of *Webb* v. *Bird* (*p*). In that case the owner of a windmill, to the working of which a current of air of course is necessary, brought an action against the defendants for erecting a school-house within twenty-five yards of the mill; whereby they obstructed the current of air which would have come from the westward; so that the working of the mill was hindered, and the mill became injured and deteriorated in value. But the Court of Exchequer Chamber, agreeing in opinion with the Court of Common Pleas, held that the right to the passage of air is not a right to an easement within the meaning of the 2 & 3 Will. IV. c. 71, s. 2. The Court were also of opinion that no presumption could arise of a grant of a right to the air from its uninterrupted enjoyment as of right for many years. The Court remarked (*q*), " In the present case it would be practically so difficult, even if not absolutely impossible, to interfere with or prevent the exercise of the right claimed, subject, as it must be, to so much variation and uncertainty, as pointed out in the judgment below, that we think it clear that no presumption of a grant, or easement in the nature of a grant, can be raised from the non-interruption of the exercise of what is called a right, by the person against whom it is claimed, as a non-interruption by one who might prevent or interrupt it." This case involves the important principle, now well recognized, that an easement cannot be gained by usage, however long, of that which is not actionable, and which cannot be prevented. On the same principle it was held, in a recent case, that a confectioner, who had for upwards of twenty years used a pestle and mortar in his back premises gained no right thereby to continue the user after his neighbour, a physician, had erected a consulting-room in his adjoining back premises, to which the noise and vibration occa-

Marginal notes:

Webb v. *Bird.*

Easement cannot be gained by usage not actionable, and which cannot be prevented.

Noise and vibration.

(*p*) 15 C. B., N. S. 841. See also *Bryant* v. *Lefevre*, L. R., 4

C. P. D. 172.
(*q*) Page 843.

sioned by the use of the pestle and mortar became then for the first time an actionable nuisance (*r*).

But the Court will prevent the mere obstruction of air to an ancient window, in cases where the obstruction would amount to a nuisance. As in the case of *Dent* v. *Auction Mart Company* (*s*), in which part of the case was this, as mentioned in the judgment of Vice-Chancellor Wood (now Lord Hatherley) (*t*) :—There was a staircase, lighted in a certain manner by windows, which when opened admitted air. The defendants were about to shut up these windows, as in a box with the lid off, by a wall about eight or nine feet distant, and some forty-five feet high; and in that circumscribed space they proposed to put three water-closets. The Court remarked there were difficulties about the case of air, as distinguished from that of light; but the Court has interfered to prevent the total obstruction of all circulation of air; and the introduction of three water-closets into a confined space of this description was, in the opinion of the Court, an interference with air, which the Court would recognize on the ground of nuisance. "This is perhaps," the Vice-Chancellor remarks, "the proper ground on which to place the interference of the Court, although in decrees the words 'light and air' are often inserted together, as if the two things went *pari passu*."

The next easement to which I wish to call your attention is that of a right to a *pew* in a parish church. In some places pews are bought and sold in a manner entirely contrary to law. In some few churches or chapels there may be special acts of parliament by which pews may be bought and sold, but such cases are very rare. The legal right is in the Ordinary to arrange the seats of the church as he thinks best for the accom-

(*r*) *Sturges* v. *Bridgman*, L. R., 11 Ch. D. 852.

(*s*) L. R., 2 Eq. 238.
(*t*) Page 252.

modation of the parishioners for whose benefit the
church is supposed to be built; but in some cases a man
may have a right to a pew by reason of a grant from Faculty.
the bishop, called a *faculty ;* and in some cases a prescrip- Prescription.
tive right to a pew, as appurtenant to an ancient mes-
suage in the parish, may undoubtedly be established by
proper evidence. The evidence, however, must consist Evidence.
not only of the occupation of the pew for a time which
will afford presumptive evidence of immemorial enjoyment, but also of proof of the repairs of the pew having Repairs.
been invariably paid for by the person who claims the
pew as appurtenant to his dwelling-house, or by his
predecessors in title. The law on this subject will be
found in the recent case of *Crisp* v. *Martin (u).* In that *Crisp* v.
case it was held that a parishioner who claims a legal *Martin.*
right by prescription to a pew in the nave of his parish
church, must, in order to displace the general right of
the Ordinary, not only show that the pew has been
occupied by him or his predecessors in title, in respect
of an ancient house in the parish, for a period more or
less extended; but must also prove, if any alteration or
repair of the pew has been necessary, that such repairs
or alterations were executed at the expense of those
who at the time claimed the prescriptive right to it.
The case of *Crisp* v. *Martin* contains some remarks of
the learned judge, Lord Penzance, with regard to the Whether
question whether the claim to a pew in the nave of a within
parish church is within the second section of the Pre- Act.
scription Act, 2 & 3 Will. IV. c. 71. In the case in
question it was immaterial whether the claim was within
or without the Act, because the objection to the prescription there was, that the evidence was only evidence
of occupancy, and nothing else, and that that alone did
not constitute evidence of prescription. But if there
had been an attempt to show that the right had not
existed from time immemorial, inasmuch as it had been

(*u*) L. R., 2 P. D. 15.

first enjoyed, say a few years later than the first year of the reign of Richard the first, then the question would have arisen whether or not a claim to a pew in a parish church is an easement within that statute. And the learned judge expressed an opinion (x) that the Prescription Act does not apply in a case like the present, or indeed he might say, in any case of a pew claimed by prescription. The point, however, has never been decided.

Right of burial in a vault.

A right similar to that of a pew is a right of burial in a particular vault, in a church or churchyard. Thus it is laid down in Comyns' Digest (y), that a man may prescribe that he is tenant of an ancient messuage, and ought to have separate burial in such a vault within the church. And in the modern case of *Bryan* v. *Whistler* (z) it was held that an exclusive right of burial in a vault is an easement, and as such an incorporeal hereditament which, according to the ordinary rule of law, cannot be granted by parol or by mere writing, without a deed.

Bryan v. *Whistler.*

Eaves.

Amongst other easements which may be referred to is that of allowing the water from an overhanging eave to drip upon a neighbour's land. The erection of a house with such an eave is a nuisance which may be abated by the neighbour, or in respect of which he may bring an action, even before any water actually falls (a).

Request must be made to alienee to reform nuisance.

But it was held in *Penruddock's case* (b) that if the house has come to the hands of an alienee, by whom the eaves were not erected, a request must be first made to him to reform the nuisance before any action can be brought against him. If no abatement be made, or

(x) Page 27.
(y) Title Cemetery (B).
(z) 8 Barn. & Cress. 288.

(a) *Fay* v. *Prentice*, 1 C. B. 828.
(b) 5 Rep. 100 b. See *Jones* v. *Williams*, 11 Mee. & Wels. 176.

action brought, an easement of dripping is in process of time created. Another easement is that of having a post, signboard, or such other chattel, erected on one's neighbour's land, or against his wall (c). Signboard.

I may add, in conclusion, that there are such things as prescriptive liabilities, as well as prescriptive rights. Thus there may be a prescriptive liability to repair a bridge. Lord Coke lays it down in his Second Institute (d), that some persons are bound to repair bridges by reason of their tenure of lands or tenements, some by reason of prescription only. But herein, he observes, is a diversity between bodies politic or corporate, spiritual or temporal, and natural persons; for bodies politic or corporate, spiritual or temporal, may be bound by usage and prescription only, because they are local and have a succession perpetual; but a natural person cannot be bound by the act of his ancestor, without a lien or binding, and assets. So a township, as distinguished from the parish of which it forms part (e), may be liable by prescription to repair all the highways within the township, of which an instance will be found in the case of *The King* v. *The Inhabitants of Sheffield* (f). So a man may be bound by prescription to repair a wall against the influx of the sea; and it was resolved in *Keighley's case* (g), that if one is bound by prescription to repair a wall *contra fluxum maris*, and he keeps the wall in good repair, and of such height and as sufficient as it was accustomed; and by the sudden and unusual increase of water, salt or fresh, the walls are broken or the water overflows the walls; that in this case no fault was in him who ought to repair the wall, and that the loss

Prescriptive liabilities.

Bridge.

Highways, repair of by township.

Sea wall.

Keighley's case.

(c) *Lancaster* v. *Eve*, 5 C. B., N. S. 717; *Hoare* v. *Metropolitan Board of Works*, L. R., 9 Q. B. 296; *Moody* v. *Steggles*, L. R., 12 Ch. D. 261. See also *Wood* v.

Hewett, 8 Q. B. 913.
(d) Page 700.
(e) *Ante*, p. 40.
(f) 2 T. Rep. 106.
(g) 10 Rep. 139.

ought to be borne rateably by all persons having lands or tenements who might sustain damage by the overflow. A man may, however, be liable by prescription to repair a sea wall, though destroyed by extraordinary tempest. This was decided in the case of *The Queen* v. *Leigh* (*h*). There is a very recent case on this subject in the Court of Appeal, namely, *Hudson* v. *Tabor* (*i*). In this case it was held that the mere fact that each frontager had always maintained the wall in front of his land, and that no one had thought it necessary to make a wall to protect his land from the water which might come from his neighbour's land, was no sufficient evidence to establish a prescriptive liability on the part of the defendant to maintain the wall for the protection of the adjoining landowners. It was also held that by the common law, apart from prescription, no liability to repair the sea wall was cast on the defendant as a frontager. The costs of a sea wall ought to fall rateably on all who need its protection, and not exclusively on the owner of land, perhaps a narrow strip, which immediately faces the sea. (*k*)

The Queen v. *Leigh.*

Hudson v. *Tabor.*

(*h*) 10 A. & E. 398.

(*i*) L. R., 2 Q. B. Div. 290.

(*k*) See *Morland* v. *Cook*, L. R., 6 Eq. 252.

INDEX.

C.

G.

I.

K.

L.

M.

N.

O.

V.

LONDON:
C. F. ROWORTH, PRINTER, BREAM'S BUILDINGS, CHANCERY LANE, E.C.

Lightning Source UK Ltd.
Milton Keynes UK
UKHW021829150219
337397UK00011B/647/P